C000245085

LONDON OBSERVED

Christchurch, Spitalfields

LONDON OBSERVED

A Polish Philosopher at Large, 1820-24

Krystyn Lach-Szyrma

Edited and annotated by Mona Kedslie McLeod

Signal Books
Oxford

This edition first published in 2009 by
Signal Books Limited
36 Minster Road
Oxford
OX4 1LY
www.signalbooks.co.uk

Introduction and notes © Mona Kedslie McLeod, 2009

Translated from Polish by Malgorzata Machnice and Agnieszka Kiersztejn

The right of Mona Kedslie McLeod to be identified as the author of this work has been asserted by her in accordance with the Copyright, Design and Patents Act, 1988.

All rights reserved. The whole of this work, including all text and illustrations, is protected by copyright. No parts of this work may be loaded, stored, manipulated, reproduced or transmitted in any form or by any means, electronic or mechanical, including photocopying and recording, or by any information, storage and retrieval system without prior written permission from the publisher, on behalf of the copyright owner.

A catalogue record for this book is available from the British Library.

ISBN 978-1-904955-64-1 Paper

The author and publishers gratefully acknowledge the support of the Polish Cultural Institute in London in the publication of this work.

Cover Design: Devdan Sen
Production: Devdan Sen
Editorial Assistance: Andrea Lucado
Cover Image: Rudolph Ackermann, A View of London from the Thames (1809). Courtesy of The Royal Institution of Great Britain, London
Printed by Bell & Bain Ltd., Glasgow

Contents

List of Illustrations

Acknowledgements

It is nearly 200 years since Krystyn Lach-Szyrma published his *Reminiscences of a Journey through England and Scotland: 1820-24.* Changes in the Polish language and European culture made translation into contemporary English a formidable task so I would like to thank Malgorzata Machnice and Agnieszka Kiersztejn and her assistants, Kalarzynska Dobrucka, Michal Janinski and Zbigniew Sabat, who, between them, produced a text on which I could base *London Observed.* Iseabael Macleod and Bruce Lenman eliminated at least some of the errors in my work and my grand daughters Shian Holt and Sarah Najani resolved recurring computer crises. Mary Burkett gave me her skilled assistance with the reproduction of the illustrations. Many of these came from Michael Oliver's copy of David Hughson's *Walks through London* and Elizabeth Barry's copy of Francis Grose's *Antiquities of England*: the portrait of Lach-Szyrma is the property of his great-grandson Francis. Neal Ascherson's enthusiasm encouraged me to edit the *Reminiscences* and my late husband Robert's support made this possible. Without the help of Aleksander Dietkow, the Consul General in Scotland of the Republic of Poland, and the very generous support of the Polish Cultural Institute publication would have been difficult. To all of these I am deeply grateful.

Foreword

This book is a window opened onto a prospect of dazzling hope – the first years of what was to become the British century. Krystyn Lach-Szyrma, a clever young Pole greedy for knowledge and mercilessly observant, saw Britain as Alexis de Tocqueville was later to see America: a land in which the world's future was being born.

For Lach-Szyrma, visiting in the mid-1820s, this was the country of mighty experiment. A quite new form of society, founded on industrialisation and agricultural improvement and drawing its resources from a colossal inrush of wealth from colonial empire, was emerging at almost uncontrollable speed. Ancient structures and practices were being overwhelmed by change, and in their place came new institutions, fresh and boundlessly ambitious plans for social and political reform.

It was a good time for a foreigner to arrive. The Napoleonic wars were over, and the period of repression and reaction which followed them was starting to dissolve. The industrial revolution was moving into top gear, and the archaic social fabric was already in tatters. These were years at once alarming and hugely optimistic; confident idealists came forward with revolutionary plans to reform almost every aspect of the social infrastructure: the poor laws, the hospitals for the sick and mentally ill, the prisons and the brutal penal system, the structure and curricula of schools and universities, and the antique and corrupt parliamentary franchise.

Lach-Szyrma spent most of his British sojourn in Scotland, exploring the 'Silver Age' of the Scottish Enlightenment, and his Scottish memoirs have already been published in *From Charlotte Square to Fingal's Cave* (Tuckwell Press, 2004). This volume records his time in London. The mid-1820s were a moment when the grim side-effects of breakneck capitalist growth – mass destitution, the disintegration of families, the spread of slums and disease – still seemed controllable if vigorous, enlightened action were taken. Lach-Szyrma's London, in other words, was not yet the terrifying 'two nations' city of squalor and abandonment alongside indifferent affluence which Mayhew was to record a few years later.

He met and befriended some of the great reformers: Robert Owen, Elizabeth Fry, the old radical Lord Erskine, the parliamentary reformer Major Cartwright, the Quaker inventor William Allen and many others. But he enjoyed himself too. A brilliantly funny chapter describes the uproar of the London theatres. Lach-Szyrma also loved impromptu singing evenings at the Cider Cellar, an early version of the karaoke pub, and he went to the packed-out 'Mathews At Home' shows in which Charles Mathews, who would now be called a stand-up comic, convulsed audiences with his commentaries on daily life.

He took notes on everything, from the complete breakfast menu at a London hotel through the prices of every variety of food to the precise output of the new steam printing-presses at *The Times*. And there was a reason for this, beyond his own natural curiosity. Krystyn Lach-Szyrma was in Britain as the tutor of three young Polish nobles who, it was hoped, would one day govern their country. Poland had been partitioned and robbed of its independence only twenty years before, but in the mid-1820s there seemed still to be a chance that the nation could modernise itself economically and socially even under foreign occupation. Every scrap of information about progress and experiment in Britain was precious.

These hopes were to prove vain. Russian repression became intolerable, and in 1830 a national uprising broke out. Lach-Szyrma, back in Poland, was one of its commanders, and after the failure of the rising he returned to Britain to spend the rest of his life in exile. His account of England and Scotland was published in his homeland, but it has taken over a century for a translation to be available in English. It is only now, through the enthusiasm and devoted editing work of Mona Kedslie McLeod, herself the descendant of Scots long settled in Poland, that this masterpiece of reportage arrives to enrich historians and delight English-speaking readers.

Neal Ascherson

Editor's Introduction

Within a few days of their arrival in London in 1820 Krystyn Lach-Szyrma and his charges, the son and two nephews of Prince Adam Jerzy Czartoryski, set out for Edinburgh. Following in the footsteps of the prince and his father, Prince Adam Kazymierz, they were committed to two years of serious study at the university before being allowed to savour the delights of London. Education was to come before pleasure.

As tutor to the princes Lach-Szyrma spent over two years in Scotland. A Scottish connection had been established in 1659 when Lady Catherine Gordon, a lady in waiting at the court of Queen Marie Louise of Poland, married into the Morsztyn family. Her daughter Izabela married Prince Kazymirz Czartoryski and, in 1757, their grandson, Prince Adam Kazimierz, was persuaded to visit Scotland by Lord Mansfield, the Scottish Lord Chief Justice of England. Like Lach-Szyrma, he fell in love with Scotland and returned with his wife, Princess Izabela Fleming. She in her turn returned with their son Adam Jerzy. On his first visit to Edinburgh in 1787 his father had written:

> The main purpose of this journey is to gather materials necessary for the moment when you are chosen to serve your country.

His second visit with Princess Izabela was in 1793. After studying the British parliamentary system at work at Westminster, he and his mother travelled north, visiting factories and 'improved' farms on their way. In Scotland Adam Jerzy attended classes at Edinburgh University, then at the height of its fame, before continuing his tour of observation. By this time Izabela was tired of industrial developments and left her son to look at more factories while she toured some of the great landscaped gardens, going as far north as Blair Castle in Perthshire and as far west as Inveraray in Argyll. On her return to Poland the Scottish gardeners whom she had recruited transformed the park round her home at Puławy, replacing parterres and formal avenues with the grottoes and waterfalls of a romantic 'English' garden.

The Palace of Puławy c.1820 Situated on the banks of the Vistula, ten miles from Warsaw, the palace became the main residence of the Czartoryski family. In 1782 it was enlarged for Prince Adam Kazimirz and the formal gardens were transformed into a magnificent park by James Savage, the landscape gardener who had been invited to Poland by Princess Izabela Czartoryska after her visit to Scotland. Her *Varied Thoughts on Ways of Designing Gardens* and Savage's romantic park set the fashion for Polish gardens for the rest of the century. A centre of culture and patronage, Puławy became known as the 'Athens of Poland'.

By 1824 there were at least 300 such gardens in Poland and the princess's book, *Varied Thoughts on Ways of Designing Gardens*, had gone into several editions.

Adam Kazimierz had created a precedent. To visit Scotland and attend lectures at Edinburgh University became a standard practice for the more enlightened members of the Polish upper classes. The Czartoryskis were among the most powerful and intelligent of these. During the eighteenth century they had built up bases of power throughout the country and there were few families of importance with whom they were not connected by marriage. Collectively they became known as 'the Familia'. Konstancja, one of the Czartoryski princesses, was the mother of Stanisław August Poniatowski, the last King of Poland. A former lover of Catherine the Great of Russia, her influence and that of the Familia had helped to secure his election in 1764.

Poland, by 1764, had become one of the most socially and economically backward countries in Europe. Social mobility, an essential ingredient in the development of a wealthy society, was rare. Agriculture declined and, with the exception of Danzig and Warsaw, life in the towns atrophied. A constitution which concentrated political power in the hands of the nobility and excluded the professional and merchant classes had reduced Poland from the great power and centre of culture she had been in the sixteenth century to an almost ungovernable state. The 'Liberum Veto' enabled the most insignificant deputy to cancel the work of a full session of the Sejm, the Polish parliament. By the eighteenth century it was being used to wreck all attempts at reform. Frontiers which provided few natural barriers to invaders left her open to attack from powerful and ambitious neighbours and wars further weakened her economy. Poniatowski set out to develop her industries and modernise her constitution. His sweeping reforms were supported by the Familia but opposed by the more reactionary of the landowners and by the Jesuit order, whose property and control of education were threatened. The Constitution of 1791 created a crisis. This freed the serfs, transferred some political power from the landowning *szlachta* to a growing middle class, and abolished the 'Liberum Veto', the cynical use of which had made a mockery of both royal and parliamentary power and had opened Polish territories to predators. The Constitution would have made Poland the most democratic state in Europe and potentially governable; Catherine the Great of Russia was determined that it should be neither. The absolute monarchies of Europe were already threatened by the French Revolution: to them the possibility that a democracy might emerge in Poland was intolerable. Catherine had had little difficulty in persuading Austria and Prussia to join her in seizing Polish territory in 1772. In January 1793, on the day of the execution of Louis XVI of France, Russia and Prussia agreed to the Second Partition. In 1795 the Third Partition wiped Poland off the map of Europe. Western powers protested but did nothing to help Poland, while the most reactionary of the Polish nobility looked to Catherine to restore their

Krystyn Lach-Szyrma (1791-1866) The portrait was probably painted during the1830 Rising when Lach-Szyrma became the leader, with the rank of colonel, of the Academic Youth of Warsaw and Cracow Universities. He is wearing a military jacket but with a civilian shirt and cloak.

privileges. Poniatowski was forced to abdicate and died, a virtual captive, in St Petersburg in 1798.

The Czartoryskis had joined the movement to resist the Partitions. Though led by Tadeusz Kosciuszko, a veteran of the American War of Independence and a brilliant commander, the Insurrections failed. The Czartoryski estates were forfeited. In order to recover them, Prince Adam Jerzy was recalled from Scotland and he and his younger brother were sent to St Petersburg as hostages for the 'good behaviour' of the family. The brothers became friends of Alexander, the idealistic crown prince who was alienated from his grandmother Catherine and disapproved of the Partitions. When, as Alexander I, he became tsar, he appointed Adam Jerzy as his foreign minister.

During the French Wars Poland was invaded and, in 1807, Napoleon created the Duchy of Warsaw out of the Russian portion. Promised a liberal constitution and the recovery of those parts of Poland still under Austrian or Prussian rule, many Poles joined Napoleon's army. They fought in Spain and Italy and, led by King Stanisław's nephew Prince Jozef Poniatowski, 10,000 marched into Russia in 1812. They shared Napoleon's final defeat and at the Congress of Vienna Poland was again partitioned. Austria and Prussia recovered territory lost during the French Wars while, out of the lion's share, Alexander created the Congress Kingdom, not as part of the Russian Empire but as his own personal domain. Adam Jerzy became his chief advisor on Polish affairs. Inspired by the British constitution, which he had admired and idealised, he helped to draft the relatively liberal constitution granted to the Poles.

When the young princes, Adam and Konstanty Czartoryski and their cousin Prince Sapieha, set off on their Grand Tour in 1820, Adam Jerzy appeared to be at the height of his power and expected to become viceroy. The young princes were to be prepared to take major roles in the government of the Congress Kingdom. But Alexander's love affair with democracy was soon over. Censorship was introduced, the reactionary Grand Duke Constantine became viceroy and the undermining of the constitution, which led to the Rising of 1830, began. Both Adam Jerzy and Lach-Szyrma played prominent parts in the Rising. On its failure they went into life-long exile; the Prince to

France and Lach-Szyrma to Britain.

But in 1820 the future still seemed full of promise. When his father sent Adam Jerzy on his first visit to Britain Prince Adam Kazimierz had written:

> I do not want you to be a light minded person – I want you to be an indispensable man and a man of charm – I do not wish you to be a kind of medicine which is extremely salubrious and effective but, Hell's Bell's, unpalatable.

Adam Jerzy was determined that the princes' education, like his own, should include a period of study at Edinburgh University. Lach-Szyrma, their recently appointed tutor, went with them. A more unlikely candidate for the post of tutor to the sons of so distinguished a family would be difficult to imagine. A protestant of peasant origins, he was born in 1790 in Wojnacy, a village in the area of Mazury on the East Prussian side of the border with Poland. His father, Adam Lach, was a small farmer. While still at primary school Krystyn began to explore prehistoric sites near his home and the insatiable curiosity, which makes his *Reminiscences of a Journey through England and Scotland* so fascinating, became apparent. At confirmation classes, when he was thirteen, the Lutheran pastor, George Schrage, noticed his exceptional ability and decided to teach him German to make it possible for him to attend the gymnasium at Königsberg. This was in Prussia but teaching was both in Polish and German. As the son of a peasant farmer, he was socially ostracised by the other boys but his ability was again recognised. When Napoleon's armies invaded Prussia and over-ran the family farm his father was no longer able to pay the gymnasium fees. Ignacy Onacewicz, one of his teachers, adopted him and drew Krystyn to the attention of Prince Adam Jerzy Czartoryski.

In his *Letters Literary and Political on Poland*, published in Edinburgh in 1823, Lach-Szyrma wrote:

> It ought here to be remarked that activity in all fields of literature has been much fostered and rendered still more universal by the liberality of the house of the Princes Czartoryski, who might be called

> the Medici of Poland. At their hospitable hearth men of letters, poets and artists found a friendly reception. In short, there existed within the last period no literary character in Poland who had not, in one way or another, stood connected with that illustrious house by receiving encouragement, benefit and support from it.

With the financial help of the prince and money earned teaching German to young ladies, he was able to attend the University of Vilnius where he studied classical Polish literature and learned English from Professor Saunders. Saunders was director of the School of Engraving and lectured on History of Art and on English Literature. Lach-Szyrma was fascinated by folk poetry and music and the Romantic Movement. Familiarity with Macpherson's *Ossian* probably laid the foundations for his love affair with Scotland. He added the noble name Szyrma to the plebeian Lach, a name given by the Prussians to Polish peasants. When a refugee in England in the 1830s he referred openly to his peasant origins but at Vilnius he was still suffering from his experiences at Königsberg. In 1813 he graduated in philosophy, with a reference from the principal as 'an exemplary young man of outstanding ability and diligence'. To his friend and adoptive father, Onacewicz, he had written in 1812:

> I desire to give myself entirely to what surprises people most: Ancient History and the study of the English language. With time I hope to be able to reap the fruit of my efforts in England or some other country and prove to the world that a Pole, though his country has lost its very name, can make that name revive the power of his own genius and that, if not superior, we are at least equal in learning to other nations.

He was 22 at the time. In spite of his protestant and peasant background Prince Adam Jerzy employed him as a tutor to some of the young princes of the Familia. He spoke Russian, Polish, German, French and Latin and could read and write English. The personality that emerges from the *Reminiscences* suggests that the Prince could not have made a better choice.

Lach-Szyrma and his three pupils reached Scotland when the embers of the Enlightenment were still glowing. The greatest of the original thinkers – men of the calibre of David Hume, Joseph Black, James Hutton, Adam Smith and William Robertson – had died, but the intellectual climate which they had created still existed. No longer perhaps a 'Hotbed of Genius', Edinburgh still merited its description as the 'Athens of the North'. It was also a social capital, for London was a long way away. The new roads created by the turnpike trusts had cut travelling time from Edinburgh from ten days to two but until the 1850s, when the railway reduced the time to twelve hours, the Scottish upper classes flocked to Edinburgh, not London, in the winter months. Polite society opened its doors to the Polish aristocrats and their tutor.

For two years, during the six months of term time, they studied medicine, economics, agriculture and philosophy. Lach-Szyrma graduated with a Doctorate in Philosophy. He delighted in an academic environment in which both teachers and students could come from a broad social spectrum and in which foreigners from every country in Europe were welcomed. They had moved in the highest echelons of Scottish society but he was no snob. He describes the appalling formality and boredom of 'At Homes' but relished the quality of conversation at dinner parties where he met men like Jeffrey, editor and one of the founders of the *Edinburgh Review* and Wilson, editor of its Tory rival, *Blackwood's Magazine*. As a romantic, devoted to folk music and poetry, he admired and revered Walter Scott but was not blind to his weaknesses. When he met tenant farmers and crofters' sons at the tables of the aristocracy he realised, from his own peasant background, that in Scotland intellectual achievement could break down barriers of class. In the summer months he visited factories, farms and institutions throughout the south and south-west and in his exploration of Argyllshire went as far as the island of Staffa. He was a shrewd observer though sometimes idealising British institutions. Walking from Loch Lomond to Oban he experienced the appalling living conditions of the Highland peasantry but he seemed unaware of the poverty of the Edinburgh poor. Nor did he comment on the severity of the post war depression which was driving thousands to emigrate.

During the years when Lach-Szyrma had been an employee of

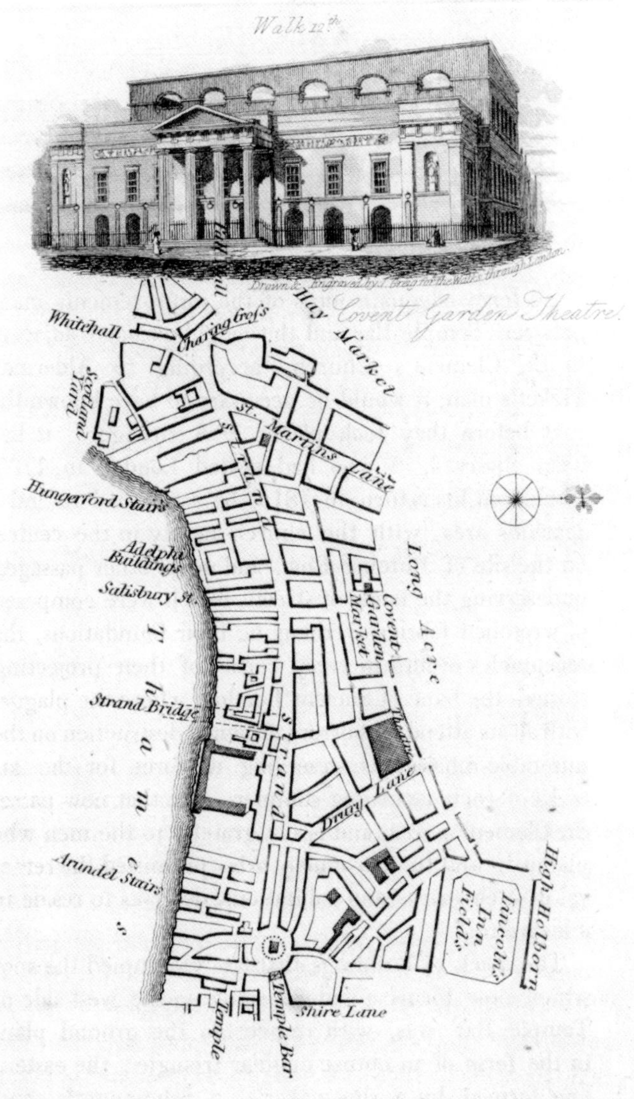

Covent Garden Theatre. Covent Garden and Drury Lane were the two theatres licensed by Walpole's Act of 1737. Burnt down in 1787 it was again burnt in 1808 and rebuilt in one year by the 27 year old Robert Smirke. Smirke's theatre was rebuilt by Barry after another fire in 1857.

the Czartoryski family he had supplemented his salary by writing. He had contributed articles to the Warsaw, Vilnius and Lwow presses and, in Britain, to English journals. Encouraged by Professor Wilson, the editor of *Blackwood's Magazine*, and assisted by the Keeper of the Signet Library, he wrote his *Letters and Tribes*. These were published by Constable in 1823. His chief aim was 'the popularisation of Poland'. He had been startled by the ignorance of people in Britain about the Slav nations, 'terra incognita' even to the most intelligent and educated. He realised that almost all western historians were unable to read Slavonic languages and depended on secondary sources. In the preface to the political letters he wrote:

> Taking all the books ever published… I find that they chiefly relate to the exterior of the people; as for instance their dress, manners, amusements and mode of living – interspersed with anecdotes, true or false no matter, if they only possessed enough singularity to amuse the majority of credulous readers. Political views, of which there was no lack, commonly ended with heavy sighs on barbarity and slavery. The moral features of the nation and still more the literary, as they have appeared in the succession of ages, remained a sealed book.

After a short tour of France, Germany and Switzerland, Lach-Szyrma and his charges returned to England. In Edinburgh they had been participants in the social as well as the intellectual life of the capital; in London there seems to have been no contact with the dissolute court of George IV or with the English aristocracy. But he was determined to explore beneath the surface of the societies he observed and was always more than an intelligent tourist. With introductions from his Scottish friends, he was guided round hospitals and asylums, prisons and schools, law courts and factories. He stayed with Elizabeth Fry and her family and met people of the calibre of Robert Owen, Major Cartwright and Lord Erskine. Reports would go back to Polish journals and to his patron, Prince Adam Jerzy Czartoryski. The decision to send a delegation of distinguished Poles to observe British industries and institutions in 1825 may well have been one of the results.

London and Edinburgh were different worlds. A pleasure ground for the rich and idle of Europe, London in the 1820s was probably the largest city and the largest port in the world as well as the capital of a vast empire. Though heavy industry was moving to the northern coal-fields, the luxuries which filled the shops were still being made in London and the City was becoming the financial and insurance centre of the world. Its population had grown from 900,000 in 1802, at the time of the census, to 1,000,000 in 1815 and 1,247,000 in 1820. With neither clean water nor covered sewers the death rate soared but, with wages fifty per cent higher than in the provinces, it attracted the ambitious as well as the unemployed. While living conditions deteriorated in the City and the East End, the West End was being transformed. In the seventeenth century the aristocracy had still owned miniature country houses near London in which they spent the winter months. These were gradually leased to speculators like Sir Thomas Bond who demolished the mansions in order to build terraces of town houses. Clarendon House was replaced by Bond Street and Bloomsbury Square was built on what had been the house and gardens of the Earl of Southampton. What is now Buckingham Palace is one of the few survivors. By the 1820s John Nash, commissioned by George IV, had created Regent's Park, the terraces surrounding it and Regent Street. The upper classes abandoned Inigo Jones' Covent Garden and moved to Bloomsbury and Mayfair. The West End was as clearly separated from the East End as Edinburgh's New Town from the Old.

Lach-Szyrma was dazzled by London but never quite lost the critical eye of a European intellectual. Westminster Abbey and the Tower were visited as a tourist but the Lord Mayor welcomed him to the Mansion House. On this occasion he would certainly have been with the princes. They are rarely mentioned in the text. Although his tour had been financed by Prince Adam Jerzy it might have been socially unacceptable to refer to his son and nephews in his *Reminiscences*. Instead he concentrated on the people he met and the cultures he observed. He twice crossed the Channel before his own return to Poland in January 1824 and some of his time in London may have been on his own. Sadly, most of England remained unexplored and the little he saw of the rest of the country had been from the windows of a coach.

After this relatively short stay in England, Lach-Szyrma returned to Poland. He was appointed to teach English language and literature at the Polytechnic Institute, and, in 1825, became the first Professor of Moral Philosophy at the newly founded University of Warsaw. But reaction had set in. By 1830 the policies of Tsar Nicholas I, who had succeeded Alexander in 1825, had driven the Poles to rebellion. With the rank of colonel, Lach-Szyrma, 'the Scottish Philospher', became the leader of the Academic Youth, the student insurgents in Warsaw and Cracow, and editor of their daily newspaper. After the failure of the Rising, Warsaw University was closed down. He and his patron Prince Adam Jerzy were exiled for life, the prince to become leader of the Polish community in Paris and Lach-Szyrma to struggle to earn a living in England.

The failure of the Rising had brought his career in Poland to an end. To his friend Professor Pillans he wrote in 1832:

> As leader of a corps I am excluded from amnesty, if an amnesty proclaimed by a Russian autocrat could deserve that name... And in fact what could I do, returning to Poland? It is impossible that I should know my former places. Universities are shut, libraries are sealed. In witnessing so many noble and patriotic efforts thwarted I would die of grief... I have come to London in order to continue to devote to my country my services in a Literary way, which is now the only one remaining, and I must think also of subsistence... Several gentlemen here are about to form a committee for the support of the Polish cause, which is also the European one. Could you not form a similar association in Edinburgh?

He was joined in England by his wife Jozefa Dzierzgowska and their two daughters. After Jozefa's death in 1837 he married Sarah Somerville, the daughter of a captain in the Royal Navy, and took British citizenship.

During the long years of exile, and until his own death in Devonport in 1866, he was an active member of a diplomatic and literary community of Poles living in London, working as a journalist and translator. Assisted by the patronage of Lord Dudley Coutts Stuart and the unfailing generosity of Prince Adam Jerzy Czartoryski, he organised charities to support Polish refugees and acted as secretary to the Literary Association of Friends of Poland. He became foreign correspondent for the Polish newspapers *Czas*, *Gazeta Warszawska* and *Gazeta Codzienna*, while the articles he contributed to British journals did something to undermine the misinformation with which the partitioning powers, Russia, Prussia and Austria, were trying to destroy the image of the country they had dismembered.

His *Reminiscences*, the first description of Britain to be published in Polish, was an immediate success. It was published in Warsaw in 1828, at a time when the Waverly novels and the Romantic Movement had made everything Scottish, from gardeners to governesses, fashionable. London, meanwhile, had become one of the wonders of the world. A fuller account of his travels was planned but never written. His *Memoir of My Life* has not been translated. It was published in London by his son, the Rev Wladyslaw Lach-Szyrma, seven years after his death. It was dedicated to 'My brave countrymen who, in such troubled times, have enriched me with their confidence and care; their memory will stay with me till my dying day.'

Helene Brochocka, who was working for the Ministry of the Interior of the exiled Polish government in London in 1940, translated the first two volumes of the *Reminiscences*. This was the basis of *From Charlotte Square to Fingal's Cave: Reminiscences of a Journey through Scotland 1820-24*, published by the Tuckwell Press in 2004. The first four chapters of Volume I, which describe the journey from Dover and the brief stay in London, were omitted. These, translated by Malgorzata Machnice, have been included in the present publication. Volume III, which describes his stay in England, has been translated in Warsaw by a team led by Agnieszka Kiersztejn.

The illustrations in the original work were portraits of such well known poets as Scott, Wordsworth and Coleridge. These have been replaced by pictures from contemporary sources. Most of the sketches of London have been reproduced from David Hughson's *Walks though*

London and those of other parts of England from Francis Grose's *Antiquities of England*.

Chapter One

Calais. Inns. Sterne's Chamber. Travellers' Characters. View of the Sea. Steamers. Packet Boats. Straits of Calais. Ship in the Sunbeams. Sea Sickness. Dover.

We arrived in Calais on 15 August 1820. Due to the large number of Englishmen settled there, the town is half English. It has many English customs and the use of the language is widespread. The place can be treated as a doorway to England, for travellers from the east and south of Europe meet at the Straits since, being the shortest, it is the most convenient crossing point. It is also possible to get to England from Ostend, Boulogne and Dieppe, but those who find long sails disagreeable choose Calais.

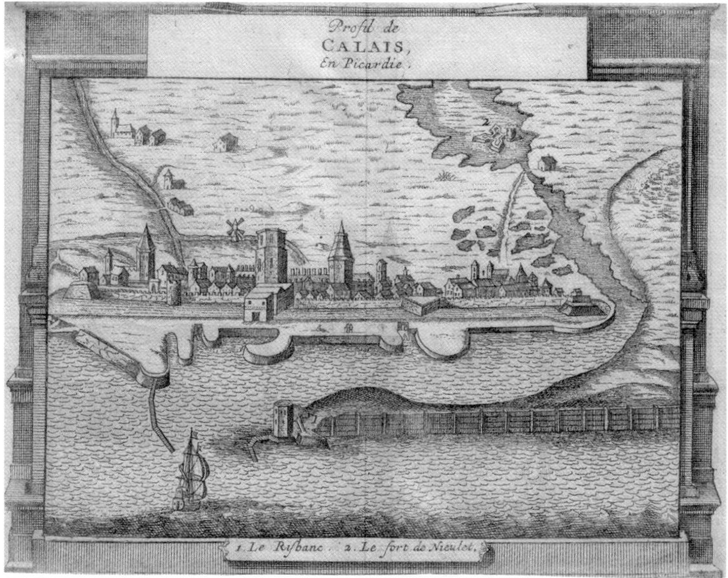

© ***The Hebrew University of Jerusalem & The Jewish National & University Library***

Calais. Only eighteen miles from Dover, Calais was built on an island and fortified in the fourteenth century. The Church of Notre Dame was built during the English occupation and Vauban's fortifications in the seventeenth century.

Circumstances made us stay for ten days in this coastal town of Picardy. Not much can be said in praise of the region, as it consists of a broad plain of chalky and stony soil, where even diligent farmers and careful cultivation have not been able to achieve much. The town itself is surrounded by high embankments in Vauban's[1] style, and has a stronghold where soldiers are stationed to protect the shore from danger. Although it seems to be large, its population is only ten thousand. It owes its growth and prosperity mostly to passing foreigners and only to a limited extent to trade which, as there is no navigable river that could make transport to and from the centre of the country easier, cannot be vast. The theatre is small and resembles a poor auditorium rather than a theatre. In place of the highbrow comedies one might expect in Molière's[2] homeland, they stage the shallow and tasteless farces for which a local audience seems to have a liking.

For over two centuries, from 1346 to as late as 1558, Calais[3] was in English hands. For that reason, as well as to improve relations with England, there are many traces of Englishness here. Public buildings are neither informative nor interesting. There are a few statues of prominent natives in one of the squares close to the harbour. They are adorned with the huge wigs and full dresses of their time, which tells one more about the inhabitants' pride in their heroes than their classical taste. Those who walk from the square alongside the stone wall shielding the harbour can see the statues which commemorate the return of the exiled Bourbons[4] to France. You can see a foot engraved in a stone to mark the place where a king, after a long exile, stepped on the soil of his ancestors for the first time.

Inns are important for travellers in Calais. Anyone who has ever travelled will admit how comforting it is to arrive at a decent inn. There are two in Calais which stand out. One of them is the Meurice, the other the Desseign. Both are furnished in the English style, with the comforts of Englishmen particularly in mind. We chose the Desseign Inn as, on an educational journey,[5] you cannot omit a place where the famous Sterne[6] had his first ideas for his *Sentimental Journey*. On entering a courtyard our first remark was: 'Where did Sterne stay?' We were shown his former accommodation, still marked with a sign on the door as 'Sterne's Chamber'. We were given that room as it was unoccupied at the time. Its windows were facing a small garden, cultivated in the English style. Flower beds were carefully kept and full of the most beautiful flowers. As it was already August some of them were nearing the end of their season, whereas others had only started theirs. It was a fascinating sight as the garden, which was undergoing changes, was rather small. However, even a small area has a certain significance! Having remembered the words of the living English poet, expressing his belief that the smallest flower coming into bloom is able to inspire thoughts which are too profound for tears, I easily understood why Sterne, who described only minor and ordinary events, was able to raise them up to such a height. His *Sentimental Journey* stands out in the history of literature more than many other works which dwell on more important themes. A genius can give the smallest object meaning and lasting significance.

We were reading Sterne's works on the site, in order to understand better his thoughts and the beauty of his writing. A public library delivered them to us for a small fee. We started with the *Sentimental Journey* and finished with his largest work, *Tristram Shandy*. Even today it is not comprehensible to all Englishmen. In the rest of our spare time we read English newspapers to prepare us for our intended further travel.

The innkeeper with whom Sterne had stayed has been dead for a long time. If he had returned to life, he would have found the courtyard of his successors as busy as it had been at the time of the gentle philosopher's stay and the philosopher would probably have found the atmosphere unchanged. Almost every moment you can hear the crack of a whip, stagecoaches and carriages coming and going and, in the ceaseless din of rattling and shouting, you have to squeeze past bundles and suitcases. In this racket the children of Great Britain are the most interesting. They are immediately recognisable by the style of their clothes, their walk, and the solemnity of their words of welcome. Even Talma[7] himself would not be able to teach a Frenchman the solemnity with which an Englishman seems to be born.

Englishmen themselves appear to differ from each other with regard to temperament, wealth and vocation. Here you can see a man who politely and without the slightest arrogance, greets and says goodbye to those present before departing in a respectable but not impressive vehicle. He is a distinguished lord who, after a parliamentary session has finished, is looking for a rest for himself and an educational tour for his eighteen year old son. He gives him the advice of his experience in order to prepare him for public life. Again, at the crack of a whip, a four-horse carriage arrives with a rattle; the horses seem to be covered with sweat. Getting out of the carriage is a short thin man of middle age in a creased hat and wearing a threadbare frock coat with a black velvet collar. He is arrogant but not distinguished and his swarthy face shows that he is an inhabitant of the tropics. Having recently returned from the riches of India,[8] he has been touring around Italy and France where, in every tavern, he has been addressed as 'milord'. Behind him is the enraged owner of two modest bundles recently confiscated by Customs officers. Talking animatedly, he is challenging the right of the French officials to confiscate his property. The penetrating look and subtle arguments are those of a newly qualified lawyer. Disappointed in his hopes of quickly becoming a chancellor, or at least a judge, he is going on a journey to foreign countries to back up his education with experience. This firm undertaking and the hope of future advancement stimulate him. God bless him! And who is that man staggering over there? There is a sweet melancholy on his pale face and the liveliness of his feelings seems to consume his frail strength. He is an admirer of the Muses but his own talent is shrivelling before it has fully opened.[9] He hurries to Italy, hoping to build up his health under its calm skies or, if not, to be buried in its classical soil.

What is that noise in the courtyard? It comes from the guest rooms. Singing, swearing and the shout: 'More wine!' are heard alternately. It is some of the very flower of John Bull's sons. They arrived in Calais to sing *Rule Britannia* under the noses of Frenchmen, to get drunk on French wine and then to return to their own island. Some of them are saturated with the punch to such an extent that the smell of them permeates the air. They are easily recognisable by their corpulence and crimson cheeks. My witty travelling companion B., having divided people into races, called them jokingly the red race. Their aim in life is to sleep and after they have awoken to relapse into a stupor.

The comely and modest daughters of Albion draw foreigners' attention to them. Though with the passage of time their originality is less striking, it is not easy to accustom one's eyes to it at first. They appear on a journey in long dark-blue dresses in which, when at home, they used to ride or go for a morning stroll. Some of them carry a riding crop which means they can ride a horse or maybe even drive from a coachman's seat. With such clothing they wear men's hats which make them look like Amazons. A black or white veil hanging from a hat weakens its masculine character. The veil, falling over a face, has a magical quality as it is transparent and you can see the delicate colouring of the skin but not the slight flaws caused by keen air or the blows delivered by merciless years. If we add those travelling for business reasons or to save money by residing in countries where the exchange rate is favourable, we will have the main characteristics of all who appear in the Desseign's courtyard.

You cannot become bored in ports; it is enough to go to a harbour to get rid of boredom. Constant movement and people's activities keep your mind awake all the time. Industry, effort and ambition, which seem to be concentrated in such places, are of great interest even to the most indifferent observer. If they are contemplative, the view of the sea itself and thoughts about what may be in its depths can give them unspeakable pleasure. If they are prepared to submit themselves to sensory impressions by watching the ships which sail to and from the harbour fully rigged or sail the seas at some distance from each other, or by listening to the murmuring impact of breakers on coastal rocks, they will experience incomprehensible rapture and their souls will be filled. For me a stroll toward the harbour was the most pleasant of experiences, particularly in the evening. Then, when the sun disappeared into the ocean, I could see with my own eyes a scene which has charmed and been described by so many poets.

The Straits of Calais are no wider than four Polish miles. Even on the sunniest days it is slightly misty. This atmosphere is common in northern seas and prevents one from seeing anything far off. A person who has good eyesight is able to see the shores of England with the naked eye. When I saw them (through a glass) they seemed to lie on the blue background of the sea like a thin, white rim: these were the

Steamboat on the Clyde. In 1788 William Symington launched the first effective steamboat on Dalswinton Loch. By 1808 Henry Bell's *Comet* provided a regular service from Glasgow to Gourock and the first Channel crossing was made in 1818. It was 1822 before Lach-Szyrma trusted himself to a steam powered vessel for his journey from Scotland to England.

calcareous rocks overlooking Dover from which England has been dubbed Albion. The word England comes much later and is said to be derived from the Angles,[10] who arrived in the island from the province of Angeln in Schleswig Holstein.

A steam ship attracted special attention in Calais at that time: it was the first that I had ever seen. I was told it was to be used on a trial basis to carry a cargo to Boulogne. Her owner, a Frenchman, wanted to establish confidence in the reliability of this new invention and invited a few members of the municipal council for a short sail on the steamer. They agreed to his request but, when it was time to go on board, they got frightened and each of them looked for an excuse not to take part in the trip. Such an important invention aroused people's anxiety in those days! Less than seven years later England had nearly two hundred of such ships.[11] In America, where they were first built, their number is even greater.

Chapter One

August 25th had come, the day of our departure from Calais. The ships which are used to cross the sea are called packet boats. They are, in general, smaller and lighter than merchant ships and are built for the travellers' convenience. They have quite a spacious cabin which is illuminated by a window in the deck. On the sides of the cabin, in two rows one above the other, there are frame-like compartments allotted for bunks. The bedclothes are clean and white, as Englishmen will not use any other. Screen curtains for the beds are green or red. French passenger ships are similarly equipped. The commanding officers are called captains. If the wind is favourable there is no day when the ships do not sail. The charge for the crossing is one guinea (forty-two Polish złotys) a person. If someone is travelling with a large family and is concerned for their comfort, they hire the whole ship. In imitation of bigger vessels each has its own name: our ship was named the 'Wellington'.

You sail from Calais when there is a low tide, as it makes sailing easier. Having sailed from the harbour, the current of water from the German Sea to the Atlantic carries the ship along the shores of France. If the wind is not quite favourable, to reach Dover safely you need skilful sailing in order not to be carried away by the strong current. Due to this current and the rarity of easterly and southerly winds, a crossing from Calais to Dover is believed to be a difficult one; the one from Dover to Calais is easier.

When you leave a harbour on board a ship, especially if for the first time, you will experience an extraordinary feeling which is difficult to describe. It is caused by the desire to experience something new. To enjoy different views and different company, different food and different drinks, we have to travel. A sea has its changes too. When we look at waves from the shore, we long to see from where they have come. Although it may be sad to leave behind you the familiar shores which are disappearing into the mist, curiosity drives you on. Separated from death and the abyss only by the walls of your ship, all you see is the sky and the sea.

The day of the crossing was bright. The sky was cloudless, the sun was shining wonderfully and sunbeams touching the surface of the slightly rocking sea produced extraordinary results. Their light, having reflected from the surface of the water and scattered in the air, created a wide space between our ship and the sun which was filled with brilliant light. There was a marvellous optical illusion when one of the many ships, which were sailing on different courses, went into that bright space. Its masts and sails got smaller and the ship itself resembled a misty shadow rather than reality; it seemed not to touch the dark waves of the ocean but to be slowly hovering in the brilliant air. This illusion lasted for a long time, for the ship was sailing towards the sun as it shone over the water. It was nearing sunset and the ship was moving closer as though, attracted by the sun, it was to be its port of call. This sight was wonderful and I would not be surprised if someone, who did not know the principles of optics, should look at it for the first time and rapturously believe, as ancient people did, that not only men, but also objects have an eternal future. Observing this ship, with its sails and its passengers undergoing such a miraculous transformation, the belief in question would become stronger.

Unpleasant reality put an end to my admiration of this phenomenon. The wind started to blow more strongly and the tilting of the ship did not allow one to stand safely or walk on deck. The ship was rolling on the waves more and more, causing the unbearable suffering called seasickness. Happy are those who can avoid it but few escape. Only deckhands and those who are used to sailing are spared. Even to describe the symptoms of the sickness is not pleasant. Sufferers have stomach cramps and are prone to vomiting. They suffer from vertigo and see coloured spots before their eyes, especially green ones. The most unpleasant feeling is when a huge breaker, having raised the ship high, brings it crashing down. Your whole body feels numb. This weakness is so tormenting, that it almost makes you lose interest in life. In case of a violent storm, it must make people insensitive to danger, thus mitigating the horror of a shipwreck. Not everyone suffers equally suddenly and with the same intensity. So far, the various precautions which have been taken to avoid the sickness have proved ineffective. However, if you want to feel some relief, the best solution is to turn yourself towards the wind, sit motionless with closed eyes or look all the time at the same point – the most commonly chosen is one on a mast. The air below deck is the most harmful so it is better

Mote's Bulwark, Dover Castle. Guarding the nearest crossing to mainland Europe, there had been lighthouses and signalling stations at Dover since the first century AD. The bailey of William the Conqueror's fort enclosed 34 acres and the bulwark was built in 1559 to strengthen the defences of the castle against invaders from the sea.

to stay on deck even if you have a cabin with a comfortable bed. If you lie, it helps a bit. Heavy dishes delay the sickness, but do not prevent it: a light meal causes sickness but at the same time makes it more bearable. For that reason you should drink tea for relief.

Fortunately, the favourable wind that accompanied our journey shortened both it and the unpleasant experience of that unbearable weakness. The crossing did not last as much as six hours. Due to a low tide it was not possible for the ship to arrive in port. We were given a boat and put down on the shore. The ship had to wait for the rising tide. And so we are in Dover.

NOTES:

1 Sebastien le prestre de Vauban (1633-1707). A French military engineer in the service of Louis XIV, the fortresses with which he surrounded France were of a revolutionary design which could withstand cannon fire.

2 Molière was the professional name of Jean-Baptiste Poquelin (1622-73). His theatre company, 'L'Illustre Théâtre', was set up in a hired tennis court in Paris in 1643. Its tours of the provinces, playing both tragedies and comedies, would have included Calais. Molière's own great comedies were written after his company came under royal patronage in 1658.

3 Edward III's claim to the throne of France led to the Hundred Years War. Calais was captured in its opening years and, under Mary Tudor, it was the last English stronghold to be lost. Her marriage to Philip II of Spain had dragged England into a disastrous war against France. English monarchs continued to claim their right to the throne and to display the fleur-de-lis on the royal coat of arms until the Treaty of Amiens in 1802.

4 Bourbon princes who took refuge in Britain included the Comte d'Artois (Charles X 1824-30) who lived at Hartwell in Buckinghamshire and then Holyrood Palace, Louis-Philippe (1830-48) at Twickenham, and Louis XVIII (1795-1820) at Hartwell. Louis had been proclaimed king on the death in prison of his brother, Louis XVII. He landed at Calais in 1814.

5 Lach-Szyrma came to Britain as tutor to two young Czartoryski princes on their Grand Tour of Europe. This culminated in two years of study at Edinburgh University.

6 Laurence Sterne (1713-68). An Irish clergyman and novelist whose success with his comic masterpiece *The Life and Opinions of Tristram Shandy* enabled him to travel abroad when his health began to fail. *A Sentimental Journey through France and Italy* was published the year of his death.

7 François-Joseph Talma (1763-1826). A French tragedian, he introduced the practice of dressing actors in costumes appropriate to the period and setting of the play.

8 Employees of the East India Company were allowed to trade privately. The few who survived the infections to which they were vulnerable returned to Britain with enormous fortunes. They were known, derisively, as 'nabobs'.

9 The Protestant cemetery in Rome is filled with memorials to British invalids who failed to recover their health.

10 Germanic invaders were attacking the south coast, the Saxon Shore, by the late fourth century. The Angles were settling in the north by the mid fifth century.

11 The first steamboat was designed by William Symington and launched on a Scottish loch in 1788. His second ship, the *Charlotte Dundas*, was the model for Robert Fulton's *Claremont*, which operated on the Hudson River. Regular steam packets crossed from Calais to Dover from 1818.

Chapter Two

Departure from Dover. Views of the Region. Canterbury. St Thomas à Becket. Rush on the High Road. Mail and Stage Coaches. Dinner at Rochester. Shooters Hill. View of London.

We stayed overnight in the Ship Inn in Dover. As we were weary our sleep was calm and sound. The sea never seemed to leave us. Even in our sleep it seemed to rock us in bed and the surf gently swished in our ears, as if we needed it to sleep better. Having had such a nurse, we enjoyed a deep sleep. Next morning, having received our bundles and passports from customs, we immediately set off on a further journey. Officers in the Customs house, who are usually strict, for some unknown reason treated us kindly and returned everything to us intact.

The Talbot Inn. Originally the Tabard Inn, it was used in Chaucer's day by wealthy pilgrims on their way to Canterbury. The Talbot was typical of the coaching inns used by Lach-Szyrma and his charges on their journey to Scotland. In London they stayed in the far grander Clarendon Hotel where some members of the Zamoyski family were in residence in 1820.

A journey from Dover to London lasts one day: it would be more, but a perfect road, flat as a table top, makes an overnight stop unnecessary. You can make this journey in a carriage or a stagecoach. The local carriage is cheap and quick and justifies Lord Byron's description:

On with the horses! Off to Canterbury!
Tramp, tramp o'er pebble, and splash, splash through puddle;
Hurrah! how swiftly speeds the post so merry!

The road is on the flatlands of Kent. It is neither wide, as Englishmen grudge the loss of good land, nor is it lined with trees, as everywhere on the mainland there is a hedge on both sides, separating the road from the fields. The soil is mainly calcareous, as in the vicinity of Calais. Some geologists speculate that France and England were formerly one land and believe that the sea made the gap between them which is now called the Straits of Calais. The soil, judging from the crops, did not seem to be fertile. The wheat which we could see from the road was thin and short and the ears were thinner and shorter than Polish ones. A lot of hops are grown and there are many orchards. Kentish cherries are famous and a pleasant cherry wine is made from them. In this region you will never see large villages or as many settlements as you would in Poland. Here and there a few houses are grouped, other houses are isolated. All the houses are of stone, roofed with brick tiles or shingles. They are very neat and pleasant, although generally speaking too small. Some of them are so small that they seem to be trinkets, to be looked at rather than to be lived in and more useful for a hermit than for a farming family. But some farmers live in somewhat bigger houses. In front of almost every house there will be a garden full of flowers. They are not planted in straight beds as in Poland, but in informal clumps, according to the owner's taste. The paths are of gravel.

Fields are divided; you would not see cornfields as extensive as those in Poland anywhere in England. Fields are like gardens: they are separated by ditches and hedges which give them, when you look down on them from a hill, a form of chessboard, coloured by the variety of the crops. You will not see forests there either but this does not mean that this part of the country is without trees. Here and there in the so called parks, the gardens of the English landowners, great trees stand out darkly. Between them one catches glimpses of wonderful mansions, with cattle and flocks of sheep grazing on the meadows in front of them. Sometimes magnificent splendour and pastoral simplicity are connected with each other so skilfully that art does not detract anything from nature's charm.

Surrounded by such charming views we arrived in Canterbury, which is a considerable town. Its origins go back to antiquity; the Romans called it Durovernum. It was the capital of Kent under the rule of Ethelred, the most powerful of the Saxon kings. The Christian faith was brought to the idolatrous Saxons in 596. They were converted by the Benedictines[1], the ruins of whose monastery you can see. The development of the city has been shaped by the course of history; today it is inhabited by merchants and craftsman. The Cathedral, of a beautiful Gothic architectural style, is worth seeing: it is considered to be one of the oldest churches in England. Erasmus[2] from Rotterdam

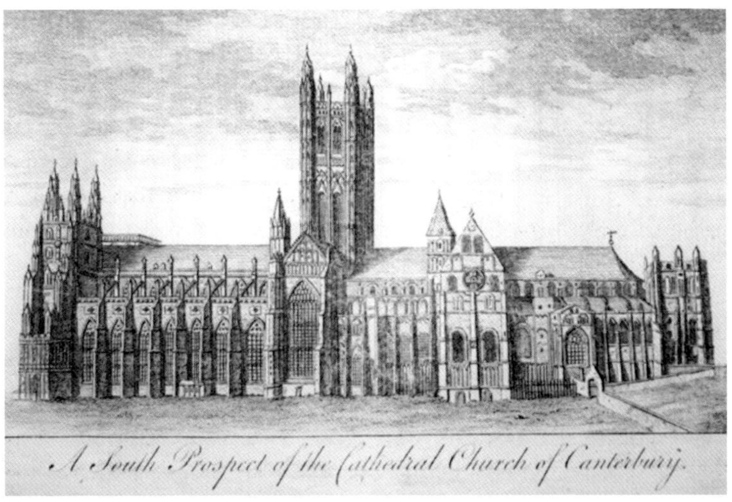

Canterbury Cathedral. There was probably a church on the site before the arrival of St Augustine in 597. The tower of the church built by Archbishop Lanfranc in the 1070s survived till 1832.

mentions it in these words: 'tanta maiestate ses erigit in coelum, ut procul etiam intuentibus religionem incutiat' (It rises up to the sky with such grandeur that even from a distance those who are looking at it are overcome by religious adoration). It was once famous for the tomb of St Thomas à Becket[3] who, in 1170, at the foot of the altar, suffered the same fate at the hands of Henry II's assassins as Stanisław Szczepanowski.[4]Later, Henry VIII, having seen in Becket's behaviour towards his predecessor an insult to the royal majesty, charged him four centuries after his death. This was a strange historical event. As the saint did not appear before the court, the king pronounced him a criminal in a legally valid judgment. As a result, his name was erased from the calendar, his corpse was burnt by an executioner and his ashes scattered to the winds. There was a time when hundreds of pilgrims came yearly to the saint's tomb; amongst them was the French King Louis VII.

The Archbishop of Canterbury is also the primate of the country. Although, during the reign of Henry VIII, the Protestant religion became the official one, the former ranks and titles of the Roman Catholic hierarchy have survived to this day. From the time of Augustine, the first Archbishop, until today there have been ninety-nine who have served as the primate, amongst them the famous Cranmer,[5] who openly supported the Reformation.

In a side chapel of the church there is the interesting tomb of Edward,[6] called the Black Prince. His statue is enormous. Cast in bronze, in royal robes, he rests his head on a helmet and puts his hands in a gesture of prayer on a sword which is so heavy that none of us would be able to lift it. We are belittled by the strength of the dead. The ancient black armour, which he used to wear in battle, hangs over the tombstone.

Halfway on the journey to London, we noticed an extraordinary increase of traffic on the road. Frequently we were passing carriages and stagecoaches; the latter were quite new to us. All of them were beautifully oil-painted and on every one was written, in gold letters, its name, place of departure and destination. Many men and women of different ages and status were sitting on top and inside them. Each coach was drawn by four splendid horses. The coachmen of the stagecoaches were dressed in wide baize frock coats, were vigorous and hearty and were driving from the coachman's box. The coachmen of the carriages were slimmer and wore yellow leather trousers. They were driving mounted on the horses and everything around them was so clean and neat that they looked like dolls. What we observed seemed to be a parade for pleasure but the serious faces and intelligent appearance of the travellers made us realize that necessity was the reason for their travel. Our surprise deepened when we were told that at least sixty such vehicles run daily between Dover and London and they reach the half waypoint at the same time. I counted, on and inside a few of the coaches, as many as fourteen to seventeen people. What incomparable activity and traffic!

It is not the custom in England to travel using your own horses, everyone travels by carriage or stagecoach. Even the wealthiest do so. In this way you go on a journey much faster and more cheaply, without wasted time arising from disabled horses or broken down vehicles and without tedious delays. Those who choose to travel by private carriage will hire two or four splendid horses but it is cheaper to go by coach. In England there are two kinds of these, mail coaches and stagecoaches. Mail coaches belong to the government and are used to carry letters; they are outnumbered by stagecoaches, which are cheaper and owned privately. In both cases a fare is fixed and there is no haggling over it. They are equally comfortable. However, mail coaches are the preferred means of transport, as they are used to facilitate correspondence and have to reach their destination on time. Whether you have a seat outside or inside determines the price. You pay more for the latter, as they are more comfortable on cold and rainy days. When the weather is good it is better, especially for foreigners, to take outside seats on a coach. If they are interested in England they should observe and study the view. At every station you pay a few pence to the driver as well as to the ostler who, as soon as you arrive, is at your beck and call and helps to un-harness and harness the horses. You do not give anyone more than the recognised tip. The horses are harnessed in no more than five minutes and then you are off again, not slowly, in a German way, but at a trot, though never at a gallop which could be damaging. The owners of carriages and coaches are often innkeepers, licensed by the government.

At change stations, a traveller is given an unusual and all too rare polite welcome. The host goes out to meet him, opens the door of the vehicle, lowers the steps and offers an arm to lean on. It is an English custom that you neither hold out your hand to a person who is getting off a vehicle nor take their arm, but, respectfully, you only offer the support of yours. A traveller does not experience less politeness from the hostess. She will be waiting in front of the door where she greets him kindly before leading him to the assigned rooms where she asks for orders. If he wishes to eat a meal before the horses have been changed he will be served with everything he orders and even if he does not want anything, the politeness of the proprietors will not be affected. With the same politeness as they received him, they walk him to the vehicle and wish him a safe journey and ask to be remembered favourably. Such a kind reception at the very beginning was a good omen for us of the hospitality of the English nation. The famous hospitality of primitive people may be compared to that of civilized countries. By carefully meeting the needs of the travellers, inn keepers prevent them from becoming a burden on anyone else. This attentiveness, as it is a salutary result of education, is at the same time a sure sign of its high level.

We stopped for dinner in Rochester. Here we had an opportunity to sample the English cuisine. We were served with a soup which was neither thick nor thin and which none of us could eat nor guess its ingredients. Unable to analyse its contents, we called it a sister of the Spartan soup of which no philologist, also due to lack of sufficient evidence, has been able to determine the ingredients. After soup they brought us roast-beef, the basis and crown of the English table. John Bull cannot imagine a good dinner without it. We expected the equivalent of Polish roast beef but it was not similar to it at all: it was a huge and beautiful chunk of fatty beef, not roasted but only scalded. When you cut it with a knife blood oozed out. Therefore, although it may have been faithfully prepared according to a London recipe, we were disgusted and had no appetite for it. So we did not eat that delicacy either. Since then, having been put off once, wherever we stopped for dinner we used to go as a delegation to the kitchen, as we wanted roast meat to be cooked longer and on a spit. I do not mention this in order to insult the English cuisine or to infer, as many writers have tried to prove, that the national enthusiasm for boxing, atrocities and murders stems from their liking for semi-raw meat dishes. Taking into account the proverb: 'Every country has its own customs' and the fact that I came to have a liking for a cuisine which I found more nourishing and healthier than more refined French and German cuisines, I mention it only to advise those who intend to travel to England to choose dishes in accordance with their national tastes before they get used to English food. You can get at every change station: delicious hams, tongues, fish, butter, and cheeses. You will find them in the entrance halls displayed behind glass in the most beautiful way. The wisest thing to do is to choose something from this selection rather than risk ordering something you are unable to eat and for which you sometimes have to pay a lot.

The price of the food is known and it is not very high. Finding wine to buy does not require a lot of effort; it is expensive due to heavy duties and you can rarely get an un-adulterated bottle. It is better to take it for granted, that the wine the natives drink themselves must be both the best and the cheapest. In this case I would advise you to follow the opinion and taste of the majority rather than your own.

Shooters Hill is a few miles away from Rochester. From its peak I saw the Thames for the first time, meandering in a wide channel towards the sea. Ships were sailing on it, as though on another road, carrying riches for England from faraway lands. You can see London from here. On the basis of what I could see, London seemed to me huge and because of its vast suburbs I did not know where its beginning and end were. It was covered by the thick and foggy atmosphere which is characteristic of England. Smoke from hard bituminous coal, which was hanging like a motionless cloud, dimmed the view. It was nearing sunset and the sun with its last beams gave the view the dirty red colour of blackened glass. I could see the hazy dome of St Paul's Church and the gothic towers of Westminster Abbey which dominated the surrounding area.

Having known that I was approaching the biggest and the wealthiest capital city in the world, I was overcome by unusual emotion. I directed my utmost attention and imagination to everything we came across on our way, especially shortly before nightfall when every outline became indistinct. Having read and heard a lot about England and Englishmen, their literature and customs, I could scarcely believe that I was already amongst them and so close to their capital city, and that soon I should see everything with my own eyes. The palaces of mighty lords and rich merchants, which I saw from the road, were wonderful in themselves; the night and the mist made them loom even larger. In my imagination I could see the splendour, luxury, virtues and misdeeds with which wealth is often associated. People walking in groups or on their own may have been thinking about attackers and robbers, but such fear of them is now groundless. The honorary guild of gentlemen called highwaymen, whose members, gun in hand, once charged travellers a fee for entrance to London, no longer exists. The vigilance of the government disarmed that band, and education of a higher quality and the spread of morality amongst the common people have stopped it from coming into existence again. If you hear anything about such a band nowadays it is from old romances or from nurses' tales, told to frighten children. The increase in population in this part of England itself contributed a lot to the disappearance of highwaymen.

It was late in the evening when we arrived in London. We were travelling fast in a closed vehicle, so it was difficult to see anything in the city apart from brilliantly illuminated streets, merchants' shops and endless numbers of houses, among which we seemed to be travelling as though in a forest. We stayed in the end in the Clarendon Hotel in Old Bond Street.

NOTES:

1 In 596 Pope Gregory I sent St Augustine and forty Benedictine monks to Kent to establish the authority of the papacy over the church in England. The Benedictines were not a missionary order and most of heathen Britain was converted to Christianity by monks of the Celtic church.

2 Desiderius Erasmus (1466-1536). A Dutch humanist and scholar, he taught at both Oxford and Cambridge. His editing of the Greek New Testament and criticism of the abuses of the Catholic Church contributed significantly to the development of the Reformation.

3 Thomas à Becket (1118-70). The first Englishman to hold high office under the Norman kings, Becket had helped to secure the accession of Henry II and, as chancellor, worked to restore royal power over the magnates. As archbishop he fought equally stubbornly to prevent the subordination of the Church to the state. By declaring himself head of the Church in England, Henry VIII succeeded where Henry II had failed.

4 St Stanisław Szczepanowski (1030-79). The Polish Bishop of Cracow, he was murdered by assassins hired by King Boleslaw Smialy on the steps of the altar of the church at Skalka. In his sermons, the bishop had been reproaching the king for his cruelty and debauchery.

5 Thomas Cranmer (1489-1556). The first Protestant Archbishop of Canterbury, Cranmer declared the marriage of Henry VIII to Catherine of Aragon null and void, over-riding the authority of the pope. He was the author of the first Prayer Book and of the 42 Articles of Religion, on which the 32 Articles are based. On the restoration of Catholicism by Mary Tudor he was burnt at the stake.

6 Edward, Prince of Wales (1330-1376). The son of Edward III, the title the Black Prince was probably first used in the sixteenth century. A brilliant general, he led his troops to victory at Crécy, Poitiers and Calais and for fourteen years was the effective ruler of Aquitaine.

Chapter Three

Hotel Clarendon. Breakfast. Stroll in a Town. Weekday in London. Sunday. Hyde Park. Cockneys.

I have already mentioned that a traveller cannot be indifferent towards any inn he might come across, therefore, in this chapter, I want to describe an English hotel. I will take as an example the Clarendon, which is said to be one of the better hotels in London.[1]

On entering a hotel a traveller will be met by a fat doorkeeper, carrying a large silver-plated staff as a symbol of his position, who will tell him if there are any rooms available. If yes, a waiter will lead him to the rooms. You go through halls and stairs covered with carpets which are so beautiful and clean that it is a pity you have to walk on them. Bedrooms are usually situated on the second floor and a drawing room on the first one. You entertain your guests there as, in England, no one of a good social position sits or is paid a visit in a bedroom. It is a private place, where no one apart from the owner is allowed to enter. Drawing rooms are spacious and richly furnished. The whole floor is covered with carpets, similar to those in the bedrooms but of better quality. There are mirrors, small tables and all the comforts a sybarite can think of. Beds are large; two or three people could sleep in them at once. People in England, especially within one family, do not flinch from this. On a bed they use mattresses and one or two flannel blankets, under which they put a sheet, so that they do not rub the body. Only the pillows are filled with down. Bed linen is changed in the presence of a guest. No one travels here with their own bedding; everyone sleeps on what is available in the place where they stay. Beds are old-fashioned in shape, supported by four tall posts from which thick red curtains hang. You can draw the curtains when it is cold because the bedrooms are commonly not heated. There are pockets for money, a watch and scents at the top of a bed. A thick rope made of cotton or silk, with a wide tassel at the end, is attached to the bottom part to help you to get up when you are in bed. Two other ropes hang from the sides of a bed to call the servants. In the drawing rooms they are on both sides of a fireplace. Sometimes they are replaced with a hidden spring – when you move it, the bell rings. The bells are in the flats below the ground floor where there are rooms for domestic servants and a kitchen. Each bell has a number by which servants identify the room in which someone rang. In three or at the most five minutes after a bell has been rung, one of the servants will be in the room and says: 'Sir?' This is the correct way for him to answer. Everything takes place in silence: you cannot hear the bell, because it is far downstairs, nor can you hear the coming servant because, when walking on the carpeted stairs wearing bootees instead of shoes, he will not make any noise. If you did not know the way bells work, you might think that it was magical and that servants were able to foresee the wishes of their masters. Therefore you can live in London as in a desert and devote your time, without being distracted, to contemplation. If the windows do not look out onto the street, you have no cause to complain as Boileau[2] did in Paris:

> Qui frappe l'air, bon Dieu! de ces lugubres cris?
> Est-ce donc pour veiller qu'on se couche à Paris?
> (Who, good God , is rending the air with gloomy cries ?
> Are we going to bed in Paris in order to lie awake?)

Servants in hotels are elegantly dressed. The owner, when taking in a servant, talks to him about the wardrobe he should have. Girls are dressed in percale[3] and on Sundays they wear beautiful muslin dresses. Lackeys wear decent black tailcoats and black silk or white cotton stockings. A foreigner, who in his own country is not used to such well dressed domestic servants, may easily mistake a servant for a master and by mistake give a servant the respect due to his master. He will then be laughed at behind his back. Servants are obedient but not obsequious and are very polite to a guest. The guest should not think that they do it for his or her pretty face. The elegant and expensive clothes in which they serve and the politeness with which they pay court to the guests have to be generously paid for. You will realise this when you are about to leave. In order that they should not be forgotten, though without bowing down, since even servants have English pride, maids, the doorkeeper and those who clean the shoes are on the watch by the door. Each of them has to be paid what they deserve. In a way it is the duty of a guest not to forget any of them, as their only income is what they receive from the travellers. This must be enough to support them and buy clothes, as the owner of the hotel does not pay them. It often happens that the servants pay the owner for giving them the opportunity to serve, as such positions, especially in big hotels, are considered to be well paid. Hoping they will be well rewarded for good service makes the service perfect. People, even if they are well paid, will be dilatory if they can expect no reward for extra effort.

Hotels are furnished in the same way as private houses, so a traveller can find in them the same comforts as they have at home. For that reason English hotels are superior to all hotels in Europe and everything which has been said about them can be said about the interiors of private houses. The only difference is the fact that the latter are furnished with the comforts necessary for family living: hotels are supplied with everything that is needed to live the most luxurious life. You can have breakfasts, dinners, suppers, drinks of all kinds, and newspapers. You can have dinner for one person or for a dozen: you only need to let the chef know when he comes every morning for orders.

The first day of our stay in London was full of very interesting experiences and from breakfast onwards aroused our curiosity. Having gone downstairs to the drawing room in the morning (because no one eats breakfast or dinner in their bedroom unless they are ill), we found a table laden with breakfast dishes. There was coffee and tea and boiling water in a large samovar on the table. Next to them, in different places but not without a certain order, were toast, bread, butter, soft-boiled eggs, cold roast beef, roast pork and ham. Preserves and ice cream were served later. At the sight of such a variety of things I thought about the Egyptian years of plenty. But no one, even with a good appetite, would be able to take advantage of such abundance. It would be difficult to eat everything, even in small amounts and, as you do not have to pay for everything, everyone eats as much as they want and only what they like. You pay only a normal fixed price for breakfast. In our country it would seem high but in England it was not exceptional. Having been in England for only a short time, we did not immediately acquire an Englishman's appetite for so many delicacies. We preferred, according to the old custom, to have a modest breakfast so we started with drinking coffee. The coffee was already made and placed on the table, but it was not good. English coffee is weaker than Polish and its taste is different because they do not roast it for long. So we could do nothing else but start to drink tea. There was a silver teapot and black and green tea in tins - they mix both kinds of tea together. You need to be very confident before you start to prepare tea in England. It is never brought on the table ready to drink; you need to make it yourself according to your companions' tastes, which is not easy when you have many companions and there might be tea experts among them. If there is a lady in a room her task is to make tea; if there are only men, he who is confident enough to please everyone makes tea. In England, in order to make tea, you have to possess appropriate knowledge and everyone tries to acquire it. Making tea is an office of honour; even a seat closer to a teapot is more honourable than one at a distance.

Shortly after breakfast, which went on for a long time because of so many delicacies, I went out. Only the unfamiliarity of that breakfast prevented me from being impatient and regretting the passing of time. I did not know where to go and I did not care. I was walking in the streets and squares, over the bridges, looking at shops, vehicles, tombs, dresses, monuments and people. Whenever I wanted to stop somewhere for longer, crowds of people, going in the same direction as I was, pushed me and took me with them as though in a flood and as if they wanted to tell me that what I had seen was nothing compared to what I was to see further on. I let the flood carry me and, at the end, came back home tired. When I was thinking about what I had come across during my walk I realised that, instead of a picture of London, I had chaos in my head. The variety of elements of which the capital consists, instead of having taught me anything, made me dizzy. I saw and knew a lot, but in the confusion of things I had seen it was impossible to find a connection and fit everything into a whole. Many things were not what they seemed to be at first glance and many more remained a puzzle to which I needed a clue. It is impossible to get to know London in one day. The outline I am presenting here was made two years later, after I had been to London three times. It concerns only the superficial form of the city.

A day in London is different from a day anywhere else. Each part, even each hour, has its own features which made it different from another. The variety of these characteristics depends on the style of life, class and vocation of its citizens. Characteristic ways of behaving have been established for so long that the appearance of London has remained almost unchanged for nearly 100 years. Today, as it was a hundred years ago, a workman and a man of fashion do not get up at the same time. When it is time for an exhausted craftsman to go to bed is when a thief should be on the alert. You do not go to a bank, the court, the theatre or an opera at the same time. These and changing occupations make London look different at different times. The streets are never completely quiet and at midnight there is more traffic in London than in many towns at midday. It is shortly before dawn before everything is quiet, when streets become empty and citizens can hear the night watchmen more clearly. Dressed in grey coats, with a rattle, torch and a truncheon in hand, the watchmen are announcing the time and predicting the state of the morning's weather; sunny, cloudy, wet or foggy. In a country where the weather is changing constantly it is helpful to receive this kind of information while still in bed.

Fishermen on the Thames begin their activities at daybreak. Their voices can be heard early in the morning at Billingsgate. The next group of people to get up are the market gardeners. They arrive on huge wagons filled with vegetables and fruit at Covent Garden[4] where, with rare skill, they display vegetables, fruit and flowers on market stalls which attract potential buyers. Because it is so early in the morning, no one with better taste than the stallholders and cooks can admire their talents. At seven o'clock it is still quiet in the streets and it is as late as eight o'clock before small shops are opened. You can see cooks here and there in front of the houses – they wipe their sleepy eyes and buy from market traders something which is similar in colour to cream but tastes different. By this time London becomes even gloomier as smoke from kitchen stoves rises from thousands of chimneys. If the weather is nice, it is like a dark cloud over the city; if the weather is rainy, it drags the soot down and makes the air full of an unpleasant smell of sulphur. Nine o'clock is the hour for breakfast and later on traffic in the streets becomes heavier. Bigger shops are opened and vehicles and stagecoaches go in various directions carrying merchants, traders, office workers and doctors. At a time when you can observe such a rush at the east end of London, people in the west part of the city are still asleep and it is as quiet there as if the sun were still over the antipodes. This is the world of the so-called great and fashionable, of people who go to bed and get up at a different time from common people. They need more time to rest after the parties, games, dances and concerts which finish late at night. Even at eleven o'clock the streets are still empty there and it is as late as one o'clock before you can see fine vehicles and elegantly dressed people in the city and traffic then becomes even heavier. At this time ladies from the west end of London go to the shops for ribbons, scents and love affairs, sometimes in order to begin a new intrigue or to finish an old one, but most often to do something to kill time. Paying visits is a wonderful way of killing time. It is done not to show friendship or respect but to conform to the fashion. 'Someone paid me a visit, I must visit him, but it would be better not to see him and not to know him: I will leave him a visiting card, it does not matter if he is at home or not, and that's that!' Many of those who go out to pay visits think and act in this way. Such visits last till four o'clock and after that the great world disappears and gossip and backbiting appear.

The normal traffic in the city is not lighter, although Bond Street, Piccadilly and Regent Street are deserted by great figures. There is still the small world left, that is the world of the rabble, living from hand to mouth. You can observe the rush hour, particularly in the City, at four o'clock. Then you must make your way between capitalists and bankers who walk slowly, thinking about interest rates on amounts of money which, lent to governments, might support or complicate the financial interests of nations. Profiteers are dependent on world-wide events. Many political economists and diplomats would be able to learn something from them.

The first to eat dinner in London are those who are the poorest, because they eat when they have finished work. The latest are those who live in the West End of London, as they are rich, have food in

Harding, Howell & Co., Pall Mall 1796-1820. A fashionable drapers, typical of the shops which dazzled visitors to London by their plate glass windows, gas lighting and gilded shelves.

excess and have to wait long before they develop an appetite. Here, between six and seven o'clock, numerous vehicles pass each other, all equally magnificent, and occupied by formally dressed ladies and gentlemen. The rattle of wheels and the noise of knockers on the doors where dinners are to be served are then unbearable. During dinner calm is restored and you can cross the streets without any problem but in three or four hours (English dinners last a long time) the carriages appear again. While plays and operas in the theatres, and balls in private houses continue, the noise lasts, with short intervals, till almost two o'clock in the morning. Even when it is getting lighter and street lamps give out a dim light, you can hear vehicles moving in the distant streets. Sometimes you see one in which the occupants are pale and swaying wearily. Women, exhausted after being up all night, wish they were back at home and had had some sleep; but the rest will only give them energy for new weariness. They live a fast but short life!

In the evening London seems to be much more beautiful than during the day. Since gas lamps[5] were introduced, it has gained much charm. However, you cannot say that London is better illuminated than Paris. They do not yet have lamps hanging over a street. Lamps, according to the old tradition, are on the posts on both sides of the street and although gaps between them are not very big, they do not light the area far from them. Most of the light in the streets comes from the shops. They have been illuminated by gas for a few years now and look like enchanted castles. You only have to look at the shop windows to find out what is being sold there. The goods are arranged in the windows in the strangest way in order to attract the attention of passers-by. For an even better effect, there are mirrors inside the shops which reflect the goods repeatedly. The most interesting for me was one of the shops in the city. All the walls and pillars were covered with mirrors and, when you entered, you did not know where the shop began and ended and it did not feel safe to walk through it. Booksellers, butchers, shoemakers, tailors, furriers and those who sell fruit, flowers, glass and crystal illuminate their shops equally impressively. Particularly charming are jewellers' shops and chemists, where there is a custom of displaying in the windows different chemical distillations in large glass jars. You can see there the jewels and colours of the world. Everything is illuminated and you can see crowds of people and vehicles in the streets. The picture is like an exceptional celebration with which only the indifference of the citizens seems out of place. What appears wonderful to a foreigner is something common and ordinary for the Londoner. You will see the biggest crowds at the theatres. The followers of Aphrodite, the goddess of Paphos,[6] will be on parade there and thieves and cutpurses will be on the watch. At midnight, those who are careful slide the second bolt across the door. Even the bravest do not feel at ease when walking in the empty streets of St Giles or on the banks of the Thames. The policing of London[7] is not of a high quality. In fact, policemen here are only watchmen and they are sometimes in league with the thieves. Everyone then must look after his own safety. For unprovoked attacks, violent thefts, or forcible entry you can be sentenced to life imprisonment. Those who go to bed last are the printers, who are preparing newspapers for the morning, and the thrifty Jews in Duke Street. The Jews are busy all night, receiving stolen goods from thieves and melting down silver and gold.

As you can see, there is no quiet moment in London. The activities of this capital city join each other at their beginnings and endings, like the snake of eternity. Fishermen are at the beginning of the snake and Jews are its end: fishermen announce what they have caught overnight but the latter are silent on what they have hidden. The most skilled writer could not encompass the whole scene. Anyone brave enough to attempt it would have to write the history of all virtues, endeavours, losses, mistakes, misfortunes, and crimes. Repeated day after day, nothing new is left for the morrow. Considering all that happens in London within twenty four hours, one could repeat Juvenal's[8] words to the descendants of Rome:

> Nil erit ulterius quod nostris moribus addat Posteritas.
> (Posterity will not add anything new to our morals)

This is the fate of all large cities that they are full of crimes and yet the home of many virtues. The picture is always the same, only the colours are different.

On weekdays London always looks the same: on Sunday it looks quite different. This is the result of the commandment: 'Remember the Lord's Day to keep it holy.' In no other country is this as strictly observed as in England, where this day is still called by the biblical word, the Sabbath. Sunday mornings are as quiet as though the people seen on weekdays had suddenly died. Closed shops detract splendour from the streets, but the streets themselves are not blocked by a mass of carriages and vehicles, or filled with offensive shouts and imprecations. Everyone, no matter who, is neatly dressed and behaves in a respectable manner. If someone were to hum a song when walking in a street on Sunday he would be judged in the public eye as a desecrator of the Lord's Day. This behaviour, which anywhere else would be considered as innocent pleasure on a rest day, is seen in England as inexcusable thoughtlessness. But silence and modesty do not last all day and later on the traffic becomes heavier. As soon as you hear the bells, the city is transformed: people leave their houses and the streets become full of those who walk or drive to church. After two hours of quiet everyone will be going home. The pattern is repeated in the afternoon, as there are two church services. When the second service is finished, that is at four o'clock, those who celebrate Sunday in a strict

Kensington Palace. Originally the home of the Earl of Nottingham, it became Kensington Palace when sold to William III. Suffering from asthma, he wanted a palace west of the stifling atmosphere of London.

way go straight home from church. They spend the rest of the day reading the Bible and studying other religious writings. Others, and they are the majority and include wealthy Londoners, go for a walk in Hyde Park.

Hyde Park is a garden in the English style. It is not perfect as it is more like a large meadow of coarse grass than a garden. It covers a considerable area and is cut by roads and paths going in many different directions, much used by vehicles and people. Here and there you can see grazing cattle, but the few isolated trees do not give enough shade to make it a pastoral scene. There is a river flowing through the park which, due to its shape, is called the Serpentine. One end flows from the adjoining Kensington Garden, which could more appropriately be called a garden. With its regular paths and lanes it is more like an old French one but, even here, you can find traces of the English style. There are plenty of trees and the citizens of London like to visit this place to enjoy the shade of the ancient elms and feed the swans swimming in the river. The swans are a great curiosity for the ordinary people who rarely go outside the city. Whenever they talk to foreigners, they never forget to ask them whether they went to Kensington Garden and saw the swans. This is an inquiry made by cockneys.

Cockney[9] is a humorous name given to Londoners living in the City within the sound of the bells of Bow Church. They rarely leave the City even once a year and they do not know anything about the world apart from their shops and offices, where they are condemned to endless work. Therefore they have odd thoughts about the outside world. There are many anecdotes circulating about them but I will write about only one, which explains the origin of the term cockney. A father from the City went one day with his son to a village in the country. They heard a horse neighing and the surprised son said: 'Father! What is that horse doing?' His father answered: 'The horse crows'. They went further and heard a cock crowing. The son again asked his father. Father! What is that cock doing?' The father answered: 'The cock neighs.' That is why those farming experts coming from London have been called cockneys.

Anyone who wants to get to know Londoners should walk in Hyde Park and Kensington Garden on Sunday. The whole area will be filled with crowds of people, vehicles and riders. The din and the diverse mixture of people will be an amusing and even informative sight. You will see there haughty lords and thrifty merchants, fat aldermen and poor workmen, people of all classes displaying their typical addictions, morals and quirks as if they were taking part in a parade. It is a panorama of London's citizens. There is no other place where you can see them gathered in larger numbers and see so closely the traits of their characters. Splendour, sentimentalism, heartiness, flirtatiousness and numerous vices typical of both sexes and divided equally among all the classes appear there as in a big show. Everyone, confident of their own perfection, carries himself or herself in a particular way, which strikes, amuses or makes an attentive spectator laugh. No person with experience of the world, although not a pupil of Lavater,[10] would have reason to complain in Hyde Park about the lack of opportunities to make observations and authors and painters will find in Hyde Park inspiration for many humorous descriptions and caricatures. Momus[11] is on the lookout.

NOTES:

1 The Clarendon was reputed to be one of the three best hotels in London and to serve the best and most expensive dinners.

2 Nicolas Boileau (1636-1711), French poet and critic.

3 Percale is a closely woven cotton fabric.

4 Covent Garden was originally the garden of the convent of St Peter's, Westminster. The piazza was designed by Inigo Jones and stalls for the sale of fruit and vegetables were being set up by 1636.

5 Gas from William Murdoch's works was being used to light a factory in Soho by the late 1770s. The Gas Light and Coke Company, which provided the gas for street lighting, received a royal charter in 1812.

6 Paphos was the ancient capital of Crete and the birthplace of the goddess of love, who rose from the foam. In the eighteenth century Crete was associated with prostitution.

7 The policing of London was not reformed till 1829 when Sir Robert Peel created a trained and adequately paid force.

8 Decimus Juvenal (c55-c140), Roman lawyer, satirist and moralist.

9 Cockney was the name given to the malformed eggs sometime laid by young hens or to babies nursed for too long by their mothers. It was used by country people to describe townsmen ignorant of country ways and was not limited to Londoners till the seventeenth century.

10 Johann Kaspar Lavater (1761-1801), Swiss physiognomist, poet and theologian who attempted to raise physiognomy to a science.

11 Momus was the Greek son of night and was the personification of censoriousness.

Chapter Four

Superficiality of London. Topography. Squares. Inscriptions on the Houses. Ways of Recommending Goods. A Loan. Interesting Places.

No matter from which direction you approach London, the respectable tenements, large suburbs, innumerable houses, and the high domes and towers of churches which a foreigner sees in front of him, indicate that he is entering a huge and wealthy capital city. I noticed that the vast size of London makes the most impression on you when you cross the Thames and see so many bridges joining the shores of the river and the crowds of people walking over them.

The appearance of London houses is not impressive and often gives an unfavourable impression. They are made of brick, of only two or three floors and are not plastered. The windows are smaller and there are fewer than one sees anywhere else. This is probably due to the severe wet climate and the burdensome tax on windows. In the majority of cases, when the houses were being built, no one took into consideration the architectural style of the exterior and thought only of comfort. People used to decorate doors, stairs and windows in the Greek style. Although superficially impressive, because the houses are made of brick of a different colour, the decorations look as though they are attached to them and do not form a harmonious whole. Bricks are not as durable as stone. Houses built of stone are rare in London and are insignificant in comparison with brick ones. Bricks can be smoothed over with stucco, which makes buildings look attractive when they are new and before rain and the soot from coal fires have stained them. Surprisingly, there are some areas, especially in the City, where there are still small and miserable houses. The new parts of the city, particularly the western ones, are wonderfully developed with houses of similar design. Joined together in terraces they create beautiful streets. Englishmen's palaces are in the country; in the capital city even the wealthiest citizens live in modest houses which are almost always built and furnished in a similar way. Even the apartments of their kings, like St James's Palace where the father of the present king used to live, are not characterised by anything special, and Carlton House,[1] one of the residences of the present king, is not even called a palace but a house. 'House' in this connection means more than an ordinary house for a citizen and less than a palace. Nevertheless, it does not make it an appropriate residence for the monarch of such a powerful country. St James's, which has been squalid and abandoned for a long time, will look better soon. They are converting it into a picture gallery, which is to be up to 190 feet long, and will be comparable with the galleries of the Louvre and the Vatican. Up till now its courtyard has been a place for military parades.

The quality of the cobbles differs according to the grandeur of the streets themselves. In the newly built parts of the city and on the wide streets it is generally good. There are pavements made of ashlar on both sides. These are so wide that between five and seven people can comfortably walk next to each other. In the City, that is in the old part of London, pavements are not good due to the narrowness of the streets, but even there the comfort of pedestrians has been taken into consideration. There are small connecting streets, the so-called lanes, which are well paved but cannot be used by horses and vehicles. In the newest parts of the city they build streets by Macadam's method.[2] When I was in London, the New Road had already been built in such a way. This is through Paddington and Islington, old villages on the northern side of London which have now been incorporated into the city. They have already started to replace cobbles with Macadam's roads in other parts. This is made easier in England by the abundance of calcareous stone. Like our black marble, it is soft and, under pressure, chippings are crushed together to form a compact surface. Because of the humid climate there are no clouds of dust over the roads and it is not necessary to spray water over them. The desire for quietness in the streets, which contributes to the comfort of life and is not possible where there are cobbles, encourages people to get rid of them. In St James's Square, which is inhabited only by rich people, they are preparing to create a Macadam road.

In order not to get lost in London you should acquaint yourself with its topography. It is not easy to get to know it. There are people who were born in London, have lived there ever since and still do not know it. Anyone who comes to the capital for the first time should get a map and familiarise himself with it before visiting the city, otherwise he will wander around like a lost sheep, asking for directions after every step. You can buy such a map in any bookshop and you should get the most recent edition, as every year a few new streets appear in London. The increase in population, industry and wealth contribute to the continuing growth of the city. In the places where forty years ago there were only large fields today you can see the most wonderful buildings. Many villages which some time ago were separate communities have been incorporated into London; other villages are linked to it. Villages which are further away, where bankers and merchants live, are now decent sized towns.

Today London is one and a half miles long and two thirds of a mile wide. The population amounts to 1,360,000. The city comprises three main parts: first the City, the core of London and its oldest part, is on the east; second Westminster which is, broadly speaking, the whole western part of London; third Southwark, the part of the city on the right bank of the Thames. The City and Southwark are inhabited by the poorer merchants, craftsmen and the common people. Hunt,[3] Cobbett[4] and Burdett[5] call the political tune among them during elections.[6] There are 23 hospitals, 95 shelters for the poor and more than 300 churches of different religious sects and denominations. Statistics are not accurate and change every year due to the continuous growth of the city. There are so many difficulties when collecting statistics that no one in recent years has written a book which might begin to satisfy your curiosity. You can find some detailed information on this subject but so far it has not been brought together.

London, as it is situated on a plain, does not have any significant and noticeable points which would help a foreigner to find directions. Therefore there is no other city in which you could so easily get lost. If you want to orientate yourself, you need to remember the main streets and squares, so that you can go to them when you are getting lost. Even someone who was born in London would have difficulty in directing you to some of the less important places. There are three rows of main streets leading towards the City, from west to east. The first is the one mentioned above, the New Road on the northern edge

Map of London. By the nineteenth century London was the largest city in the world and growing fast. An up-to-date map was essential for visitors exploring it.

LONDON,
and its
ENVIRONS.
ESSEX ROAD
MILE END ROAD
STEPNEY
COMMERCIAL ROAD
LIMEHOUSE
IX
XIV
Canal to Croydon &c.
Sun Tavern Fields
Ground belonging to the London Dock Company
Footpath to Stepney and Limehouse
Limehouse and Bromley Cut
THAMES

of London. The second one is Oxford Street, one of the longest, which is extended by Holborn, Newgate, Cheapside, and Cornhill, which then forks into Bishopsgate and Leadenhall Street. The third row of streets is along the Thames: Westminster, the Strand, Fleet Street and Thames Street. They, as main roads, are crossed by side streets in the shape of ribs. Among them, the longest are St John's Street and Tottenham Court Road, and the most beautiful are Pall-Mall and Piccadilly, Regent Street with its colonnade and Portland Place. Some streets, like the last one, are called places due to their width.

The Thames, which meanders through London, may also help one to find one's bearings. There are five bridges over it, namely: London Bridge which is the first one when coming from the sea. This may become the second one, if the tunnel under the Thames[7] is successful. The other bridges, after London Bridge, are: Southwark, Blackfriars, Waterloo and Westminster. Waterloo Bridge, as the name suggests, has been built in memory of the victory and opened in 1817 to the ringing of bells and firing of cannons. Wellington, mounted on the horse which had carried him during the war, was the first to cross. The whole bridge is made of iron and is the work of the architect Rennie.[8] It was financed by a few shareholders who were hoping to have some profit from it, and not by the government. Toll charges for using the bridge were meant to reimburse them but never did. The citizens preferred to use two other bridges in this area, for which they do not have to pay. There is a unique mechanism by the Waterloo Bridge, introduced to prevent evasion of charges. There are separate barriers for pedestrians and vehicles which will only be lifted when you throw a token into a box. Outside London is the Vauxhall Bridge, another made of iron. It is named after the beautiful village and the lovely gardens where Londoners used to go to breathe fresh air.

When taking short strolls in the city, squares may be helpful to you in finding the right direction. They are surrounded by buildings and take their names from their shapes. They are ornaments to the city, as people build the most beautiful houses near them. Some of them are quite big. The square at Lincoln's Inn Fields, where there is a school of law, is about seven acres. The length of its sides is equal to the base of the largest pyramid in Egypt, which was the pattern for the square. Of a similar size though slightly smaller, are the following squares: Russell, Bedford, Grosvenor, Berkeley, Cavendish, Portman and Leicester. Recently it has become fashionable to build houses around streets of a different shape – crescents and circuses. The most beautiful example is the wonderful Regent Circus. Among squares you can find gardens surrounded by iron railings. You can see there smooth lawns, gravel paths, and trees which are small enough not to obscure the view or block the circulation of the air. Around the trees there are beautifully cared for flowerbeds. Unfortunately, everything is blackened because of soot from the coal fires so the verdure and flowers do not have their natural colours. Only the owners of the houses built near the squares have the right to use the gardens; they have the keys to the gates and pay fees to maintain the gardens.

In spite of the fact that the gardens are full of charm and, in such a huge city, they should be attractive, no one makes use of them and you can rarely see anyone in them. English people, and especially Englishwomen, like to have some privacy; therefore they avoid everything, which would bring them into the limelight. According to public opinion, which is quite strict, a woman cannot sit by the window without arousing suspicion. Even such an innocent activity as displaying flowers in the window may cause trouble for the family and attract importunate fancy men. The use of the gardens in the squares is left to the children and their nannies, which is convenient, as you cannot lose sight of your children there. Many of these gardens contain the monuments of famous men – Pitt, Fox, or Bedford – set on high bases on which their deeds are commemorated in golden letters. Children playing around them from their early childhood must absorb a feeling for greatness and enthusiasm for fame will be aroused. At one of these monuments I once saw a nanny teaching a child its letters.

Despite the fact that London is a great city, it is easy to find anyone you are looking for: all you need to know is the street and the number of the house. Every house has not only a number, but also a brass plate attached to the door with the name of the owner or the occupant. This way of marking the houses is common and is used even in small, English towns, which is very convenient for a foreigner. In

Scotland, where it is customary for several tenants to rent a house, you may see three or four names on one door. However, there are also some people who prefer to live incognito and do not attach their names to the door. If you want to visit these hermits, you need to find them solely on the basis of the house number.

This practice does not apply only to private houses. Warehouses, shops and stalls also have their notices on which you can read what is for sale. If the goods are displayed in the windows, labels with prices are attached to them. The houses of craftsmen display large numbers of notices, written in red and black. Many of them are placed on the third and fourth floors and written in large letters so that, from a distance, they are legible. You can read on them the quality and kind of services offered and at times the name of a patron. It is the ambition of craftsmen to serve or supply the Court. Then they can claim to be saddler to the Prince of York, jeweller or tailor of the king or even shoemaker to the Duke of Wellington. Sometimes these inscriptions refer to such humble matters that they arouse laughter: one I saw read 'Pest destroyer to Her Majesty the Queen'. The use of such titles must be beneficial since craftsmen will even pay for permission to use them. The quality of the goods being sold is often assessed by taking into consideration the reputation of the people and the neighbourhood in which they work. Every house where a good craftsman or a merchant used to live becomes famous and therefore has a higher value. Anyone who wants to buy such a house will have to pay more for it. A craftsman working under someone else's well-known name, even if his own work is not good, will do well. Those who always buy goods in the same shop are called customers; lower prices usually apply to them. Craftsmen and merchants try to have as many regular customers as possible, as in this way they have a regular income. Apart from the above mentioned notices and the practice of displaying goods in the windows in order to encourage prospective buyers, there are also other ways of recommending goods – advertisements in newspapers or on the long poles carried in the streets. The latter are used mainly by the doctors known as quack doctors. They want to sell their universal medicines. It seems that if people were to believe them and bought the medicines, there would be no illnesses in the world and people would not die. If you buy even a small thing in a shop, you will get it wrapped in a large piece of paper, on which all the goods available in the shop are listed.

It will also be stated that credit facilities are available. In fact, they keep their word. You cannot complain that you cannot buy anything on credit, as I know from my own experience when I did not wish to pay immediately. Having agreed on the price of a commodity I would tell the shopkeeper my name and address and the purchase would be sent to my lodging. If by chance I were not at home, the landlord would accept delivery for me. Sometimes a few weeks (in Scotland even a year) passed before someone came to collect the money. A shop owner knows that if someone buys on credit, they will do it again on the same account. There is nothing to lose for the shop owner as, according to their custom, the landlord who confirmed that I was staying with him became my guarantor. If I were to go away without having paid the bill, he would have to pay instead. Therefore landlords make sure that those who are moving out do not leave any debts behind. Sometimes the transfer of responsibility goes too far, as in the following example. My tailor brings me a tailcoat. Then someone pays me a visit, likes the tailcoat and asks the tailor to make a similar one for him. The tailor does so, but my acquaintance is a bad payer and goes away without having paid. The tailor has his eye on me and I have to pay someone else's bill. The legal basis for my responsibility in this case is based on the fact that the agreement between my acquaintance and the tailor had been reached at my place, in my presence and, as I remained silent, it meant that I gave permission for that agreement. If you do not want to have this kind of trouble, you should let the tailor know that he should watch a client, as you do not want to stand surety for him. You may be exposed to such troubles for any recommendations or orders.

It is advantageous when you can trust somebody's word in such a commercial and industrial country and it is easier if you can do small-scale business without wasting time on written formalities. The huge credit system, for which England is world famous, is connected with and developed on that trust. However, even in small business transactions people act carefully. Goods bought on credit are written down in a book and, as soon as you pay for them, they will be crossed off in the book. You will receive a receipt that you have paid the amount due. You should keep this receipt as, if your debt has not been crossed off in the book – by negligence or on purpose – you have to pay again. This happens rarely but, in the eyes of the law, the accuracy of the information in traders' books is not questioned. After one year receipts can be destroyed, as then a debt in the books has to be deleted.

Each street represents a part of the general picture of London, but gives only fragmentary and general information. However, there are some places – public and private – in which many curiosities are gathered together and in many respects they are closely connected with the condition of the whole country. I tried to get to know them as far as I could. One of them is Westminster Hall and the adjoining buildings, where the English parliament and several high tribunals hold their meetings. The other one is Westminster Abbey where they crown and bury kings, where there are monuments to legislators, poets, philosophers, and heroes. When we were passing Charing Cross, we saw the monument to Charles I. Whitehall – once the residence of

Charing Cross. In 1633 Edward I's memorial to his wife Eleanor was moved and replaced by Le Souer's bronze statue of Charles I. Ordered by the Commonwealth government to break it up, John River, a brazier, buried the statue. It was re-erected on Grinling Gibbons' pedestal in 1678.

Cromwell, who had not hesitated to give orders for Charles's execution – is not far from there. We visited the magnificent St Paul's Cathedral built in imitation of St Peter's Church in Rome. Because of the many memorials, St Paul's may be considered as the second English Pantheon. We also visited the Tower, where political prisoners used to be kept and executed, Somerset House, the seat of administration, and the British Museum. This houses a rich collection from various cultures, a library with extensive collections of books, and many Greek and Egyptian antiquities. We went to the Mint, a bank, and to the theatres at Drury Lane and Covent Garden. We saw a few picture galleries and the Whitbread porter brewery, which is said to be the biggest one and to be mainly powered by steam. We have also visited some places near London: shipyards, Richmond, and Kew Gardens. But I will write more about them later, now I only mention them by the way. My first stay in London was too short to see and judge everything properly. The distances between them did not let me visit even half of the places which I later managed to get to know thoroughly.

Whitehall. An episcopal palace till the Reformation, it was ceded to Henry VIII by Cardinal Wolsey. Inigo Jones' Banqueting Hall replaced the hall destroyed by fire in 1618 but John Webb's plan to incorporate it in a palace which would have extended across Whitehall was never realised.

NOTES:

1 Carlton House had been the main residence of the Prince of Wales since his coming of age in 1783. Five architects had been employed and the equivalent of millions of pounds spent on enlarging and decorating it in a mixture of classical, Gothic and Chinese styles. A Throne Room was added in 1819 while his father George III was still alive. Alterations to Buckingham House were started in 1820 but not completed till after the death of George IV in 1830.

2 John Loudon McAdam (1756-1836), Scottish engineer and inventor. His roads were made of small chipped stones bound by gravel and raised to improve drainage. These were later waterproofed by spraying with tar. They were cheaper to build than Metcalf's and Telford's which, like Roman roads, required heavy stone foundations.

3 Henry Hunt (1773-1835). An English radical, known as 'Orator Hunt', he was a leading advocate of parliamentary reform and the abolition of the Corn Laws. Imprisoned for three years after the Peterloo Massacre, he was MP for Preston from 1831-33.

4 William Cobbett (1763-1835). An English writer and radical, his *Political Register* was founded in 1802 as a Tory weekly but rapidly became the leading Radical paper. In 1806 he initiated the reporting of parliamentary debates, later taken over by Hansard. He is best known for his *Rural Rides*.

5 Sir Frances Burdett (1770-1844), English politician and liberal, was in France during the Revolution and became an advocate of parliamentary reform and freedom of speech. Like Hunt and Cobbett, he was imprisoned for his criticisms of the savagely reactionary policies of the government.

6 Before the Reform Act of 1832 Westminster was one of the few boroughs in which there was a substantial popular vote.

7 The Thames tunnel, from Rotherhithe to Wapping, was started by Marc Isambard Brunel in 1825 but not completed till 1843.

8 John Rennie (1761-1821), Scottish civil engineer, famous as a designer of bridges, docks and canals.

Chapter Five

The Journey from London. York. Durham. Newcastle. Alnwick. Dunbar. Haddington. Edinburgh. The Parthenon.

Our stay in England should be called a passing through rather than a journey. Six days after our arrival in London we started for Scotland. The weather served us well which was all the more desirable for the appreciation of the surrounding countryside. It should be noted that the sky is seldom really blue in Great Britain, nothing compared with the deep azure of the Italian or even our Polish skies. It is greyish here, mostly cloudy. The clouds move about or sometimes seem to stand quite still as though a fleece had been thrown over them. The British poets call them fleecy clouds. They look lovely in moonlight; the sky then seems truly soft. I travelled quickly for the roads are excellent.[1] From time to time we had to stop at turnpikes for the toll to be levied but this never lasted long, for the moment the coach was seen in the distance they made ready to let us pass as quickly as possible. The upkeep of the roads is in private hands and the Government has nothing to do with it.

We passed through several charming and prosperous towns about which, however, not a great deal may be said. In each flourished some industry or handicraft, for such is the main characteristic of all English towns. The canals which criss-cross the whole country enormously facilitate trade and communications; their length is estimated at some 500 miles. Our road took us through Stilton, a place famous for its cheeses, which are known by the same name, and then through Grantham where Newton[2] was first introduced to the sciences. Her inhabitants were fully aware of the fact and told us of it. O happy nation that knows its great men! Doncaster, at first sight, appears to offer little to the traveller. It is well built, full of life and has numerous horses at pasture on her level ground. This includes an enormous enclosed area where races are held.

To the right lies York, one of the ancient towns of England with her magnificent Minster which, in terms of size, might rank second amongst the greatest churches of Europe. According to experts, York

Ouse Bridge, York. In spite of frequent floods, the medieval bridge survived till the nineteenth century.

Minster is an excellent example of Gothic architecture. Particularly remarkable is the size of the columns which support the ceiling and the lancet windows alongside, which are some 57 feet tall but only five feet wide. A music festival is held here every year at which, besides numerous citizens and connoisseurs from all parts, there are usually up to 200 artists. One year they even included the famous Catalani.[3] The main compositions of Mozart, Haydn, Handel and Beethoven are performed here. At the trumpeting of the words 'Tuba mirum spargens sonum' Mozart's Requiem fills one's eyes with tears. The music creates such an indescribable impression throughout the vast and imposing Minster that it seems the very earth itself is passing judgement on the dead. At York there is also a hospital for lunatics which is said to be exemplary. It was founded by the subscriptions of the Quakers and is also supervised by them. It bears the gentle name of The Retreat. Gone are the bolted doors and rattling manacles; instead there is a beautiful home farm with a garden intended for the use of the afflicted. The sweetness of being able to stroll around it, together with the fine diet it provides, is considered an essential principle of treatment. Banished also is the letting of blood, while warm baths are used to alleviate melancholy.

We passed by Durham, a small town said to be the poorest in England, yet in a beautiful setting the massive walls of her cathedral provide a picturesque quality. Of an age contemporary with the cathedral is the castle built by William I and now in ruins. According to Scottish chroniclers, it was into these very fastnesses brave Wallace[4] entered, dressed as a bard, in order to decide with Robert the Bruce who was imprisoned there, the destiny of his native land. In this place the passer-by may wonder at the high bridge slung from cliffs between whose shady banks flow the waters of the Weare.

The bishopric of Durham is supposed to be the richest in the land, bringing to the bishop an income of no less than £9,000 if not more. A tidy sum and that with little work and fewer still privations! He has beneath him deacons and canons and they too are well recompensed. All live happily doing precious little, like the gods in Homer's plays, with the one difference that the clerics become old and must make way for successors. By virtue of his high rank the Bishop of Durham is also a Justice of the Peace; there is surely no lay position which combines more suitably with the dignity of a cleric. In Durham Borulawski,[5] the famous dwarf from the time of Stanislaw August, still lives. He is aged almost 80 but remains in rude health and

Count Borulawski. John Kay's sketch of the advocate, Neil Ferguson, with Borulawski was made in Edinburgh in 1788. Though never a count he was supported by a pension from the last king of Poland and the patronage of many European aristocrats. He rarely had to raise money by exhibiting his minute 3 foot 3 inch stature. Retiring to Durham, he died in his 92nd year.

was still considered to be a notable wit. Welcomed into the homes of the country's foremost families, he was described by them as a count.

The road led farther to Sunderland where we crossed by the famous iron bridge. It is formed of a single arch, a full 100 feet high and 236 feet long. Under it masted ships pass with ease. Arriving into the district of Newcastle one might easily believe one had entered the land of Vulcan. Wherever one looks, nothing can be seen but smoking foundries and flaming furnaces in which iron is being smelted. The people rushing around are as black as in the land of Negroes. Everything is done here by machines driven by steam. Here too are the famous coalmines whose produce is said to be of the finest and hardest quality. It is extracted in such quantity that it suffices for practically all of London. Everything local is connected in some way to fire and coal. Thus it is easy to conceive that this land, whose very bowels are being torn out, can scarcely present anything of beauty to the human eye. I also saw iron roads for the first time. These are in fact iron rails on which run wheels and there is no iron where the horses have to go. Newcastle is also the birthplace of Captain Cook[6] who sailed the globe. Beyond lies the Picts' Dyke[7] which runs from here to Carlisle, in other words to the Irish Sea. In the year 121 the Emperor Adrian ordered its erection so as to keep out the incursions of the northern Picts and Scots from his newly conquered province. At distances of equal measure along the wall stood guard the tough and experienced soldiers of the emperor's legions.

Further along our route we passed Alnwick with its enormous castle, seat of the Duke of Northumberland. It surpasses in magnificence all other such monuments in England, or at least those which are still inhabited, with the single exception of the royal palace at Windsor. Alnwick stands on a promontory above the river Alne and within is divided into three courtyards. Its upper parts are designed in the style of all old castles, with bastions and towers whose interiors are filled with suits of armour. All in different positions, as though ready for battle, they will certainly not conquer this fortress. Below ground are dungeons dating from feudal times. Today everything has a gentle appearance; no longer violence but benevolence and respect reign supreme. The Duke of Northumberland is universally known for his charity. In the year 1810 he built a school in the town for 100 poor boys. Near the highway, on a hill, we saw a column some 80 feet high erected in his honour by grateful tenants.

Having left Alnwick near Branxton, I visited the Field of Flodden.[8] There is a cross at the roadside, marking the fatal spot where in 1513 James IV, the greatest of all the kings of Scotland, fell with the flower of Scottish knights. From thence we came to Berwick which is the last English town and lies on the very frontier of Scotland. It was fortified in ancient times and has resisted many an invasion. But today the ramparts are only used by the inhabitants for walking. The river Tweed and the Cheviot Hills mark the boundaries of England and Scotland.

The nearer we drew to Scotland the more hilly became the landscape and the more varied it appeared, for fertile fields and pastures were also seen. The hills became more and more like mountains and their outlines were sharper and bolder. Flocks of sheep were grazing on the steep slopes. In one place we saw gypsies, busy with the camp which they were preparing for the night. They were lighting numerous fires. The road followed deep valleys and climbed up steep hills from whence the sea could be seen. We saw the ruins of the castle of the Douglases,[9] lonely among the gloomy firs. A stone bridge, a single arch 120 feet over a roaring stream, seemed to be the only entrance to that fortified place. Further on the views increased in beauty and at night, when clouds passed dreamily over the shining face of the moon, I felt indeed that I had reached the country of Ossian,[10] and that I had breathed the same air as that father of all song did breathe. Near Dunbar the view of the sea is simply splendid. The whole shore is lined by cliffs and their shape is so strange that one wonders what uncanny evolutions of the earth have formed them that way.[11] The pounding of the waves, for the sea is very stormy there, is heard at a great distance. A mist like a constant drizzle arises from the foaming breakers.

The fields of Haddingtonshire are pleasant to observe and they are known in the whole of Scotland as the best cultivated. John Knox[12] was born at Haddington. The remains of a twelfth-century Franciscan church may yet be seen; it was ruined during the Reformation and most of it is roofless now. In the less damaged part, a service is still held on Sundays. Driving farther I admired the Firth of Forth, Arthur's Seat, and the Calton Hill. I passed through Prestonpans where the Pretender won a victory in 1745. Then through Musselburgh and Portobello, meaningless little towns, known only for sea bathing and military barracks.

To enjoy the finest view of Edinburgh, one should always approach by the road from the Calton Hill. There is no town with more marvellous and impressive surroundings. The road was cut through the rocks at great expense. To the right one sees the sea and Leith Harbour and to the left Arthur's Seat, 850 feet high. The Salisbury Crags touch it, and at their feet are Holyrood and the ruins of the Gothic Chapel. Not very distant is the churchyard in which Adam Smith and Doctor Gregory are buried.[13] One sees the whole Old Town and the cathedral church with its steeple like a crown. In the background towers a castle on a steep hill; a banner waving over it and clouds often pass across. The least sensitive spectator is bound to be charmed by so many beautiful things. The present British king, when he came to visit Scotland in 1822, also arrived by that road. Seized with admiration, he exclaimed: 'God what a sight.' And I do not wonder at his emotion. Anyone who knows the history and the fate of a great nation must be touched deeply at seeing the places where all of this happened.

The suburbs of Edinburgh are not wild and neglected as are those of Paris or London. The approach to the city is through a wide, rich and beautiful street which provides ample food for thought. Nelson's monument, the Observatory, the Penitentiary, the Jail, David Hume's monument, the Picture Gallery, hotels, chemists, the Post Office, the Regent's Bridge and the Theatre were passed. How numerous and varied are the types of life represented here. Though all this is contained in a comparatively small space, yet it is so disposed that it does not give the effect of being crowded. It is a place fit for meditation.

Prince's Street, straight as an arrow and almost three-quarters of a mile long, begins behind the theatre. A deep valley to the left, over which two bridges are thrown, divides the Old Town from the New, the Scottish from the Anglicised. The former is as old as Scotland herself; the houses are narrow, some eight or ten storeys high, with closes for pedestrians between them. In the latter part, built much later, everything is as in an average English town; the same squares, crescents and even such gardens as could be found in the very centre of London. The streets are wide and the pavements excellent, made of stone cut in the shape of bricks. This gives the impression that they are paved with a recumbent wall. Each stone prepared for paving costs the town the equivalent of one Polish zloty. Some of the streets have a wonderful view of the sea. The houses are much more impressive than in London for they are built of stone, not brick. This stone is quarried near the town. When new it is straw coloured, but it becomes grey under the influence of the air. It contains mica and owing to this it shines in the sun and the houses seem to be stuck with diamonds. The roofs are mostly made of stone shingles. The houses are healthy and dry for the stone does not let damp through. In Scotland, as in England, they are heated only by open fires, but here they are much warmer. Though there are no double windows and no stoves, the walls are much thicker. Watching new houses being built and huge stones being hoisted up, I thought that in Scotland they seem to be making houses for eternity. The very greyness, which covers them in time, makes them somewhat similar to the eternal granite rocks of the Alps.

For the exceptional beauty of its position, travellers compare Edinburgh to the most famous towns of Europe: Lisbon, Naples and Constantinople. But to the Scots, imbued as they are by the poetical spirit which has chosen their country as its home, cold comparisons are not enough. They speak of their native town in parables and with great sentiment. The common people call it: 'The City of Palaces'; sentimentalists, in accord with the ballads, 'The favoured Seat of Edina'; the romantics, led by Sir Walter Scott, 'Our romantic town'. The classicists find that it is like Athens and, disregarding whether or not they will meet with general approval, they call it 'The Athens of the North'. The likeness is indeed striking. Like Athens, Edinburgh is beautified by a bay, for the Firth of Forth is certainly worth the Aegean Sea; Leith is good enough to take the place of the Piraeus; the castle on the rock that of the Acropolis. The Parthenon alone seems to be missing but even this is to be erected. The consent of Parliament was obtained in 1822, and during the King's stay the foundation stone was laid, in the King's name, by the Duke of Hamilton, Scotland's first peer and the Grand Master of the Scottish Free Masons. The plan and the dimensions of this Scottish Parthenon have been taken from the Minerva Temple at Athens. It will be dedicated to the memory of Scottish men and will be called the National Monument. It will be erected on the top of Calton Hill and, as there is not enough room for it, the monument of Nelson will have to go. This is certainly not a pity, as it is nothing but a satire on the lack of taste of the Athenians of the North. It consists of a round tower on a square basement, with winding stairs inside. Having paid, one could go up these stairs to admire the view. In the basement there was a café and several rooms for guests. What a singular idea, for the monument of a hero! How indecent and how ridiculous, thus to make money from such lofty things! Monuments erected to the dead should be solely for the dead. Turned into a means of bringing profit to the living, they are an insult to those departed.

Edinburgh from the Calton Hill. Lach-Szyrma and his pupils were to spend over two years in Edinburgh, dividing their time between serious study at the University and the social life of the New Town.

I am told that the foundation stone of a school has also been laid on Calton Hill. Formerly the situation of the High School in the Old Town was too enclosed and unhealthy. It was impossible to choose a more appropriate place for the education of the young than this spot, so near the future temple of fame and facing such beauty of nature. Genius is sure to develop here, and future generations will think of this place as one of the most memorable.

NOTES:

1 The quality of the roads built for Turnpike Trusts by John Metcalfe (1717-1810), Thomas Telford (1757-1834) and John McAdam (1756-1836) reduced travelling time from London to Edinburgh from ten days in the 1750s to two in the 1820s.

2 Sir Isaac Newton (1642-1727), English scientist and mathematician.

3 Angelica Catalani (1779-1849), Italian singer of international renown whom Lach-Szyrma may have heard in Poland in 1819.

4 Sir William Wallace (1274-1309), Scottish patriot and, with Sir Andrew de Moray, leader of the Scots against the English in the early years of the Wars of Independence. He was a supporter of John Baliol. Robert the Bruce opposed the Baliol cause and paid homage to Edward I in 1296, 1297 and 1299. There is no evidence that he was ever imprisoned in Durham Castle.

5 Jozef Borulawski (1739-1837), had been King Stanislaw August's court dwarf. He came to Britain in 1782 and was not a count.

6 Captain James Cook (1728-79), the British navigator and explorer who charted the coasts of New Zealand and eastern Australia and claimed Australia for Britain. The Dutch had sighted it a century earlier.

7 Hadrian's Wall became the northern frontier of the Roman Empire and protected it from the Picts and the Scots until 383 AD.

8 War with England had been intermittent since 1296. When Henry VIII attacked Scotland's ally France, James IV invaded England and was killed at the battle of Flodden Field.

9 Tantallon Castle fell to General Monk in 1652.

10 In 1760 James Macpherson (1736-96), published *Fragments of Ancient Verse collected in the Highlands*. These were accepted as genuine translations from ancient Gaelic poetry by Edinburgh's literati, some of whom financed Macpherson's search for further ballads. *Fingal, an epic poem in Six Books* was followed by *Temora, an epic poem in Eight Books*. The validity of his sources was questioned by some of his contemporaries and it is now generally believed that his 'translations; were increasingly his own composition, though based on scraps of ancient Gaelic poetry. As a Romantic, deeply interested in folklore, Lach-Szyrma had studied these while a student at Vilnius University.

11 Lach-Szyrma's route took him near Siccar Point where observation of the configuration of the rocks led James Hutton (1726-97) to develop the ideas about the age of the earth's crust which became the foundation of the science of geology. His *A Theory of the Earth* was published in 1785.

12 John Knox (1513-73) was the most influential figure in the development of the Protestant Reformation in Scotland.

13 Canongate churchyard is the burial ground of many of the leading figures of the Scottish Enlightenment. These include the economist Adam Smith (1723-90) and Dr John Gregory, one of the third generation of distinguished doctors and mathematicians connected with Edinburgh University.

Chapter Six

The Way to London by Carlisle. Steam Vessels. Rainbows. Scarbrough. Spanish Armada. Movement of the Sea. The Thames. Hanged People. Trip to the Mainland.

Travellers going by land from Edinburgh to London usually head for Carlisle, an English town near the Scottish border and from there to the romantic mountains and lakes of Westmoreland, renowned as the home of poets like Southey and Wordsworth, the main representatives of a modern school of poets called the Lake School.[1] It is characterised by its ability to express deep feeling with the greatest simplicity of style. The most common of things, normally excluded from poetry by their ordinary nature, become the source of inspiration. No other school has created such poetry. It has a freedom comparable to the freedom of rustic life and is as clear as the air of the mountains and the surface of the lakes among which, away from the bustle of the world, the poets have chosen to make their homes. Their poetry is the poetry of nature and the heart an anthem to creation. What Sterne's *Sentimental Journey* is in prose, their writings are in verse; they differ only because of the individuality of the poets. The school included a few good romantic authors who created philosophical idylls. The lakes, Windermere and Grasmere, the town of Keswick and the mountain Helvellyn play a significant role in their writing.

However, not all foreigners go as far as this secluded area of reclusive poets which is visited by the admirers of genius and the beauty of nature. Most travellers head for Liverpool, Manchester or Birmingham to wonder at the factories and to calculate the origins of the wealth and power which nations can only achieve by education and industry. In this context these cities are central. No traveller who wishes his journey to be instructive should omit them.

The rest of the journey he may shape according to his preference and fancy. Anyone who wishes to get to know the characteristic features of nations which are rooted in their distant past crosses over to Ireland and from there to Wales, where the ancestral features of the Celts can still be observed. Anyone who loves social life and the amusements of the capital, removed to the peace of the country, will visit the baths in Matlock, Hotwell, Bath, Cheltenham, and Bristol.[2] But his health, instead of being improved, is likely to be impaired. A lover of scholarship will visit its honorable institutions in Oxford and Cambridge, their origins lost in the mists of time. Those who like to visit the birth-places of important people will make their way to Lichfield, the home of Johnson, the greatest of English critics, or turn towards Stratford on Avon to see the home of Shakespeare and the church which houses all that was mortal of him. Antiquarians visit the fabulous Stonehenge on Salisbury Plain to see the mysterious monument of stone columns, the remains of a gigantic construction of the Druids.[3] Nor do they omit Castleton[4] with its ruins of England's oldest castle. Built on a vertical rock, it had already been ruined at the time of the Romans' arrival and, due to its fortified character, was called by the common people Arx Diaboli. In this area a curious traveller may go down into an enormous underground cave called Peak's Hole. There, just as if he had sunk into the underworld of Erebos, he finds a cold black river across which he is transported in a boat as though by Charon,[5] across the dark and silent River Styx.

I did not have an opportunity to see these important places, about which so much has been written and so many stories have been told. I have travelled three times from Edinburgh to London but always by sea. This means of transport is the least expensive and, since the introduction of the steamship,[6] it is also the fastest and often a pleasant one. It is used both by those who are thrifty and by the wealthiest. As for me, I have always found most enjoyment at sea. Thus, each time I had the choice of travelling by stagecoach or by boat I have always chosen the latter. The undulation of the sea over the depths of the abyss and the sense of losing oneself in the infinity of the ocean brings extraordinary pleasure. One who has never been in the limitless expanse of an ocean and has never lost sight of everything, apart from the sky and the water, cannot have an accurate idea of infinity. To exist in this limitless area has a charm which is inexplicable.

Thus I did not agree and did not regret disagreeing with Cato the Censor,[7] who could not forgive himself three things: having wasted a day doing nothing, having entrusted a woman with a secret, and having chosen to travel by sea when a journey by land had been possible. As to the final point, the Censor would not be so harsh on himself had he seen our passenger ships, by comparison with which the praised triremes and quadriremes seemed childish inventions. It is no wonder then, that Cato found travelling on them unwise and the very thought of the consequences of a sea journey makes many of us feel nauseated. They were miserable boats driven by the winds, the servants of Aeolus,[8] wherever they wished. By comparison with our steamships they are as nothing. They are not governed by the weakness of oars or the instability of sails; they are full of powerful steam, the daughter of fire and water. These forces, according to Thales,[9] brought the world out of chaos, creating life and spirit in its endlessly varying forms. A ship now seems to be an animate creature. The power of steam flows through its veins and puts it into motion, with its prow it defeats the hostile winds and with its sides it dashes through the fierce billows. But for the lack of speech, it would be equal to the Argonaut's[10] ship which, as we are persuaded by the poets, was to have spoken and even prophesied. Had Cato travelled on our ship he would not have suffered from colic, which was the case each time he travelled on his chariot or quadriga. Rather, he would sit as if in his palace in Rome and, without noticing his progress, he would suddenly find himself miraculously at his destination. At the same time he would eat and drink as Lucullus[11] and, enjoying the music at his table, would fall into a sybaritic sleep. On the soft cushions of his curtained bed he would be rocked as once was young Achilles whose mother Tethis, would sing to him about Pythagoras' celestial spheres.

To sail nowadays at sea is no different from being in an enchanted castle. The ancients did not know this delight; it is the triumph our navigation has scored over theirs. In these journeys on England's main water route we find convenience and luxury and the satisfaction of the most sophisticated needs. It is combined with intellectual refinement, enlightening conversation with people of various social and national origins and the pleasures of companionship and kindness in intercourse. Those who love dignified entertainment sit in the ship's cabin at a serious game of chess; someone who loves poetry escapes with Walter Scott to the romantic age of chivalry or with the Irish

Anacreon (Moore)[12] to the lands of love and joyful feasting. He will find their works in the ship's library. One who is totally absorbed by his own thoughts and pursues original ideas writes whatever comes to his mind in his pocket book. These jottings may then be published in literary memoirs or constitute the pages of a profound work. One who enjoys idleness more than anything else, looks at the smoke that soars away from the mast as if he were trying to observe where the wind would drive it, or follows with his eyes the sea birds, wheeling and calling as they are frightened off the coastal rocks. One who is burdened by sorrow watches the waves chasing one another and disappearing or, at night-time and in solitude, follows the silver road towards the pale moon. The lingering memories of the past turn the sailor's thoughts to the places he leaves and then to the places he is heading for and the hope of a safe end to his journey. And so in his soul intertwine the worlds of joy, sorrow, hope and contemplation.

Such are the main features of the companionship one may encounter on a passenger ship. An active mind is sure to find an occupation in any place, but in no other place is it more awake and more eagerly captures impressions from objects as it does at sea. Endless space sets no limits to his thoughts. Faced by the vastness of nature, material considerations fade and only thought is significant for, in the face of the magnitude of creation, vanity and thoughtlessness are inappropriate. As I pondered these ideas it often came to my mind that the seriousness in the character of the English, as well as the profundity of thought in their writings, is predominantly the result of their frequent contact with the sea. They are enriched in two ways; the earth and the sea unite as if in a covenant to provide them with objects for thought, a covenant of which a nation living at a distance from the sea must be deprived. Where the eye does not have in front of it the variety and the vastness of creation, it is harder for the mind to have significant ideas. As a consequence, both the nations living close to the sea and those settled in the mountains have won more fame due to their learning and power than the nations settled in the lowlands. Tyre, Carthage, Greece, Rome, and Switzerland are examples.

These were the kind of thoughts I was busy with while at sea between Edinburgh and London. The steamship I sailed in this time was called the *Walter Scott*, a name so popular, that it is used to refer to stagecoaches, hotels etc. It is not only through monuments that the English commemorate the memory of great people; they attach their names to the most common objects of everyday use and this contributes to the growth of their fame. Not only Walter Scott, but also many other men of merit and some of the most significant historical events, have been honoured in this way At first a foreigner finds it odd to sail in the *Walter Scott*, drink punch 'at Shakespeare's, walk on the Waterloo Bridge' and wear 'wellingtons', but this feeling disappears with time. He approves of this custom and finds it worth imitating.

The interior of steamships does not differ much from the interior of ordinary ships: they are just wider, bigger, have a flat bottom and carry a heavier load. They are used mainly to transport people and are usually more comfortably furnished. There are two chambers in them, one for women and one for men. The latter is bigger; twenty steps long and eight steps wide, lit from above by a window in the shape of a half-sphere, with iron bars added on the outside for safety. All around the room there are beds placed in the walls as if in niches. There are three rows of them, one above the other. In each there are the finest and whitest of sheets and they are so spacious one can comfortably sit, lie and stretch oneself on them, but they are too low to allow standing up. Each of them has curtains of green or crimson silk, which, as they hang loose, give the impression of creating a separate room. It is also where the traveller's most private possessions are stored. Bigger packs are registered and handed over to the steward who, with the help of two to three servants and a cook, provides service to the guests. The beds are numbered on the passenger's ticket to avoid misunderstandings as to which belongs to whom.

There are two classes of travellers: those with beds and those without. The first pay four guineas for transport from Edinburgh to London and a place at the table; the latter, the servants and the poor, pay barely one fourth of this. They have to stay on deck all the time and they do not sit at the common table. The first group eats together. The served meals were: breakfast, dinner and tea; anyone who wished could also receive supper. Porter, wine and rum are available in any quantity for an additional charge. At the table there is the utmost politeness and absolute equality. The captain of the ship does the honours and if any one has a dish in front of him, he follows the English custom and serves it to others. It once happened that we sailed with Captain Maitland, to whose frigate, as is commonly known, Napoleon surrendered. He was not treated with greater courtesy than other commanders, nor did he seem to expect it in any way. He was unfailingly polite to everyone and always seemed to know some anecdote with which to entertain the company. It is an innate feature of the English character not to assert one's superiority over others. It was as if everyone was convinced that what he had done was just a matter of a citizen's duty and nothing for which to claim gratitude. I have discovered that this captain has published the history of the life and surrender of his captive.

Another positive fact about the owners of passenger ships is that they not only supply their ships with products which satisfy physical needs but also with intellectual entertainment, which may prove useful to passengers during a monotonous journey. The most common game is the game of chess. Cards are rather disliked in such places and the English generally play with them less than other nations. As I have already mentioned, the ship has a library which consists of the writings of the most prominent authors, among others the works of Byron, Walter Scott, Moore, Campbell and Burns. Nor has music been forgotten. The Scottish ships usually have a piper playing the national instrument, the bagpipes, in a Caledonian dress. We had one of them on our ship. He gave the signal to leave the shore and, as we sailed away, he played a farewell to the Highlands. As the hills slowly disappeared from our eyes, the company joined in to sing a well-known national song, *Highland Laddies.*

Where the Firth of Forth opens into the sea the shore adopts the wildest contours. Great natural distortions must have taken place there.[13] Single and grouped massive black rocks, or rather mountains, projected from the surface of the ocean. One of them had a hole into which the foaming sea forced its way with a great uproar. The biggest of them all was the Bass Rock on which were the ruins of an old castle. Today it is only the nesting place of solan geese. As we approached we sailed into a heavy drizzle, the so-called Scottish mist. It

Tantallon Castle and the Bass Rock. Built by the Ist Earl of Douglas c1370, the castle fell to General Monk's cannons in 1652. The Bass Rock is home to one of the world's largest gannetries.

created in front of us a rainbow with one end on the sea, splitting the light into thousands of colours and shades and the other illuminating the Bass Rock. It was an extraordinary sight, especially as our ship sailed under it as if under a triumphal arch that grew fainter as we sailed towards it and finally disappeared in the air. The falling rain caused an even more extraordinary phenomenon. The sun's rays seemed to curve in the rain and poured blinding light into the sky while raindrops fell like liquid silver, fine and delicate.

Before it grew dark we sailed toward a massive coastal rock on which, in the dim dusk, one could see some buildings. The rock was a peninsula protruding into the sea and on it lay the town of Scarborough with its castle standing on its very edge, 300 feet above sea level. This was where the ship stopped in order to disembark a few men whose journey's destination was not London. A few others had come out in the same boat to take their places. The evening was beautiful, the wind dropped and the sea was completely tranquil. Such conditions are ideal for steamships; allowing their paddles to engage the water more deeply and steadily than when it is rough. The ship gathered speed. The stars sparkled in the canopy of the heavens and the moon gleamed palely over of the dark background of the sea. Our Caledonian piper played on the deck and an energetic team of sailors danced lively reels. Subsequently everything calmed down, everyone retired, the sole helmsman stayed awake and so did I. I had decided to spend a sleepless night and in the morning to see the sunrise at sea. And so I saw this magnificent and indescribable picture.

On the next day we did not sail along the shore any more but so far out to sea that one could hardly see the land in the distance. Generally speaking, the coasts of the east of England do not create such striking views as do the coasts of Scotland; they are too low and flat to be called beautiful. It is dangerous to come close to land due to the frequent shallows. Although, unlike sailing ships, steamships do not have deep draught, when we sailed quite near the sailors frequently lowered a lead into the sea to check the depth. The shallows are most numerous at the mouth of the Thames. I was shown the place where the famous fleet of Philip II, called the Armada, was defeated. This was in the year 1588, during the reign of Elizabeth. After this defeat the Spanish navy never recovered and hegemony at sea went over to England.

The closer we came to the mouth of the Thames, the heavier became the sea traffic. Ships sailed ahead and behind us at a distance, others went close past and they were so numerous that the sea looked like a wide road, bringing wealth to England from all over the world. By paying for them with her own produce she seemed to join people from the farthest states and nations with a chain of reciprocal trade. It was a wonderful sight to see these enormous ships at sea, almost motionless in their quiet tranquility, yet able to awaken with their stately images the deepest of feelings. Nothing can equal the activity of the English at sea; by comparison any land traffic, on the most important of roads, is nothing. At a single glance I have seen more ships there than breaks and vehicles on any of the busiest trade routes. This scene was brought to life most beautifully by people on passenger ships. Standing on the decks of the ships that sailed past, the fashionably dressed men and women greeted each other, acquaintances waved their handkerchiefs, some glanced through field glasses at the gracious figures of the daughters of Albion and the ships' captains talked with each other through megaphones. It created a picture of celebration and holiday rather than of a day in an active and strenuous life. Our Caledonian Amphion also shared this joy and, as if ignorant of his national ballads and caught by the common feeling of the whole nation, he played from the deck of the ship 'Rule, Britannia' A few young midshipmen who have been sailing with us joined him and added words to the music. The genius of Britain, which in its greatness seemed to be soaring over this scene, must have rejoiced in its power and delighted in the expectation of its even greater growth. As someone rightly observed, the English owe a great part of their maritime power to this song: it is sung by sailors in both good times and bad.

We sailed along the Thames. The river has made London the warehouse of the world's riches. Its twists and turns in the capital have been accurately compared to the squirming coils of a dragon reluc-

The Shipping Entrance, London Docks. To ease congestion on the Thames estuary, London Docks were excavated in 1802. Lined by warehouses, they could hold 550 ships.

tant to leave it. We sailed past ships going here and there, sailing past us in all directions on this turbulent water. The docks were like a vast orchard, ropes hanging tangled from the masts, the furled sails making them look like thick canes, and the occasional ship with sails set, playing with the wind, enlivening this tranquil scene. There is nothing special about the Thames. It flows slowly in a wide bed: its right bank is flat and fertile the left one is a little hilly, with here and there mansions appearing amongst their parks.

It was here that we saw a horrid example of how justice had been dispensed. Three men hung on gallows; they had been sailors. They had been sentenced to this shameful death for mutiny and killing their captain. Their bodies had already fallen apart; still hanging were the bones and the clothes, which had been left as a warning to other sailors. Then we sailed past Greenwich Palace, the magnificent hospital for sailors of long standing. The rest of the buildings on the shore are of little significance. In the capital only the poorest classes live by the Thames.

In two days, two nights and four hours we had come from Edinburgh to London. This time our stay in this capital was not long. We decided we would go on an excursion to Switzerland first and then spend more time in London on the way back. I shall not undertake the task of describing this journey during which we passed through some of the provinces of the Netherlands, the German states, France and the charming Rhineland area. These countries are far better known by my countrymen and I am unwilling to allow any more mature opinions I might have to be preceded by the publishing of some inaccurate and superficial observations made on this journey. I am thus returning to my initial intention from which I could be distracted by a description of this short excursion. I am leaving the Continent and going back to England. I am in the little coast town of Dieppe in France, where I shall have a longer distance to travel by sea than on my previous crossing from Calais to Dover.

NOTES:

1 The Lake Poets, Robert Southey (1774-1843), William Wordsworth (1770-1850) and Samuel Taylor Coleridge (1772-1834), were drawn together as students by their early Jacobin sympathies and belief in the dignity of the common man. They settled near each other in the Lake District and only Coleridge returned to London.

2 From the mid-eighteenth century, when improved roads made travelling easier, visiting the spas which developed round springs of mineral waters became fashionable for men and women of all ages. They flourished in the early years of the nineteenth century when the Grand Tour, a male preserve, was made impossible by the French Wars.

3 Druids were active in Celtic Britain at the time of the Roman occupation. Stonehenge is now believed to have been erected in the late Neolithic Age, about 3,000 years earlier.

4 Castleton, the Castle of the Peak in North Derbyshire, was built soon after the Norman Conquest by William Peverell. It replaced an Anglo Saxon castle on what was probably the site of an Iron Age fort and was made famous by Scott's novel, *Peveril of the Peak*.

5 In Greek mythology Charon was the boatman who ferried the dead across the Styx, the boundary of the underworld

6 Henry Bell's paddle boat, the *Comet*, provided a regular service on the Clyde from 1808. The first Channel crossing under steam was in 1818.

7 Marcus Porcius Cato (c119-57 BC), Roman statesman and orator who advocated the rejection of luxuries and a return to simple living.

8 In Greek mythology Aeolus was the god of the winds.

9 Thales (624-545 BC). A natural philosopher, geometer, astronomer and founder of Greek philosophy, he identified water and heat as the sources of the universe.

10 In Greek mythology the Argonauts were those who sailed in search of the Golden Fleece

11 Lucius Licinius Lucullus (c119-57 BC), Roman soldier, statesman and patron of the arts, he acquired so much wealth that, living in luxury in retirement, his name has been used as an epithet for luxurious food.

12 Thomas Moore (1779-1852), Irish romantic poet and translator into verse of *Anacreon*.

13 The *Walter Scott* would have sailed near enough to the coast to see Siccar Point. The juxtaposition of vertical and horizontal strata exposed here provided James Hutton (1726-87) with proof of his theories of the formation of the earth. His *Theory of the Earth* denied the Biblical theory of Creation and formed the basis of modern geology.

Chapter Seven

Dieppe. Character of a Particular Englishman. Englishmen's Voyages. Brighton. Spas. Masters of Ceremonies. Coming Back to London.

From Dieppe one travels to Brighton. In Dieppe, as in Calais and Boulogne, there are so many Englishmen that they may be treated as though they were the suburbs of England. It is curious that French channel ports become so English, while on the opposite coast each town is as English as though there were no French in the neighbourhood or even in the whole world. We had to wait three days in Dieppe because of an extraordinary storm at sea.

In moments of shared adventure the participants usually get closer to each other and make one another's acquaintance. So it happened on this occasion. We got to know Mr W., an Englishman who had travelled with us from Rouen to Dieppe, much better. He was of such a height that he and a Patagonian could easily have supported the roof. No matter whether we stood or sat beside him, all our company looked only slightly taller than Lilliputians. He seemed to surpass us in everything. To his great stature he added unprecedented originality. He was aware of this and did not try to conceal it. When asked for his opinion he usually began by announcing that his ideas were unusual or quirky or romantic and, with such an introduction, he prepared us for answers which would be untypical or even bizarre. And indeed, he rarely let down our expectations. I will quote only one of his announcements here. When the wind began to change slightly, which was an omen of a change in the weather, it remained violent and the sea was as rough as before. Many people hesitated whether to go or to wait longer. Mr W. spoke up in the stentorian voice which was typical of him: 'As for me, I don't care about myself and the world cares little for me. There are two or at most three people on earth who may care whether I am drowned or hanged.' This statement was one of his frequent outbursts of misanthropy. What in somebody else would be the blustering of a braggart, in him emerged from his principles and character. He was one of those people who say 'your homeland is where you feel happy' and is proud to call themselves cosmopolitans, the citizens of the world. Each time he used this word, and he used it often, you could hear the pleasure he derived from the conviction that he was able to rise above the prejudices and superstitions of the commoners.

He had seen a lot in his voyages and what he had seen he could describe well. He dealt mostly with natural science (of course in terms of being an amateur rather than a professional), but about some of them he spoke as profoundly as a scholar. He submerged himself in politics as many Englishmen do who think that by the right of birth (*politicus natus*) they are destined to be politicians. However, he acquired information from newspapers rather than from research and experience. He worshiped Napoleon and he owned a little bronze statue of him. When, after landing at Brighton, many of his possessions were confiscated by customs officers, he comforted himself for their loss by the fact that Napoleon's statue had escaped their watchful eyes. He did not like his own country, something almost unheard-of among Englishmen, but he praised the politeness of the French and the Italians, confessing that he had often experienced their generosity in circumstances in which the behaviour of his own countrymen might have made him ashamed. He was coming back to England only to leave it as quickly as possible. He wished to move to Italy for good, as many of his countrymen had done. At that time up to 100,000 of them lived abroad and were in no hurry to return to their homeland. Travelling through France, Switzerland and Italy you may see many beautiful country houses inhabited by English families. They settle there for many reasons: to benefit their health, for the education of their children, to live under sunnier skies, or to enjoy the wonders of art and nature. But for the majority the motivation is economic. It is cheaper to live on the Continent than at home. Many soldiers, who left the army as half pay officers when peace was declared, settled in France or Germany.

These journeys abroad not only give the Englishmen pleasure and financial benefits but also widen their culture and their understanding of science. Getting to know the conventions and laws of other countries helps them to lose their inveterate national prejudices and their belief that there is nothing good outside England. The upper classes, who travel a lot, have already shaken off these misconceptions but in the lower classes there has been little change. There is nothing more ignorant and defiant than a real John Bull or a London Cockney. The spirit of enquiry, which in Englishmen is almost innate and is being encouraged by developments in the educational system, enhances knowledge and science by research. Some collect relics of ancient cultures from different parts of the world, others visit arctic regions and discover unknown lands; others scramble up inaccessible mountain peaks, if not for scientific reasons, than just for the joy of reaching the summit. Once, in the valley of Chamonix in Savoy, I witnessed a couple of English women preparing for a dangerous journey across crevasse seamed glaciers to reach the valleys around Mont Blanc. I also saw others who, despite the discomforts and difficulties, were travelling on foot or on mules all through the mountainous regions of Switzerland.

Usually a good thing will be linked with a bad one and this is also true in the case of these journeys. People who care about their country look at these journeys with disapproval. The economists, who watch over the nation's wealth, complain about the drain of money. The travellers' expenses seem to be a large contribution that England unwittingly pays to other countries, including its rival, France. The farmers complain that they must sell their crops at a lower price, hardly enough to pay their rent, than they would sell them if the 100,000 people who go abroad stayed at home and had to be fed. The craftsmen complain that there is no market for their products because of the lack of these wealthy and luxury-loving citizens who also do harm by buying things elsewhere. By supporting foreign craftsmen they cause their native ones to go bankrupt. Even the most tolerant Englishman is saddened by his fellow countrymen's passion for travel, which he sees as weakening their sense of nationality, the basis of their literary and political superiority. In the history of the human race there is no nation that achieved such twofold fame without a strong sense of nationality. Nationality is the holy fire of Vesta[1] and the existence of nations depends on it. But not only does travelling diminish the love of homeland; it also weakens the willingness to carry out civil duties. For what is the co-called citizen of the world? He is a man who pursues his pleasures, with no concern for the country in which he was born and brought up and which is still the source of his wealth. A licence for the citizenship of the world makes a man alien to one country and unhelpful to all others and generally leads to idleness and sponging: one who uses such a passport is a passive creature, taking from a society but adding nothing to it. A man who wants to be a citizen everywhere is a citizen nowhere; he is nowhere at home and everywhere a foreigner. In a dark hour neither the country in which such a man chooses to dwell, nor the homeland which he had scorned, may count on his concern or strength. Having left his own home; he will leave any other and settle where his egotism will enjoy both safety and pleasure. This company of travellers are like migrant birds that nest in a different place every year and have no interest in the future of their nesting places. How useless are those who live abroad! I once

Mermaids at Brighton W.H.Heath. In 1780 William IV, not yet of age, was forbidden by his father George III to visit Brighton because of its reputation as a raffish spa. Dr Russell had succeeded in persuading the vulnerable that drinking and bathing in sea water would cure anything from rheumatism to rabies. In the words of his son:

Brighthelmstone was confessed by all
T'abound with females fair
But more so since fam'd Russell has
Preferred the waters there.

heard an accurate assessment made by one of our own more enlightened officials who believed that a mayor in a small town did more for his country than a senator who remained abroad. But let us go back to our journey.

After quite a rough voyage, which was particularly distressing for women who are not used to sailing, we landed in Brighton. It is a middle-sized town well known for its beautiful setting by the sea and for sea bathing. Forty years ago it was only a fishermen's village called Brightelmstone; today it is ashamed of its old name and calls itself Brighton. It owes its fame to a skilful doctor[2] who was living there and who encouraged some wealthy families to come and bathe there under his supervision. The success of the treatment brought more patients the following year and then a new fashion established this town as one of the most popular of bathing places. Finally, it became the favourite place of the present King of England, who started to go there when he was the Regent in order to bathe, or rather for sailing, which was believed to be good for his health. He has a beautiful palace there, the Royal Pavilion,[3] and large stables, for he enjoys breeding horses and often enters them in races. What Windsor was to earlier kings, Brighton is to the present one. It is noticeably growing in buildings and wealth and the frequent presence of the court increases the circulation of money.[4] The truth of the Polish proverb: 'Under the master's eye the horse is fed' is illustrated here.

Besides Brighton there are other places where people go bathing; every town lying by the sea may take advantage of its position. However, there are places which have become popular, not because of the properties of their waters but for some whim of fashion. These are Brighton and Ramsgate for sea bathing; Cheltenham, Bath, Clifton, and Matlock for their mineral waters and hot baths. The latter two were no more than villages but now have many substantial houses and, in the shops, you may buy everything just as in the biggest English cities. Matlock lies in an enchanting valley where the beauty of the place and the social life probably do more for the sick than the waters themselves. I say really sick ones, for there are many people who go there and do not need the healing touch of Aesculapius' staff.[5] The waters are warm and the spring has this curious property that it petrifies anything put in it and, if the object stays there long enough, it will be turned into stone. A wig and a brush that have been petrified after being kept in the spring for some time are shown to visitors. The waters in Cheltenham are supposed to be good for scurvy. During the reign of Edward the Confessor these areas were royal lands which paid a tax of three thousand loaves of bread for the king's hounds. Often in Poland tenants paid their taxes in game. Since hunting ceased to be a major occupation of kings, Cheltenham's canine tax has been commuted for a money payment and in Poland the corvée has replaced the game tax.

The waters in Bath, Bristol and Clifton are good for pulmonary consumption which, due to the ever-changing weather, kills more people here, particularly of the fair sex, than anywhere else. Usually it is the youngest and most gentle who are struck down by this merciless illness but, before they die, they are graced with an ethereal beauty, just as a rose, penetrated to its centre by a worm, blooms and fades before its time. It is sad to look on those youthful and delicate creatures, already halfway to the other world, as they wander like shadows under the branching elms of the graveyard, treading unsteadily on the grass which so soon will cover them. Looking at the graveyard, in which lie so many of those who preceded them, only increases our pity. On the rows of tombstones you may read the names of this country's most distinguished families, names which death did not respect. The age of the dead, usually from eighteen to twenty-five years, shows that most of the people buried there were taken from this world in the spring of their lives. In Cheltenham, because of its peculiar planning, those going for a walk or to bathe have to walk through the churchyard, as though they were to be familiarized with the grave in this manner.

Reminders of death are not always separated from the places of healing. Equally sad is the impression made by Bristol: firstly, because those suffering from incurable illnesses sometimes go there as a last resort, secondly, because it was once a place connected with the infamous slave trade. Bristol lies on the Avon, surrounded, like Rome, the conqueror of the world, by seven hills. The quay in the harbour is the most beautiful one in the world but its stones are stained with the tears of thousands of men who took their last breaths as free men here. The slave trade, which the European countries shamefully practised for a long time, was finally abolished, but it still exists in America and the colonies, making the governments endeavours ineffective.[6] Laws may act as breaks for many things but against human greed they are no stronger than a spider's web. A wise government, in the upbringing of the young, should root out greed and encourage noble feelings. Only in this way will there be respect for justice and its enforcement. Unlawful deeds must be crushed in the bud and the wounds of ill-doers be healed with mercy.

The most famous of the spas is Bath. Bath is the English Karlsbad or Warmbrunn. The water is hot; there are three springs, one hotter then the other. The sick start, as in Karlsbad, in the coolest. The water must cool for three hours before it may be used for bathing. The bathing season lasts throughout the winter: it starts in December and ends in May. Its efficacy was known to the Romans: they called it 'thermae sudatae, aquae calidae'. The Anglo-Saxons called Bath Akemanceaster, the village of cripples. One needs to be neither crippled nor sick to go to a watering place; people come not only for health but also for entertainment. The sick minister to their health with the waters; those who are accompanying them rescue themselves from boredom with balls, concerts, theatre, games and horse racing. Many come to health resorts for the same reasons they go to the Continent, which is to save money. Chevaliers de Fortune, the majority of whom are Irish soldiers, have come to find wealthy wives, for in watering place shared suffering inclines people to romance. Quite a number of heiresses have been able to escape the watchful eyes of aunts or guardians and have had the good or ill fortune to elope to Gretna Green with the sweet Adonis of their choice.

Spas are pleasant for their very setting, as they have often developed in the most beautiful landscapes: they would be even more pleasant if there were more spontaneity and less emphasis on etiquette. An Englishman is serious by nature so strict adherence to rules of behaviour will prevent him from enjoying himself. The resulting lethargy and idleness cause boredom. An Englishman may be seen having a good time only in his private life, whereas in public life he appears lifeless. Thus one can easily agree with a Frenchman who, when asked by a friend on his return from England: 'How do the English amuse themselves?' answered 'Ils s'amusent tristement.'

Like everywhere else the pleasant atmosphere of the spas is spoiled by prejudices about birth and wealth. The so-called upper classes are afraid of the commoners and avoid them wherever it is possible; while the lower classes avoid the upper because they find it pointless to expose themselves to humiliation. It would be a great mistake to think that everyone who is able to pay may go to a ball or a concert: the majority of the visitors are not admitted and those who are treat it as an honour. Hence the big difference between 'a select party' and 'mixed society': only the first of these is fashionable and acceptable. There is even a separate official to select the company and act as a Master of Ceremonies. This high office fell into the hands of a true adventurer[7] who made himself comfortable in the upper echelons of society. In addition to superficial politeness he had the rare advantage that he knew by heart the genealogies of the most important families in England. He was the one to whom the visitors reported on arrival. He was the marshal of all, and a gold medal on his chest marked his office. He planned the balls and concerts, kept order and peace and settled the arguments arising from the statutes, which are displayed in every room. He also arranged music for the visitors to listen to during their baths and on the walks, which they call 'the morning parade'. All this music, however, usually ends with 'God save the King' or 'Rule Britannia', with which Englishmen are never bored. They cherish these above any composition by a Rossini, Cherubini or Mozart. For such labours he collected a generous salary from the guests, sufficient for a life of comfort and luxury. Richard Nash, the first of such masters of ceremonies, travelled only in a four in hand. He died in 1761 and was buried in splendour. During his lifetime he was honoured with a statue which to this day stands in the great reception room. It is interesting to read the regulations for guests written by this master, whose services for Bath were so great. These regulations were established in 1742 and were passed by common agreement. They begin with an article insisting on courtesy towards the master:

1. From a lady of the upper classes nothing more is required than paying one visit on arrival and a second one before leaving – unless she is ill-mannered.
2. At balls ladies should order their servants to come for them on time – unless they wish to give themselves or others trouble.
3. In the morning men should not visit ladies in their bathrobes and nightcaps – if they do not wish to appear uneducated.
4. Only the conceited will bear ill will towards a friend who visits someone else to play cards or take breakfast in the morning.
5. Men should give tickets for balls only to honest women – unless they know none.
6. Only those men who think the world revolves around them will sin against courtesy by standing in front of a lady and blocking her view.
7. No man and no woman should feel abused if another couple is invited to lead the dance – other than those who should not be dancing at all.
8. Elderly ladies and children should be so kind as to seat themselves in the second row of benches at the balls – for the first, the time for dancing has passed and, for the second, it has not yet arrived.
9. Young ladies should always bear in mind the numerous eyes that look at them – but coquettes are exempted from this rule.
10. A person spreading gossip and slander should be taken for their author – he will be believed and accepted in society only by those like himself.

The rules of Bath's legislator are so clear and they have so much practical use that they should satisfy even the most experienced man of the world. They are displayed on the wall in the main reception room and they are legally binding to this day. I do not see why they should not be, for the warnings they contain are so prudent and sensible that neglecting them could cause embarrassment and trouble anywhere.

The office of the Master of Ceremonies, which is honoured with the title: 'the King of Bath', has passed through different hands. After the famous Beau Nash (for fame has so many origins!) it was given to Mr Collet, who held it for a short time and resigned voluntarily. He was succeeded by Mr Derwick. After his death two candidates ran for the office; this divided the elegant world so much that it would have come to a civil war if they had not given up the office to a third person. However, in 1777 the office was divided; since then two people have shared this once absolute power. I do not know what duo holds the sceptre now, but a few years ago it was Tyson and King.

After being examined at Brighton's customhouse, which, as in all customhouses, tends to be unpleasant and the search for contraband so rigorous that they even take off your shoes, we set out the next day for London in a stagecoach. Constant rain darkened the surrounding countryside which seemed to be beautiful; cared for as though it were a garden suburb of the capital and built-up with mansions, fine houses and farms. However, from the covered coach they could not be clearly

London from Greenwich Park. Just visible through the trees are Inigo Jones's Queen's House, built c.1616 for James I's wife, and Wren's Naval Hospital. Originally a royal palace, it was converted into a home for retired sailors by Queen Anne.

seen. The people travelling with us, apparently merchants, were taciturn as if busy with calculations, so that it seemed rude to interrupt them with questions. Thus I have nothing important to say about this journey. At four o'clock we were in London.

After Paris there was so little movement on the streets that London seemed dead to us. But the part of the city we were travelling through was not the City, where at this hour it is difficult to get through the crowds of people. Each part of London comes to life at a different time of the day and this depends on the status, the way of life and the professions of the people residing there. In Paris there is no such division of residents from their occupations and everything there is still mixed. Because of this, the same noise, shouting, commotion and rush of traffic continue throughout the streets of the city.

NOTES:

1 Vesta was the Roman goddess of the hearth. In primitive tribes responsibility for keeping alive the sacred fire which was essential to welfare was given to the young daughters of the chiefs. In Rome responsibility rested with the Vestal Virgins.

2 Dr Richard Russell was a Sussex doctor whose treatise on the beneficial effect of salt watter in the treatment of tumours, insanity, impotence, consumption and rabies brought hundreds of patients to Brighton. His son identified it with love and pleasure:

> Then fly that dangerous town ye swains
> For fear ye shall endure
> A pain from some bright sparkling eye
> Which Russell's skill can't cure.

3 Brighton Pavillion. Between 1793 and 1818 Henry Holland's classical villa was converted into John Nash's oriental extravaganza. It was equipped with every contemporary improvement in plumbing, heating and lighting.

4 In the first decade of the nineteenth century Brighton's population doubled and the number of houses tripled.

5 Aesculpius is the Latin form of the Greek god of medicine, Asklepios, who was believed to have been brought to Rome in the third century BC in the form of a serpent. A serpent coiled round a staff has become a symbol of the medical profession. Temples dedicated to the god were often erected near healing springs.

6 Bristol shipowners made fortunes out of the slave trade but few slaves can have landed at the quay. Most victims were shipped directly from Africa to the West Indies. The trade was made illegal in 1807 but slavery in the British Empire was not abolished until 1833.

7 Richard Nash (1674-1762). A Welsh lawyer, soldier, gambler and dandy, he was appointed Master of Ceremonies at Bath in 1704. His influence on the development of the town as well as on the manners of visitors made it the most fashionable watering place in Britain.

Chapter Eight

Foreigners' Lodgings. Description of the Most Convenient One. Food Prices. Westminster Hall. The Lower House. The Upper House. The King. The Parliament. The Royal Court.

Having described my journeys across the country, I would now like to draw the reader's attention to London and its vicinities. From now on the aim of my recollections is to complete the image I have already begun to sketch of this great capital.

People who intend to settle in London for a long time and are wealthy enough may stay in an hotel, which is costly, or rent a detached house. This is common practice among newcomers who come with their families and are concerned about expense. Foreigners who come alone and do not wish to live in an hotel may rent furnished lodgings. These vary enormously in price. The landlord or landlady of the house remains in charge of the kitchen and other amenities. They respond to the tenant's wishes and collect the rent either weekly or monthly. But lodgings of this kind are not the most rewarding for a foreigner who is curious, or one who is perhaps carrying out some research and would be glad to associate with the natives. If he wants to spend time profitably, he needs company in his lodgings unless he has many connections in the city, which is rather unlikely. It would be best for him to board with an honest family should he meet one. Throughout my whole stay in England and Scotland I lived in this fashion. Such houses, called 'pensions' in France, are run by impoverished families, commonly tradesmen's, lawyers' or clergymen's widows who, living on interest from what money they have left, eagerly enter into undertakings which will increase their humble incomes. A boarder in such a house seems to be part of the family and his stay is often both pleasant and rewarding, especially if a few boarders live together and they are well matched. Sometimes you can meet whole families living in this way. The more boarders the better. It makes it easier to choose between them, and their number itself indicates the quality of the establishment. Information about such boarding houses can be obtained from signboards exposed in windows or nailed to doors or else from the notices at the Royal Exchange, where I once saw a wall completely pasted with advertisements. In order not to be disappointed the best way to find a house is by recommendation. However, in order to be accepted you too have to be recommended, which provides the household with a guarantee of the honesty of your character and your reliability as a rent payer. Such houses are a kind of hotel, where guests not only have their separate bedchamber but also the use of public rooms where they can get together and receive visitors. They sit at the common table – much like à table d'hôte – with the slight difference that boarders, seeing each other every day, get to know and trust each other. Anyone seeing them for the first time at the table or in the drawing room would believe they were a group of close friends.

In the boarding house in London where I used to live, there were three families, about twenty people of various ages. These included the family of Admiral Frazer, a Scotsman who lived there with his wife and daughter. Some boarders had lived there for several years and the longer they had been there, the more prestigious the seats they took at the table. These were those nearest to the landlady who sat at the head of the table. These rules were followed so strictly that when the Admiral arrived a week after me a council had to be summoned and it was eagerly agreed that, out of respect, the most prestigious places should be given up to him and his family. But as they were about to come to the table he refused to take the prestigious seat and instead he and his family took seats, as befitted them from the beginning, at the bottom of the table, next to the door. Then he declared, and I remember his exact words, that he would be most delighted to follow all the rules of the house. Great is the nation in which a senior official does not assert his superiority except when performing his duty!

My stay there was pleasant and rewarding. I associated myself with people of various ages, standing and occupations. A few of them had spent several years in America or India, and some had travelled to many different countries. One man, by the name of Evans, was a well-known writer and was working on the publication of the history of the fundamental rights of all nations. Associating with them, whether in a serious or light-hearted mood, was always educational and interesting. They recommended to me sites worth visiting and facilitated my admission to these whenever they could. It is a significant help in a city where a newcomer does not at first know where to turn and what to see: proper guidelines can spare him time and money.

Apart from these obvious advantages, living in such a house is the cheapest way for a foreigner to live. Even though living in London is so expensive, I did not pay more than £7 sterling a month for board and lodging, whereas in Edinburgh I used to pay ten. Generally speaking, living in such houses in London would be incomparably more comfortable and cheaper if it were not for some extra expenses, such as servants, drinks and desserts, which the boarders buy for themselves. Living frugally they totalled £2 pounds sterling a month but, depending upon the spirit of the company with which you lived, they could amount to more. Although you could sometimes avoid these expenses, it is not always seemly to exclude yourself from the activities of others without damaging your own image. Even though in such communities frugality is a common goal, even frugality has limits which should not be crossed. There are households where you could live and dine for as little as £4 sterling but by saving the money you could lose more than you gained. Such a loss is irredeemable for a foreigner and such a loss cannot be recovered. Nowhere are the profits resulting from good company as valued as in England. When English gentlemen send their sons to school they will give £50 sterling and more to have them placed in households where they can benefit from the company of bright and intelligent people and further their social education. A foreigner who wishes to benefit from a short stay should choose his accommodation equally carefully.

Let us now consider how life in these houses is organised. Every tenant has a single bedroom with a carpet. The room has all the necessary furniture and bedding and sheets are changed every week. The price of the rooms depends on their size and position, on the first or second floor. At nine o'clock in the morning there is breakfast. It is served in the dining room where everybody gathers. For breakfast, according to the English custom, there is tea, toast bread with butter, soft-boiled eggs, some beef or some cold roast meat. Everybody eats and drinks to their heart's content. Because English breakfasts are lavish, you can have a rest and read one of the newspapers which will be lying on the table, often still damp with ink as they have just come off the press. The boarders subscribe to them individually or together. Having discovered what is new around the globe, what changes have taken place in governments or nations, what storms raged at sea, what fires and thefts took place in the capital, and what robberies in the outskirts, satiated and entertained, having commented on what they have read, as if adding some salt and pepper to their meal, the boarders go off to their affairs. Breakfast is the time when servants tidy the bedrooms: their presence at breakfast would be unnecessary, as they carry out their duties at the table beforehand. Around one o'clock there is lunch, which consists of some cold meat, cheese and bread, but it is rarely attended: some are detained by their affairs, others by lack of appetite. Lunch is served in the drawing room.

The dinner commences at five. At this time people gather from every quarter of the house: you can hear the repeated sound of knocking and the opening and shutting of doors until everyone is assembled. Just a quarter of an hour is given for dressing. Everybody walks down neatly dressed, the women quite smartly, and they all sit down in the usual order and in their own seats. The dinner, a typically English one, is without delicacies but healthy and composed of five dishes. Nothing is in excess but everything is in abundance. The fish which we had every day was especially delicious. The dinner ended with cheese. Desserts and drinks, other than beer, were the responsibility of the boarders. Dinners last quite long, because by dinner time the day's activities have ended and then everyone takes a rest. Nobody leaves the table until the landlady gets up and, following a national custom, takes all the ladies with her. Men stay with the wine some time longer; everyone keeps his bottle in front of him or shares it with his neighbour. They recount anecdotes, hum convivial songs and usually end standing to sing the national anthem: 'God Save King George'.[1] On one occasion a young Frenchman rented a room in this house. He had recently come to England and whenever this tune was sung he left the table. Once he stayed but did not stand up. This outraged the English patriots and, even though they were unwilling to break the hospitality code and disturb the peace of the house, they gave their word that they would show him the door if he dared to repeat this insult. I left soon after so I do not know what fate befell him as the result of his patriotism. After the singing, chatting and jokes one goes for a cup of tea to the drawing room where visitors to the boarders may join the company. Here the presence of the ladies invites more decorum, conversations are not as noisy, and sometimes books are read or music is played. Only rarely are cards played and then the stakes would be either non-existent or very low. And so one day follows another: the slightest change would create general confusion in the household: servants and guests would be unable to find their way in the chaos. Everything has its time and place here and, since there are not many servants, there is a general readiness to help.

For the information of my fellow countrymen who may happen to travel to England at some time or another I have listed here the usual price of board, lodging, and amenities in the inns and eating-houses. (6 pence = 1 zloty, 1 shilling = 2 zloty, 1 pound = 40 zloty)

Coffee or tea for breakfast is 1/- 6d to 3/-: Dinner: 3/- to14/-: Tea at eight o'clock: 1/- 6d to 2/- 6d. A bed: 2/- 6d to 5/- And servants' beds: 1/- 6d to 2/-. A bottle of porter: 9d to 1/- (its ordinary price 1/- 6d). A bottle of port wine or sherry: 5/- to 6/- Madeira: 8/- to 10/- Claret or Burgundy wine: 13/- to 14/-. Hock (from Rheingau) and champagne up to 16s. If a guest demands a private sitting room, the expenses increase by 2/- to 3/- a day. A waiter costs 1/- or 1/- 6d a day and a chambermaid 1s. In the better hotels drawing rooms and bedchambers cost 10/- to £1 1/- a day, and just a bedchamber 4/- or 5/-. Breakfasts and dinners are also more expensive in inns and hotels. In the eating-houses, where people only come to dine, the prices are not too high, as can be seen from this board. You can order from the menu:

	/-	d
Mock turtle soup	–	10
Oxtail soup	–	8
Broth	–	6
Pea soup	–	6

	s.	d.
Potato soup with lamb	–	6
Fish with gravy	1	–
Piece of meat	–	9
Ragout	–	5
Game in aspic	–	6
Green peas	–	9
Rump steaks	–	10
Stewed meat	–	10
Lamb chops	–	5
Pork or mutton chops	–	5
Veal cutlets with ham	–	10
Liver with ham	–	9
Veal head with ham	–	9
Minced meat with ham	–	9
Mutton with peas	–	10
Roasted pork loin	1	–
Roasted goose	1	–
Roasted duck	1	–
Capon or roasted chicken	1	–
Roasted turkey	1	–
Roasted rabbit	1	–
Chicken pâté	1	–
Pigeon pâté	1	–
Poultry pâté	1	–
Eel pâté	1	–
Plum pudding	–	4
Bread and butter pudding	–	4
Rice pudding	–	4
Fruit cream	–	4
Peas, broad beans, beans	–	1
Potatoes and greens, etc.	–	1
Carrots and parsnip	–	1
Lettuce	–	2
Lettuce with eggs and olive oil	–	6
Bread	–	1
Cheese	–	1

A week or a month will not suffice for visitors to London to try to get to know its peculiarities. In chapters I and IV I drew a rough picture of London's characteristics. It now remains to become acquainted with its most significant buildings and institutions and to understand their organisation and history. Where we begin is a matter of no importance. Let us start with Westminster Hall.[2]

This edifice is deemed the most beautiful in Europe. It is 270 feet long, 74 feet wide, the ceiling structure rising to 90 feet. It is worth observing that no pillar supports it. Richard II held a feast there for which 2,000 cooks cooked the dinner and 10,000 guests were invited to the table. The present king held a ceremonial banquet in the Hall after his coronation. This building houses a few courts where lords of the realm are tried for crimes that carry the death penalty. Here the unfortunate Charles I was tried.

From the Hall a dark corridor and stairs took us to the Lower House, the House of Commons.[3] Its appearance does not reflect the importance of its use. It is a hall made from a former chapel and is

Westminster Hall. Originally the banqueting hall of William Rufus's palace, the hall was rebuilt in 1397 to house the courts of Chancery, Common Pleas, King's Bench and Exchequer. These had previously been ambulatory, accompanying the kings on their progresses through their domains.

cramped and dirty. On both sides there are rows of seats, gradually rising above each other and upholstered with green morocco. They are designed for the Members of Parliament. At some distance there is a place where, on a high chair, sits the Speaker, the equivalent of a Polish Marshal of the Sejm,[4] who is elected by the House and confirmed in this office by the King. Members taking the floor address their speeches to him. Before him rests the Mace, a symbol of his high authority, which he lifts onto the table when he opens a session and places under the table when a session is adjourned or closed. Bills, the intended legislation, are filed on the table where two assistants and one clerk sit. Opposite the Speaker's chair there is a gallery for strangers but it holds no more than 130 people. Access is available by a letter of introduction from a Member of Parliament or, less legally, by giving the doorman a silver half-crown (5 Polish złotys). The sight of this is surely dearer to him than a sheet of white paper, albeit it bears the name of a most respectable Member of Parliament. In this gallery sit shorthand writers who record even the smallest events and every word being said in the House and immediately pass their notes to the papers. These are printed so quickly that the next morning, at eight o'clock, the public can read what had been passed at two or three am. Descriptions of these debates can occupy a whole long paper. I say long because these newspapers are printed on sheets as big as tablecloths and with very small print. Typesetters work all night to compose them. It is hard to grasp how they can manage with such a task, which is always done on time. What a furore there would be if just once the newspaper failed and the post came without delivering it. It would be unprecedented.

Under the Lower Chamber there is an undercroft where, in 1605, concealed gunpowder, supposedly intended to blow up the Houses, was discovered. The conspiracy was called the Gunpowder Plot[5] and the perpetrators are unknown to this day. Its discovery caused such terror that even now, as a precaution, a party is sent to inspect the undercroft before every sitting of Parliament.

I did not have an opportunity to observe this House during the session. Proceedings during which the Queen Consort [6] was tried were too stormy, and the crowd was too great, to make entry possible. Moreover, I did not then know any political figures, and so these sessions did not interest me much. Later on I did not have the opportunity to be in London when they were held. I have heard that the Members of the House disappoint one's high expectations. Those who have watched them marvelled, not at the gravity, but rather the rhetoric with which some members supported their bills. Only the Speaker, whose symbols of authority are respected by all, impresses by his gravity. He is dressed in a long black robe, wears a wig and has a hat on his head. The Members do not wear a distinguishing uniform. Each of them dresses as he pleases: he can wear a frock-coat or boots with spurs, sometimes he holds a whip, as if he has just dismounted from a horse, and they all wear some headgear. Many of them can be seen in the most informal poses and, especially when the sitting is very long, some can be spotted eating what they have brought in their pockets. A lot of them talk so loudly that it is difficult to hear the voices of those taking the floor and the Speaker, by virtue of his office, is sometimes compelled to ask for order in the House. There are 658 Members, but if the subject matter of proceedings is unimportant, merely a tenth of that number will be present. Many come only to vote. At least 40 Members are necessary for the House to function, and for a committee eight is enough. Elections are held every seven years. Despite the unimpressive appearance of the House and the extravagance which is inseparable from its proceedings, no one can fail to notice a certain feeling of exhilaration when present within these walls. Here the affairs of this and other countries are resolved, and here resounded the eloquence of the most famous orators who rose to speak about the welfare of their country and mankind. Here spoke Pitt, Fox, Burke and Canning. Here Lord Chatham[7] was brought in on crutches to make his last speech in the House of Lords – a speech which culminated in the words 'Let us at least make one effort and, if we must fall, let us fall as men.'

On the same day we visited the House of Lords. This is usually called the Upper, because it lies higher than the other and to reach it you have to go up a flight of stairs. The Upper House is neither bigger nor more embellished than the Lower House. Its walls are decorated with faded tapestries which commemorate the victory over the

Spanish Armada. At the far end of the House towers the Throne from which the King opens or adjourns the sessions. The Lord Chancellor, who sits before the Throne on the Woolsack, can do this on his behalf. The Lord Chancellor presides over the House of Lords in the Sovereign's absence and his functions in the Upper House are much like the Speaker's in the Lower House. There are 377 Lords in the House but their number is not limited because the King can create new peers. During Queen Anne's reign, in order to create a majority in the House, twelve new peers were created on a single occasion in 1711. Only the number of the Lords Spiritual is fixed: there are two archbishops and twenty-four bishops. Among the Lords Temporal are noblemen of high rank, namely dukes, marquises, earls, viscounts, and barons. Some of them sit by descent from the old families, others by recent creation and the rest by election. Sixteen Scottish peers represent their country and 28 peers, one archbishop and three bishops represent Ireland. The place where the Lords sit is enclosed by a bar. The bills that have been passed in the Lower House are submitted by a delegation to the bar for the consideration of the House of Lords, which has the power to accept or reject them. Once rejected they can go no further.

Before it becomes law every bill is put to the vote in both Houses and the outcome may vary. In the Upper House a vote cast in the affirmative is called 'content' and a negative one 'non content', whereas in the Lower House votes for the bill are called 'yeas' and those against 'nays'. When such a bill has been passed in both Chambers it is sent to the King as the supreme authority for Royal Assent, otherwise it would not become law. In this situation the King can exercise his power personally or devolve it upon three or more peers of his choice. If the bill receives Royal Assent and it concerns the wellbeing of the whole country, a clerk announces the King's will with the words 'Le roi le veut', and if it concerns a private person, he says, 'Soit fait comme il est désiré'. If a money bill is concerned, he says, 'Le roi remercie ses loyaux sujets accepte leur bénevolence, et aussi le veut' and, if the King deems the bill passed in the Houses to be inconsistent with the interest of the country, the clerk says, 'Le roi s'avisera' (the King will consider it), which is a gentle type of refusal. It is strange that in the most important cases the King of England addresses his nation in a foreign language but it is difficult to alter a tradition established in the reign of William I. The numerous French expressions in legal documents were introduced by the Normans who, having conquered England, became its legislators.

This is what the British call its Parliament. It combines threefold powers: that of the King, the aristocracy and the nation. How these separate powers interact and affect each other cannot be enlarged upon within this description of a journey. This could prove a lengthy work in itself since the English regard the balancing of the powers to be of supreme importance. Such a work, to be of any value, would have to deal not only with the legislative branch but also the executive one. These subjects were fully explored by Blackstone[8], Miller, Lolme and Cottu. Further elucidation can be found in the journals of Dupin and de Staël (a son of the still more famous mother),[9] both of whom travelled to England during my stay there. But now I will say a few more words about the Royal Court.

By the Royal Court I do not understand the persons attached to the King's household, of whom there are many whose positions are survivors from the medieval courts and are still held by members of the first families in the country. I refer to courtly ceremonies attached to the royal majesty, generally bearing the name Court. The most important events are the coronation ceremony, the King's birthday, drawing rooms, audiences and other days which we call ceremonial days. The courtly Gazette provides information on drawing rooms and audiences. It is almost entirely devoted to and filled with declarations of homage, respect and congratulations to the King from nobles, clergy and higher officials. Then it is customary to introduce to the King the young of the great houses, sons and daughters alike. Their presentation is generally treated as an introduction to high life and society as it is believed that a person introduced to the King has the entree to any company. The introduction is usually performed by the parents, a close relative or a distinguished member of the family. A person introduced to the Queen receives a light kiss on the cheek and formerly Kings did this as well. He or she might then kiss the King's hand. The ladies can also be introduced by the ladies of the

Court. Persons striving for this honour have to wear court dress or full ceremonial order, either national or pertaining to the person's office. There are strict rules regarding this and almost everything else in the Court. You are told by those who have been introduced to the King that there is nothing more magnificent than seeing the King of England in purple and on the throne, surrounded by a large retinue of courtiers, scrupulously following the etiquette of the Middle Ages in the shrine of the luxuries and comforts of modern civilisation.

NOTES:

1 First publically performed after the defeat of the Jacobite Rising in 1745, 'God Save the King' became the National Anthem in the early nineteenth century.

2 Westminster Hall was built in 1099, during the reign of William Rufus, and the timber ceiling was erected for Richard II in 1394.

3 The Palace of Westminster was founded by Edward the Confessor. St Stephen's Chapel was added a century later during the reign of King Stephen. Abandoned as a royal chapel after a fire in 1512, the Commons, who had previously met in the Chapter House of Wetminster Abbey, moved to the Chapel in 1547. The Lords met in another chamber in the Palace.

4 The Sejm, the Polish Parliament or Diet, consisted of the Senate, in which the elected king, the bishops and highest officers of state met, and the Chamber of Deputies in which only landowners were represented. In 1823, when Lach-Szyrma was in London, the Congress Kingdom was under Russian domination and the Sejm no longer met.

5 Gunpowder was discovered under the vaults below the Upper, not the Lower House. Guy Fawkes, who was on guard, disclosed under torture the names of seven of the conspirators. They were all hanged, drawn and quartered.

6 Princess Caroline of Brunswick-Wolfenbuttel was married to the Prince Regent in 1795. They hated each other, rapidly separated and led almost equally dissolute lives. Their only child, Charlotte, died in 1817. On the death of George III in 1820 Caroline returned to England but was refused admission to the coronation ceremony. A bill to dissolve the marriage was passed by the Lords but George IV's unpopularity in London was reflected by such strong opposition in the Commons that the bill was dropped.

7 William Pitt, 1st Earl of Chatham (1708-80), had been a successful war minister during the Seven Years War. He had been an opponent of the harsh measures taken against the colonists which led to the American Revolution but was not prepared to make peace at any price. His death immediately after his last speech contributed to the narrow defeat of the motion to do so.

8 Sir William Blackstone (1723-80). Jurist and first professor of Law at Oxford, his *Commentaries on the Laws of England* became the most influential exposition of the structure and principles of English law.

9 Anne-Louise Germaine, Madame de Staël (1766-1817) was the daughter of Francis Necker, the French financier and statesman, and wife of Baron de Staël-Holstein, the Swedish ambassador in Paris. A novelist, brilliant hostess and political writer, her complete works were published by her son and daughter in 1820-21.

Chapter Nine

The Institute of Arts. Paintings by Barry. Caricatures and Allegories. The Royal Academy. Admission Fees for Exhibitions. Scientific and Artistic Societies. Technical Schools. University of London. The Guildhall. The Polish Prisoner. The Mayor of London. Mansion House. The Room at the Guildhall. The Monument.

In the previous chapter we considered the splendour of the court; let us now proceed to the Institute of Arts, Handicraft and Trade. To these England owes her affluence. Called the Society of Arts, it is situated in the part of the city which is commonly known as the Adelphi.[1] Those who wish to enter it must obtain a letter of introduction from one of the Institute's members to its secretary, who at that time was John Aikin. Nobody is allowed in without a recommendation. The Institute has numerous models representing technical inventions dating from the earliest days to the present. This collection is invaluable for those interested in the arts and in the work of craftsmen and it is worth not only visiting but also studying the models. Above all, the enthusiasm of the Society should be lauded. Since 1754, the year it was established, it has set a shining example by rewarding at its own expense the development of new and the improvement of existing inventions. It already has 1,700 members and the Duke of Sussex, the King's brother, is its chairman.

The hall where meetings are held and a number of the adjacent rooms are decorated with historical and allegorical paintings by James Barry,[2] a member of the said Society. The paintings represent the origins of the arts and sciences and the men who, over the centuries, contributed to their growth and development. There are six great pictures, full of meaning and created with exceptional powers of imagination, but the sixth, which represents the Elysian Fields and thus the final reward, is the most interesting one – it seems to have been inspired by the following passage from the *Aeneid*:

> Here patriots live, who, for their country's good,
> In fighting fields, were prodigal of blood:

Priests of unblemished lives here make abode,
And poets worthy their inspiring god;
And searching wits, of more mechanic parts,
Who graced their age with new-invented arts:
Those who to worth their bounty did extend,
And those who knew that bounty to commend.
  The heads of these with holy fillets bound,
And all their temples were with garlands crown'd.

The painter, looking back over so many past centuries, represented the characters of the inventors and reformers, surrounding them with insignia by means of which it is easy to recognise the identity of a given person. At the bottom, under a palm tree, there is a pelican feeding its children with its own blood, symbolising the men who, in serving humanity, had to endanger their lives and face hardship. The whole picture was divided into groups or circles. In one we have Thales, Archimedes, Descartes; in the second Bacon, Copernicus, Galileo and Newton are peering at the solar system, whose secrets are being unveiled by two angels. At the angel's feet the humiliated Columbus[3] is drawing a map of his voyages to America. Next to him there are Epaminondas[4] with a shield, Socrates, Cato, Brutus, and Thomas More. The painting also includes groups of legislators, sages, poets, painters, and patrons of science, for the artist wanted to depict in his picture the most eminent sons of mankind. The legislators he represents in an exceptional manner: he places Alfred the Great leaning upon the arm of William Penn, while he, the peaceful founder of Pennsylvania, is showing the book of his laws to Lycurgus[5]. Separated by centuries, ideas have brought these legislators together! There is also a place here for women renowned for their virtues who, in their daily lives, created homes in which charity reigned and tensions were resolved. The painting is crowned by the artist's conception of the origins of the Universe. Stars surrounded by their planets revolve round its First Cause and angels represent the Higher Wisdom. Infinity is suggested.

But if good deeds are to be rewarded then bad ones should be punished. The painter tried to represent it by depicting Tartarus. Thus, at the very bottom of the picture, he depicted the fiery abyss dimmed by clouds of smoke and, above it, two mighty hands hurling into it monsters tied with serpents representing envy, pride, ambition, gluttony, harlotry, prodigality and avarice. Immersed in this sea of flames are duplicity, hypocrisy, oppression, cruelty, and war. The observer cannot be mistaken about the significance of these horrors; the painter aptly imparted each with the characteristics which distinguish it from the others.

One might suggest that English artists, more than others, are deeply interested in moral allegories. Artists of other nations usually appeal to the instinctive response of the senses while the English appeal to reason. Leaving much to the imagination, they transport the thought into infinity. Their poetry, especially modern poetry, bears the same characteristics. This must certainly be the result of better moral education and the versatile development of intellectual faculties. For this reason English caricatures are considered to be the best, for who could understand the ugliness of vice and evil deeds better than someone who recognised the charm of virtue and the abysmal difference between vice and virtue? The sharply marked features in their caricatures are a testimony to their clear concepts of morality.

The English are simply the only nation that has a corpus of caricatures and allegories. The former serve to condemn vice, the latter to immortalise the deeds of their sages, heroes and outstanding citizens. The impressive edifices of their cathedrals, churches and institutions are full of monuments surrounded by allegorical figures. The facades of public buildings are adorned with them. The people, understanding their significance, are given a visual history of their country.

I would have spent the whole day looking at Mr Barry's paintings and drawing inferences from them had it not been for the impatience of my guide, who was determined to shorten my sojourn by noisily walking up and down, stamping on the floor, drumming his fingers on the window panes and deliberately moving the furniture around. It is a great pity that, when visiting local institutions, one is not allowed enough time by the guides to look around properly. Finding oneself amongst a multitude of objects, but before managing to catch more than a glimpse of them, one has to leave. Therefore, to visit such an institution only once is pointless. For a better understanding it should be visited several times and, since such visits are expensive, for one has to pay wherever one goes, it is sensible to do so in the company of others. All the efforts and works of the Society of Arts seem to illustrate the truth expressed by one of its members in his writings. He asserted that man, living among his fellows and wanting to reach the level suitable to his destiny, to ensure his own and posterity's success, should begin by determining his own strengths and directing them appropriately.

As important as this Institute is the Royal Academy in Somerset House. It is not an academy as we know it but rather an institute devoted to painting, woodcarving and architecture. It has existed since 1769, the year when it was opened by the famous painter Joshua Reynolds, the first chairman of the Academy. He was followed by West [6] and, since 1820, Lawrence. There are forty members who bear the title of Royal Academicians. Of these four are professors of painting, anatomy, perspective and architecture. Their remuneration is only £30 sterling a year, but the scope of their duties is also fairly narrow – they give a mere six lectures a year. Every year in May a public exhibition of new works is organised there. On such occasions the galleries are filled with the fashionable, with high society, and with experts and critics, of whom all are charged one shilling for admission. And thus a sum of sometimes more than £6,000 accumulates, which is spent partly on awards and encouragement for the artists and partly to cover costs related to the Institute. When the painting by Mr Barry was exhibited, more than £1,000 was collected.

Our government cannot be praised enough for not charging citizens who visit exhibitions, but I would venture to say that introducing a small fee would not seriously diminish its generosity, nor would the public interpret it as a burden. It would, however, be of some considerable benefit: first of all, public money could be saved for awards or at least some additional capital for that purpose collected. Secondly, the crowds of idle people who attend such exhibitions, not for the sake of art or the government's protection of it, but exclusively for social reasons, would thin out. Thirdly, the artists and craftsmen themselves would benefit. Those attending an exhibition who had been required to pay an admission fee would be more likely to stay longer, examine more detail and observe everything more thoroughly, instead of rushing through, as is the case today, and thinking that if they do not manage to see something today, they will do so tomorrow – usually never to return. Such flying visits should be prevented, and since they cannot be fully prevented, they ought to be discouraged, for neither art nor the fame of artists will benefit from them. The works of art and industry need to be studied and there is no point in observing them superficially. And finally, the intended favour done to the public results in the undervaluing of exhibitions, for people value something only if they have to pay for it and usually the more they pay for it, the more they value it. It is a regrettable aspect of human character but that is just how things are. For this very reason in England, and almost everywhere abroad, people are charged for admission to exhibitions. And since the value of money is a relative matter and what is a burden for a craftsman would be a mere trifle for a wealthy merchant or aristocrat, the difficulty would consist in specifying an appropriate fee for each person. Ideally this would be left to the generosity of the rich. But that is only by way of digression.

In Somerset House there are both the Society of Antiquaries and the Royal Society, whose aim is to promulgate natural sciences and inventions. Its chairman used to be Banks[7] and now it is Sir Humphry Davy.[8] The whole capital abounds in useful scientific societies. For the application of scientific methods to arts and crafts there is the Royal Institution, a kind of technical school, where the above-mentioned Davy used to give lectures on chemistry and now Brande[9] lectures in his stead. There is also the Society of Literature, founded in 1823 for the enhancement of literature by the discovery and publication of hitherto unknown literary works, and the Royal Academy of Music founded for the improvement of music. Apart from these, there are numerous art galleries, exhibitions, public libraries, and societies for reading newspapers; in sum – various societies concerned with sciences, skills and craftsmanship.

Particularly numerous are institutes for the promotion of useful knowledge among craftsmen, founded in accordance with Birkbeck's[10] plan for his Mechanics' Institution. This Institution was a model for several schools established in various parts of the capital. In 1828 there were 78 such schools around the country. What a huge step towards further progress in industry and crafts, as well as in morality, when craftsmen, weary after a whole day's toil at a workshop, do not seek repose in physical rest nor intoxicate their senses with liquor but study the theory of their crafts and examine relationships between specific and general laws of nature! Just how many new modifications and improvements in workshops may this bring and how many new inventions and discoveries! Technical schools have received of late a great deal of encouragement from a society established by eminent scientists and citizens of the country, the aim of which is the enlightenment of craftsmen by publishing appropriate periodicals encompassing not only different fields of science, but also the moral education of the people. Those periodicals appear monthly and are sold for nearly nothing.

But surely, of all the scientific institutions the most important is the University of London[11] in which, in the year 1828, scientific courses are to commence. The schedule of the University reveals some novel elements: public lectures will be held and students are supposed to spend much of their time teaching one another. This method, which elsewhere is applied only in primary schools, seems to gain acceptance here even in the highest scientific institutions. Professors will not have permanent salaries but they will be remunerated from the fees paid by students attending their classes. The funds requisite to establish the University were accumulated by means of a collection. To complete the endeavour £300,000 sterling is required. Time alone will tell whether the appeal succeeds.

The Guildhall is the name of the old Town Hall of London, where the mayor of the City, the Lord Mayor, is elected and where a number of trials which are within the scope of his jurisdiction are held. Once I visited one of the courtrooms where two boys, aged ten and thirteen, were being interrogated on a charge of theft, an offence severely punished in England. The boys, though, escaped retribution due to the lack of evidence. The judge merely reprimanded them publicly and ordered them to behave so as to clear themselves of such dis-

The Guildhall. The fifteenth-century hall was given a neo-Gothic facelift in 1818. In the great hall the Lord Mayor sat in front of a statue of the reigning monarch. The chapel, on the right of the etching, was used by the Court of Requests.

honourable suspicions and avoid any misdeed which could be punished with deportation or even the death penalty. The judge put it in most appropriate terms and, desiring that the children should understand the gravity of his reprimand, asked their parents to explain to the boys what transportation meant and to look after them more carefully. Many a time did I witness this paternal solicitude for the accused on the part of judges: the leniency which was evinced did not impair the dignity of high office. Quite the contrary, by showing humanity they often imparted it with more glory.

I arrived there not out of mere curiosity but because of special circumstances. As I mentioned elsewhere, at the house where I was staying people usually read newspapers at breakfast. One day a companion of mine handed me his paper, pointing to a passage which would, as he said, interest me. From it I learnt that there was a Pole sentenced to imprisonment at the Guildhall. The editor of the paper presented him as a helpless wretch who 'used to know better days', condoling with him at the same time. The article was couched in such strong words, even reproaching the judges, that it must have attracted every reader's attention, and mine in particular. On the very same day I repaired to the Guildhall intending to learn more about him and his plight. Perhaps I knew his family in Poland and might be able to aid him in some manner? Having informed the judge of the reason for my coming and my desire to see the prisoner, I was most courteously permitted to enter the jail at Giltspur Street Compter and, since it was situated nearby, I was guided there by a court servant. On presenting to a warder a note from the judge, the prisoner was summoned. I spoke to him in Polish, which confused him so much that I had to wait a while before he mustered enough courage to venture an answer in the same language which, it was apparent, he had forgotten. He tried to comprehend the reason for my visit. I answered that it was his present situation, which surely could not be regarded as enviable. Having received such a reply he asked me to talk to him without witnesses. I rejoined that there was no reason for that; after all we were speaking a language which no one understood in that place. After a few minutes' conversation I managed to understand everything and he, having realised that my curiosity was satisfied, added finally: 'I do not demand anything of you, for I have not deserved any grace. All I ask of you is to take pity on me, as any good man would on a prisoner.' Hereupon I handed him half a crown and departed. But readers would probably wish to learn who the prisoner was. As he himself revealed to me, he was a Polish Jew from Płock. At that time he had been in London for several years and, not having any decent work, as so often happens in Poland, he led an idle life, frequently loafing about in the streets at night and being taken to court for vagrancy by the police. He knew the prison very well for it was his second stay there and, by professing to be a Polish exile, he inspired so much pity in the public that even the newspapers began to defend him.

The following day I was a witness to the election of the Mayor of London. It takes place each year on Michaelmas Day, which thus becomes a day of great celebration in London. The guilds and companies gather at the Guildhall for the election. Ten days later the new Mayor, accompanied by music and a colourful parade of guildsmen, repairs to Westminster to take his oath. Part of this journey is on the Thames and part by land through a most numerous mob of common people. His carriage is old-fashioned, gilded and covered with the coats of arms of the guilds, and he is surrounded with servants in livery that is equally old-fashioned. City councillors, sheriffs and other clerks accompany him on this parade. The whole pageantry evinces more splendour than good taste. In days of yore it used to include some additional queer ceremonies, which have been abandoned lately.

The mayor is elected from among the city councillors and, should he shrink from accepting the post, he must pay a fine of £500 and the election will be repeated. Usually affluent citizens are elected. And since wealth in mercantile countries is not always inherited and even the poor can acquire it, it should come as no surprise that many mayors were not of aristocratic origin. At the time of which I am writing Waithman, a cloth merchant, was elected. Wood, who held this post in 1817, was a weaver's son, and it has been this way from time immemorial. This is reflected in the ancient song 'Bells of London' which wet-nurses used to hum when feeding merchants' children. It tells the following story: Whittington, the son of a poor countryman, came to London without anything to live on and not knowing what to do, decided to leave the city. As he reached the city gates, the bells of Bow Church began to toll and he imagined he heard them say:

> 'Come, come Whittington,
> Lord Mayor of London'

He then returned and was admitted to a merchant shop on which he served for many long years. Later he joined a group of partners who decided to organise an expedition to overseas countries. One of them sent a ship, the others goods, money, etc. Being very poor, he could send nothing but his cat. But there was a plague of mice in a distant overseas country – let us assume it was Poland during Popiel's[12] reign – and the cat was bought for a great deal of money. Whittington became so rich that he was elected Lord Mayor of London, and thus the prophecy of the bells was fulfilled. And there is indeed a person with this name on the list of city mayors. He founded a school for merchants' children and a few almshouses. His remains are buried in St Michael's Church and there was a monument erected to commemorate him and his cat.

The story, which has some elements of a fable, bears testimony to the fact that London owes a large part of its affluence to the guilds and to the endeavours of the merchants. There was an Anglo-Saxon law by which the title of thane was awarded to a person who undertook a journey to an overseas country at his own expense.[13] The habit of sending a journeyman on a journey used to be very common in England;[14] apparently it is still preserved in Germany. Nevertheless, even now only the City companies have the right to elect the mayor. There are 91 of them and they include tobacco pipe makers and tobacco blenders, fan makers, launderers and carriers. However, I doubt if a member of any of these would have a chance of becoming the mayor. The most important guilds were those of the mercers and drapers. The latter were subject to some extraordinary laws: for example, if a weaver apprentice was proved to have stolen a wisp of wool he was to be sentenced to death. On account of its severity, this law is not executed any more. Nobody would wish to exact the death penalty for stealing a wisp of wool, but it could still be strictly enforced if an owner of a workshop insisted on it after having caught the culprit. It is primarily to the wool industry that England owes her affluence and, in recognition of this, the Lord Chancellor's seat in the House of Lords is a sack stuffed with wool.

The dwelling of the Mayor is in the Mansion House, which impresses one more with its immensity than its architectural merits. Its erection cost £45,000. I visited the interior of the building which is the object of the ambition and endeavours of so many London merchants. The Lord Mayor himself showed us round the residence. It would be his for one year only but the memory will certainly linger on in his family for several centuries. It contains a room called the Egyptian Hall, in which mayors give dinners after their election. In an adjacent room we saw a king-size bed, in which they sleep after the election. It is very impressive and gilded throughout, and is said to have cost the City £3,000. What pleasant dreams must one have when sleeping in such an expensive bed! The mayor is remunerated with £6,000 for his year of office but usually this sum does not suffice and he has to spend a few thousand from his private resources. The insignia of the Mayor's power are the mace and the sword, which are carried in front of him at celebrations, and when he processes a page carries the train of his robe. While in office, he is referred to as 'Lord' and enjoys a great deal of respect. His jurisdiction includes several courts: he himself presides every day except Sunday at the Town Hall court, and apart from that he has to be present at the court of the Old Bailey for every criminal case. The Mayor has other miscellaneous duties, of which, however, he can be relieved by his subordinates. He is in charge of the police in the City and on the River Thames. But he possesses no power over the part of London which is called Westminster, for which there is another mayor, referred to as the High Steward, who is not elected in the fashion of the Lord Mayor but is appointed by the Westminster chapter. This post is held for life.

During the monarchs' sojourn in London in 1814[15] the City gave in their honour a magnificent dinner at the Guildhall. I will not venture to describe the splendour with which that feast was organised, the precious service used, the amount of wine consumed, the number of toasts raised or how many thousands of pounds sterling it all cost. My guide, a London merchant, still vividly remembered and enumerated it all, even though eight years had passed since the day of the dinner. The hall is commodious and lofty and, as is always the case with old town halls, adorned with Gothic sculpture. It was not very impressive perhaps because, at the time, it was being repaired. It can accommodate up to 7,000 people. On one side it is embellished with statues of Nelson, Chatham, Pitt and Beckford, the mayor most eager to defend the City's liberties. On the other side it is disfigured with two colossal giants: Gog and Magog, strangely attired and holding two gigantic halberds in their hands. They are so horrific that London dry-nurses scare children with them, just as we in Poland scare children with wolves and the Romans in Martial's days used to do the same with the statue of a potter:

> 'rufi persona Batavi
> Quae tu derides, haec timet ora puer.'

In the councillors' chamber, which abuts onto the great hall, there are several historical paintings of some quality which would be even better were it not for the humdrum flavour pervading the chamber. Under pressure from the patriotic enthusiasm of my guide, I had to express my delight at the painting representing the English royal family and even seat myself upon the chair where the Mayor is seated during a session. The middle classes are everywhere the same: they evince identical prejudices, conceit and boastfulness. Their taste is exaggerated and they have a propensity for grandiosity, revelling in guild emblems and bombastic inscriptions. The Town Hall clock is embellished with the four cardinal virtues: Justice, Prudence, Temperance and Fortitude and above them the flag, the symbol of inconstancy, is fluttering. They are guarded by the figure of Time and their vigilance is aroused by the crowing of two cocks.

Going from there towards the Thames I beheld the Monument erected to commemorate the Fire of London. Within there is a flight of stairs made of black marble, which leads to the very top, from which

The Monument. Designed by Wren to commemorate the Fire of 1666 and erected by Robert Hooke, the 202 foot column was, in its day, the tallest in Europe. Removed by James II, it was restored during the reign of William and Mary and not erased till 1830.

there is a wonderful panorama of London. Its base is adorned with various allegorical figures which are connected with the fire. The architect of the Monument was Christopher Wren, to whom London owes many of its magnificent edifices. This one is 200 feet high and is believed to be one of the tallest of its kind in Europe. The Column of Antonius Pius, said to be the tallest built by the Romans, is only 172 feet high. The column on Vendôme Square in Paris, upon which Napoleon's statue used to stand, is merely 140 feet high. According to the inscription on the base the Catholics were believed to have caused this horrific fire, in which 89 churches and 13,200 houses burnt. It is, nevertheless, a matter of controversy. An eminent poet Alexander Pope, a Catholic himself, refutes this allegation in his witty poem:

> 'Where London's column, pointing at the skies
> Like a tall bully, lifts the head, and lies.'

NOTES:

1 Designed by the Adam brothers on a series of arches and vaults above the Thames, the Adelphi was one of the finest pieces of street architecture in London. The Royal Society of Arts has survived but most of the Adam houses were pulled down in the 1940s.

2 James Barry (1741-1806), Irish historical painter and professor of painting at the Royal Academy.

3 Christopher Columbus (1451-1504). The Genoese discoverer of the New World, he reached the Bahamas in 1492, believing that the islands were off the coast of Japan. From his third journey (1498-1500) when he landed on the mainland of South America, he was sent back in irons, having quarelled with the newly appointed Spanish governor. He was restored to favour by Ferdinand of Aragon and Isabella of Castile.

4 Epaminondas (c418-362). Theban general and statesman and a man of high culture and integrity. His innovative tactics made a major contribution to the overthrow of Sparta in the Peloponnese

5 Lycurgas (c 390- c 325). Athenian orator and statesman, distinguished for his architectural works and integrity as manager of the public revenue.

6 Benjamin West (1738-1830). Born in Pennsylvania, he studied in Rome before settling in London in 1765 under the patronage of George III.

7 Sir Joseph Banks (1744-1820), English botanist. He accompanied Cook on his voyage round the world (1768-71) and equipped *The Endeavour* at his own expense. He founded the Africa Society, visited Newfoundland, the Hebrides and Iceland and was one of the founders of New South Wales.

8 Sir Humphry Davy (1778-1829). English chemist and populariser of science. The safety lamp which he invented in 1815 reduced the danger of working deep seams in coal mines.

9 William Thomas Brande (1788-1866), English chemist.

10 George Birkbeck (1776-1829). An English physician and educationist, he gave free lectures to working-class students when professor of Natural Philosophy at Anderson's College in Glasow. In 1824 he founded the Mechanic's Institute in London. This was later incorporated into London University as Birkbeck College.

11 Dissenters were excluded from Oxford and Cambridge. University College London (1828) was the first university in England in which there were neither religious tests nor teaching.

12 Popiel was a legendary Polish king who was believed to have been pestered and finally eaten by mice.

13 Lach-Szyrma had been misinformed. A thane had judicial authority over land held directly from the king and was ranked between a freeman and a nobleman.

14 Another error. Journeymen were craftsmen who had served a full apprenticeship and were originally employed on a daily basis.

15 To celebrate Napoleon's abdication and exile to Elba in April 1814, the victorious sovereigns paid state visits to London during the summer months. The restored Louis XVIII was joined by the Tsar of Russia, the King of Prussia, Prince Metternich of Austria, General Blücher and numerous minor

princes and generals. Londoners went mad, paying fifty guineas to hire a balcony from which to view the processions and a hundred guineas for a ticket to attend a celebratory ball at Devonshire House.

Chapter Ten

The East India House. Trade Companies. The Custom House. The Bank. The Stock Exchange. Lloyd's. The Postal System. Stagecoach Fares. The Book Trade. Periodicals and Newspapers. The Market Place. Burlington Arcade. Whitbread's Brewery.

It is a most interesting experience to visit the magnificent East India House, which belongs to the East India Company.[1] It houses a vast stock of Indian wares, which, I openly confess, I did not see, even though I could have, for I had an introduction from one of the Company's members to its main secretary. But I deemed inspecting the wealth of nabobs, which had certainly been amassed through oppression of the hapless Indians, a waste of time.

The building accommodates a collection of books and a museum. The library contains not only original Indian works but also all volumes dealing with India. I was staggered by the sight of two large rooms filled from floor to ceiling with books of Eastern wisdom written in Chinese, Sanskrit and modern Indian dialects. I had not anticipated such riches. I sincerely regretted that I lacked the ability of the learned Schlegel,[2] who at the time was poring over them like a bookworm. He was preoccupied with the translation of an Indian poem which preceded by a few centuries Homer's songs and was reputed to be equal in beauty to the Iliad. I do not know whether his work has already been published. He was accompanied by an assistant, an expert Sanskritist like himself, who had been assigned to him by the Prussian government. The post of librarian is occupied by Dr Wilkins,[3] the author of a grammar and a dictionary of Sanskrit, a learned, courteous and civil man. He was surprised when I told him and explained by examples how similar are Slavonic dialects and Sanskrit and that, in Poland, we have a comparative grammar written by Majewski.[4]

The museum collection of Indian antiquities is not as extensive as it is rich, but one needs a deeper understanding of Eastern culture to respond to it. Statues of Indians do not appeal to the intellect and imagination as clearly as Greek ones; they are shrouded in dark mysticism and obscured by the transformations of deities and inexplicable allegories. One needs at least a few days to find one's bearings amongst them. The Indian deities are not presented, as is the case with the Greeks, as statues in human form but rather as a collection of the various figures which they assumed in their transformations or incarnations. These might represent the four-headed Brahma, Buddha or Krishna, but now the object of vain curiosity rather than worship. How the change of location can alter the significance even of the gods! The Thames is no substitute for the Ganges. Looking at these deities, London begins to resemble ancient Rome, where the gods of the subjugated peoples were gathered in the Pantheon in order to keep their worshippers safely under the yoke. The bright Surya, the revered Sun of the Indians, stands astonished by the foggy atmosphere of England, holding in her hand a lotus flower. She is preceded by Aurora who, riding on the seven steeds which stand for either seven planets or seven days of the week, heralds the dawn. Her son is Light who carries a beam like the bow of Apollo. Cold and Penury are huddled behind the rocks, some distance away from the Sun. How many new concepts are expressed which Greek mythology did not attach to the Sun! There is also another beautiful image of the Sun called Surra Wahona, but it is only a copy of the original which is in Delhi.

On the walls I beheld several landscapes of India painted by the famous Ward.[5] One of them represents a wedding, the other an Indian funeral. At the wedding people are dressed in black, at the funeral in white. The third one depicts the national celebration of the Indians, the Lantern Festival, the fourth is of the rock called Trichonopoly. On its 330 feet high peak there is an Indian temple to which Brahmins, preceded by trumpeters, carry holy water in vessels. The fifth represents Vera Malis, a rock situated forty miles from Trichonopoly. On its top there are gigantic boulders, or rather rocky mountains, looking as though they had been rolled there by some tremendous force. The sixth depicts a mandarin en route to Tartary. It is especially interesting, for it was painted by an Indian painter and gives an excellent notion of winter in that country. The seventh picture is charming: it portrays the city of Calcutta, the second, Eastern capital of England, with its picturesque environs, lush vegetation and delightful hills. On their tops are shady trees and groves and the fortresses erected by the English to subdue the indigenous population.

Among those antiquities and works of art are hung naval flags captured in battles with Spain and France. Amidst them there was a flag of the unfortunate Tippoo Sahib,[6] the king of Mysore, who, unable to withstand the might of England, had fallen in Seringapatam, the capital of his country. On display there is also the gold head of a tiger which used to stand by his throne. Its teeth are made of the most dazzling diamonds. There was also a wooden full-sized tiger painted so realistically that it seemed to be alive. It was strangling a man and concealed inside was a musical instrument which produced the roar of an animal tormenting its prey. There were many other curiosities there as well: one was a staff decorated with two huge agate stones which had been carried in front of foreign envoys in recognition of their importance. Another was the Koran, rolled like a ribbon and not thicker than the middle finger and written on silk paper in a neat, small script with gilt ornamentation. Then there was a musical instrument from Java, a kind of piano with eleven keys or brass plates, which are hit by the player with two hammers. Instead of a case, the amplification and embellishment of the sound was achieved by copper pipes, which were situated under each key and had apertures which could expand and contract. When fully opened, the purest and longest tones are heard. The music thus produced is said to be pleasant, somewhat slow and bearing a semblance to that of a harmonica.

In the hall filled with Indian birds and animals the most peculiar exhibit was a tapir from Sumatra. As tall as a donkey but in its build more like a stout, fat cow, it also has a trunk like that of an elephant but shorter. Its meat is eaten by the local populace. I also saw a meteor weighing 25 pounds which fell from the sky in the East Indies in 1815. It dropped at noon on a clear day and penetrated five feet into the ground. During its fall a sound similar to that made by a cannonball was heard. There are also a few stones and bricks brought from the ruins of Babylon with inscriptions which no one can decipher. The script appears to be irretrievable but humanity will certainly be better off without it, for the construction of the Tower of Babel has bred more than enough tongues.

The East India Company consists of affluent merchants who possess exclusive rights to trade with the East Indies. The Company has its origins in the time of Queen Elizabeth. At first it traded with Arabia, China and the adjacent Indian islands. In exchange for various loans made to the government it subsequently acquired numerous privileges and liberties which aroused the general envy of merchants and led to complaints about its monopoly of trade with the wealthiest English colony. As the conquest of India progressed the Company reaped more and more profits. As a result of these remonstrances, Parliament, in the year 1814, restricted the exclusive trading rights of the Company. Some parts of India were opened to all traders but there were certain conditions and a license had to be obtained from the Company. However, one category of trade, the tea trade, was reserved for the Company because of the large profits resulting from the immense consumption of this beverage in Britain. There were also regulations connected with England's obligations towards the Indians in matters relating to moral education, the promulgation of Christianity and the provision of schooling. People who work in India in these fields were given government support and encouragement. The subsequent achievements of the English missionaries should be praised. Their Christian efforts, as well as the humaneness of English laws, have alleviated the predicament of the Indians and restrained rapacity and cruelty.

In England there are many trade companies similar to the East India Company and, with the gradual expansion of trade, their number increases. We in Poland trade with the Baltic Company but there is no company which has as many foes as the Indian one. It may be observed that for several years the nation has been demonstrably struggling to abolish these privileges and introduce freedom of trade. But there are various obstacles which are not easy to overcome. Much will depend on the year 1834, the year in which the contract for the East India Company expires. Will it be able to retain its former privileges? Hitherto it has been *statum in statu,* has maintained its own network of agents, both official and secret, has kept an army which, even though English, has been in its pay, and, as political analysts emphasise, of little or no benefit to the country. The protection it enjoys has proved to be a burden. The growing affluence and power of this company may one day become a threat to its own country if not restricted.

There are certain buildings in London which a foreigner visits not for the sake of their architecture or for the curiosities amassed within but because they are at the centre of everything of importance in trade and finance. The first of these is the Custom House. This is an enormous building by the Thames with a spacious hall in which one can see merchants from all nations doing business, while groups of customs officers stroll along the banks of the river. Although I have been in the hall several times I am not at all clear about what happens there since it is the fate of all customs houses that the corrupt merchants of all five continents plot to cheat them. Not all wares brought to this place are dutiable. Those meant for further transport and temporarily stored in warehouses are duty-free. Only those meant for consumption within the country are taxable. Similarly, duty is not paid on goods produced in England and intended for export: only those sold within the country are chargeable. With the duties so high, the price of the products of their own country are excessive. This is why their domestic products such as woollen cloth, muslin, iron products and porter, as well as colonial wares like tea, sugar and coffee are sold in our country at prices lower than those in England. Taking into account the distance and the dangers of transport, they are even lower.

An important role in trade is played by the Bank of England.[7] There is nothing special about the building; on the outside it is not much different from Newgate prison. Its architecture is confused; the walls are enormous and the dome is modelled on the temple in Tivoli where the light falls into the dome through the windows in the roof. In the lower parts of the building there are underground vaults, where Plutus sits on a throne over bars of gold and silver. Despite all the security measures and caution, thefts still take place. Where force fails, cunning will succeed: the lure of gold can tempt man to commit any crime. During my stay in London, on a misty day, a thief sneaked into the accounting chamber where he grasped a sack of gold, ran into the street and disappeared into the fog. The autumn and winter days are sometimes so misty that one can hardly see a few feet ahead and ever since the time of Homer the fog has been an element favourable to the thieves' fellowship. There is no sign of silver in the bank, just gold, and it is not counted but weighed. Although it is not a government bank, the Bank issues notes which circulate in the entire country, and like those of our bank, are accepted for tax purposes and are on bearer's demand fully exchangeable for gold or silver. This condition is the only guarantee of their security! The number of banknotes is unlimited, the bank may issue as many as it decides, but it should not issue more than it can exchange. However, it is commonly believed that for the £30,000,000 worth of gold deposited, there are more banknotes in circulation than the actual capital deposited in the Bank. Despite this, its credit is stable and, due to the ease with which it can be transported, which is quite important for a trading country, paper money is more desirable than gold itself, and it is almost more valued. Upon accepting notes one needs to be very careful, for many are forged and one should not accept them from just anybody. In suspicious cases one should demand the owner's signature. This advice should be followed carefully, particularly by foreigners, since they are the ones who are most often offered counterfeit bank notes. The Bank of England has existed since 1694. In the old days banking was in the hands of jewellers; now the Bank consists of shareholders who won their charter by making loans to the Government. It is controlled by a Governor and twenty-four Directors who are elected annually from among the subscribers. Apart from this bank Great Britain has another five privileged banks and 868 private ones. We observed earlier that trade was in the hands of trading companies; here we see that money, the means by which buying and selling are facilitated, remains in private hands. The inter-relationships of the Government and the people are innumerable. If it tried to handle money and business alone, without any help from subjects, it would fail. The English people and their Government form the most complex machine with each of its elements performing its task smoothly and without obstruction.

Not far from the Bank is the Royal Exchange, a meeting place for merchants and their trading partners founded by Gresham.[8] In the courtyard there is a monument to Charles II. The set time for activity is between two and four o'clock. As the clock strikes four, all busi-

Royal Exchange. Modelled on the Exchange in Antwerp, the Royal Exchange was built for the Elizabethan financier Sir Thomas Gresham. It was rebuilt after the Fire by the City Surveyor, Jerman, and refaced by Dance in 1767. One of the rooms became Lloyd's Coffee House, the birthplace of the insurance company.

ness is finished since it is the merchants' dinner time. The Royal Exchange clock is said to be so punctual it has become the reference clock for other clocks in the capital, for trade depends on punctuality. To facilitate business, each trade has its own meeting place for merchants from various nations and religions. The rich are united by Fortuna; the only thing she detests is fraternity with the poor. I was shown the pillar where her favourite, Rothschild,[9] stands when he concludes contracts worth millions.

It is this building, dedicated to Fortuna, that houses Lloyd's[10] Coffee House which, however, is not a coffee house. It is the place for trading stocks, the securities of public and private trusts lending money to the Government. These constitute what we actually call England's national debt. The sum of the debt is believed to be so enormous that the possibility of repayment seems doubtful, and the variety of interest upon it is a reason for much speculation. The buying and selling of these funds and their transfer from one person to another are so complicated that their owners are no longer able to perform these actions by themselves without the help of proficient stockbrokers. Every morning in the meeting chamber a qualified official announces the value of these trusts. This will depend upon various circumstances such as war, peace, victory, the deaths of monarchs, riots etc. They obtain the news about these events either from the newspapers or from the agents employed in various countries. Trade is connected to political affairs and, before the Government itself, traders are the first to hear news about the events and possible changes in government. News from Lloyd's is considered certain and reliable. The extent to which speculation is pushed can be observed in the main hall where there is a clock which indicates not only the time but also the direction of the winds. Since not all winds are equally favourable for sailing and some may blow ships aground, while others may wreck them or delay their arrival, their direction has to be taken into account and may either increase or destroy the chances of a ship's safe arrival. It seems that you could not go any further in speculation than to consider the direction of the winds. The idealism of philosophers is entirely annihilated here; space and time become realities that are evaluated in terms of money. The number of members of Lloyd's is unlimited. Upon entering one pays £40 and then £4 annually.

A different kind of dealer and of a lower rank are the stockjobbers, who are not involved in the handling of such funds. They conclude contracts in which they state that in a specified number of days, weeks or months they will be able to transfer a certain amount of money to a client at a fixed interest. It proceeds as follows: person A concludes a contract with person B to supply bank stock worth £10,000, which is to be transferred as the sum of £12,000 in twenty days. But A does not possess this property. Suppose however that the price of bank stock on the day of transfer is 118%, it would be easy to buy bank stock for £11,800 to carry out the contract and he would thus gain £900. If, however, the price of the bank stock jumped to 115% he would lose as the result of this contract £500. And since A and B know that they are neither in possession of nor likely to possess such an amount of money, what they are after is the profit and loss difference resulting from the mutual agreement. This theft of imaginary money is highly developed and does not merely concern public trusts and insurance, but may encompass any material or product. In many respects it is similar to betting that an event must occur within a particular time span, or to a game of cards, where professional card-sharpers are allowed to declare a sum of money instead of staking it. They also call it gambling. A loss is a debt of honour which may not be legally claimed; one pays it in order not to loose the credit of being trustworthy. The stockjobbers use a specific language: a buying person is called a 'bull', a selling person is called a 'bear' and someone who is unable to pay is called a 'lame duck'.

Naturally, in a country with so many trade relations, the postal system is worth examining. The Post Office is close to the Royal Exchange, for this is indeed where it is most needed. Domestic mail goes out every day, the external mail two or more times a week and the mail to overseas settlements once a month. Due to England's unique relations with all the nations of the world, the London post is almost the central point for any correspondence on the globe. It is through it that letters to and from America, Africa, India, China, Australia and around the Equator are sent and collected. Letters going abroad are franked, letters within the country are paid for by the addressee. They are collected at a post office in the simplest manner; they are thrown into a post box made for this purpose. From there they are picked up an hour before the mail's departure, counted and stamped to indicate the price to be paid and the date of posting. The charge for England is not too excessive. A letter which goes no further than fifteen English miles costs five pence (twenty-five groszy), a letter which goes between fifteen and thirty miles, six pence (one Polish złoty), from thirty to fifty miles, seven pence, from fifty to eighty miles, eight pence, from eighty to 120 miles, nine pence etc. The Members of Parliament have the right to send their own and other letters free of charge and they pay nothing for collecting mail from the post office. Letters are not weighed, for it would be too time-consuming. A one-sheet letter is considered single and any slip of paper, a sample of gauze, or anything which could be recognized by the postal workers' fingers, doubles the cost. Therefore it is not a good idea to send letters to England in envelopes, for no matter how thin they are the charge will always be double. The English themselves do not use envelopes; most people receive letters on single sheets and close acquaintances often write crosswise. Should one mistakenly pay a double charge for a single letter, upon showing it, the post returns the charge without any demur. What a mark of good faith! The post itself is absolutely trustworthy. One can send large sums of money unregistered and be sure of safe delivery. Punctuality and absolute honesty are essential in a mercantile country, where so much depends on rapid correspondence. The letters are carried by mail-coaches, which travel at the speed of one and a half Polish miles an hour.

This Post Office is the main one in London and has sixty agencies to collect letters in distant parts of the city. Additionally, before dusk, there are men who walk the streets with a bell and pick up letters at a charge of a penny per letter. Apart from the main post there is the two-penny post, which facilitates correspondence within London and in its vicinity. It also has sub-offices. It departs every two hours and, just as in the main Post Office the postmark marked the day, here it marks the hour of posting. The system is a great boon for an industrialized and commercial country where fast communication is essential and few servants are employed. As yet there is no need for such a frequent and speedy post in Warsaw except, that is, for New Year's Day, when so many greeting cards need to be delivered. The average number of letters posted in London is one and a half million a week. In the year 1825 the Post Office brought £2,268,619 in revenue to the Government. Since this is an increase on the previous years it must now be bringing in over £2,500,000.

This revenue is produced only by the post; it does not include the revenue from stage-coaches and the numerous vehicles and carts used for the transport of people and commodities, all of which pay the Government. The stage-coaches which travel only within the capital are called hackney-coaches and serve to carry people in all directions within and outside the city. Written on them in big letters is information about their destinations and places of departure. At set times they stop at a particular place where they can always be found but they also pick up passengers on their way. In addition, there is a postilion who stands at the back and is on the look-out for passers-by whose haste or concentrated expression suggests that they might wish to take the coach. From a distance he gives a sign to indicate that there are free spaces and, as he draws nearer, he stops the coachman and asks the person wishing to travel whether he chooses to sit inside or on the top, showing him the ladder. Vehicles of this sort have the shape of stage-coaches and replace them in the city. The fares are fixed and there is no haggling. There are still others that may be hired. Their charges depend either on the distance or on the number of hours travelled. They do not make advance bookings for there is no need. Such vehicles can be found at any time and at any place in and around London. In order to satisfy curiosity I shall cite their usual prices. Measured by distance the price would be 1/- for 1 mile to 11/- for 9 miles or, by the time taken, 10d for 30 minutes to £1-7-6 for 4 hours.

The book trade is not an insignificant source of national wealth and, regardless of the influence that it has on the morality of this and other nations, it deserves our attention. Its influence spreads to every part of the globe, for it is difficult to find a corner where the English have not settled. Lots of books are sold in the United States and on the continent, where English literature is increasingly read, but the profits

Ackermann's Repository of Arts, Literature and Commerce. Born in Saxony, Rudolf Ackermann opened his print shop in 1795. His best known publication is a set of coloured engravings of London.

from this trade are not easy to calculate. The booksellers are secretive and authors are bound by their contracts not to disclose details. They have a commercial stake in this. The scale and profits of the trade must be assessed not just by the huge royalties earned by the finest authors but also by the number of booksellers and printers who earn their living by it. In order to understand how significant they are one has only to pass St Paul's Church Yard, Paternoster Row and Ave-Maria Lane, where the bookshops are located one after the other, and to notice how many other bookshops and reading-rooms there are in London.

One has to sympathise with those authors who support so many people, many of them rich, while living in poverty themselves. Each year up to 700 new works are released in England, excluding pamphlets, diaries and newspapers. Out of these only twenty works see a second edition; there are very few like Moore's *Lalla Rookh*,[11] which had eight editions in one year. Works as popular as Walter Scott's romances sell a few thousand copies every day. A novel as long as his, in three volumes, usually costs £1 on the first few days, later the price drops. The booksellers are not printers; typography is the lowest branch of the industry and the highest rank in the trade are the publishers. In London these are: Baldwin, Longman, Hurst, Whittaker and Murray, who published the works of Lord Byron, and in Edinburgh Constable, the publisher of the works of Walter Scott. These and their like are wholesale tradesmen and have agencies at home and abroad. Every academic subject, the law, medicine and theology, has its booksellers and publishers. Apart from these there are many others who sell books second-hand or, like peddlers, by auction. For the printing of expensive editions, many of which are published in Britain, several booksellers club together and their names are then written at the bottom of the frontispiece. There are strict laws which protect the author's and publisher's copyrights. The author sells his script and the right to use it for fourteen years to the publisher. After the expiry date copyright returns to the author who can sell it again. On the author's death the right is transferred to his successors who can resume the process every fourteen years. This law is not only just; it can prevent the families of authors, honoured but not financially rewarded by their country, from facing poverty.

Popular writings are much sought after and well paid. The works of Byron are assessed not by pages but by the number of verses; for each verse the publisher pays £1. Walter Scott did not make his fortune on poetry but rather on his novels, which are better and more popular. Recently, the fruits of his pen, although widely read, seem to have less charm and passion. He inspired many competitors in this field; amongst the most successful are Washington Irving,[12] Wilson,[13] Galt[14] and Lockhart,[15] Scott's son-in-law. There are also many female novelists. Miss Edgeworth[16] holds the first place amongst them; she is as famed for her works on the upbringing of children as is the authoress of *Rozrywki*[17] in Poland.

When a publisher obtains some important work, he tries to draw the public attention to it by advertising that a work bearing such-and-such a title is being prepared for print; that it is being printed; that printing is almost completed; that it will be finished in a few days; and, eventually, that it has been released. This continues for a month or two in all journals and papers. Such advertisements bring substantial profits to newsagents and they are usually expensive. Forty pounds would be a small price to pay for a well placed advertisement. The best work, without costly advertising, will lie on the shelves indefinitely because no one will know about it. The sale of a new work will also be promoted by being reviewed in some scientific journal or literary paper, no matter whether the review is good or bad. The effect of the review is as follows: a work praised in the dailies is in great demand because it is widely acclaimed; one which is criticised is also in demand because it may be supported by the Tories or the Whigs and it may be very good. To be neither praised nor criticised is the worst possible fate and the bookseller will lose on it. The public hates the 'amphibians'. Just as there are two parties in Parliament, so the periodicals, journals, dailies and papers support either the Tories or the Whigs. Both parties wage an unceasing literary battle and, since each author acts as a wrestler for one side or the other, it is difficult to be a popular writer in England unless one writes anonymously. That was the reason why Walter Scott, known to be a Tory, for a long time did not acknowledge his writings. Lots of others do the same, not from modesty but for the sake of peace and money.

An extraordinary number of periodicals are issued. I have counted 117 academic ones of various kinds. Five hundred newspapers are published. Their boards consist of the editor and the contributors, who are paid from £200 to £800. The editor's responsibility is to write leading articles which are of a political or economic nature. The junior editor prepares smaller articles, arranges publication and, if need be, defends the paper against other people's attacks. Each paper also has reporters and translators of foreign magazines, who are paid £200 to £300 each. The number of printed copies of the papers can be estimated by the stamp duty. In March 1814, when the demand for news was high because of the war being waged in France, 2,384,026 newspapers were stamped, which brought the government £34,767 in just one month. In 1821, the government got £358,100 from the stamp duty, and in 1826 it was £390,684. Comparing these years with the previous ones, it is clear that the number of readers was growing significantly year by year. The stamp duty is high because it exceeds half of the newspaper's value: a paper costs four pence, but the public gets the paper for seven. To ensure high-speed printing of the papers they do not use ordinary printing presses but steam-driven machines. I have seen one of these sophisticated machines at the printing-house of *The Times*. It is a cylinder almost a fathom in diameter. At first this machine printed 1,100 sheets per hour on one side only; now, printing on both sides, it produces 2,000 copies per hour. The machine has been in use since 1814. It was invented by König,[18] who originated from Saxony.

It is important for a foreigner to know where he can make minor purchases for a moderate price. The best place is the market at Soho Square, where products are sold for the benefit of the poor. They are mainly handmade by the finest daughters of Albion, who work on them in the winter so that they can donate them in April. In spacious rooms, hung with beautiful pictures, decorated with red cloth and filled with mahogany tables, these charitable gifts are placed. The price of each item is pinned on a tag and remains fixed. Selling is entrusted to twelve poor women who, in this way, can earn their livings. Every day, from three till five, one can see so many carriages arriving and such throngs of buyers, that it is difficult to pass through the crowd. Many people come just out of curiosity, to see and be seen. High society only frequents places dedicated to fashion, and the market is just such a place. A similar sight can be seen in Burlington Arcade[19] in Bond Street, which is built in the shape of a long gallery lined on both sides with shops. The roof of the gallery consists of glass through which light enters, while the passers-by are sheltered from the rain. Two doormen stand at the entrance and deny entry to dirty or dangerous customers.

Establishments worth visiting are the porter breweries. Of these I have seen only Whitbread's. Everything is done there with machines powered by steam. A steam-driven machine hoists the grain, moves the mill for grinding malt, tempers the malt in the tub, etc. Porter is cooled in large flat tanks, ponds of warm steaming liquid only six inches deep. We were told that, taken together, they would cover seven acres of land. The porter has to be kept there for six hours until it is cooled and then it crosses the street in canals to enter another vast and lofty building where it is poured into large tuns. It is kept in these for a few months in order to improve the flavour. We counted forty-six of such fermenting tuns or gyles. The largest were twenty-two feet in cross section and twenty-seven in height. They had a balcony reached by a staircase. These tuns are made of timber planks encircled by mighty iron hoops, which are denser and thicker at the bottom where the pressure is greatest. The late King once visited this brewery with the whole of his family. For the reception of the honoured guests Whitbread gave a breakfast in one of the tuns, which cost him £1,500. When the King asked him how many barrels of porter he had, he replied that he had so many he could block the way from London to Windsor with them. Windsor is the summer residence of the King, twenty-two miles from London. This brewery has 200 workers. The enormous numbers of horses used for transporting porter are of a distinct breed that I have never seen before. They tend to be slow by nature and are used to transport heavy weights, such as coal, stones and metal. They are given malt to eat and their horseshoes weigh twenty-five pounds. The other equally famous brewery is Barclay's. Last year (1827) its gyles of porter held enough to fill 380,580 barrels. Each year Barclay pays £200,000 just as a tax on porter. There are twelve such big breweries in London, apart from many smaller ones. Breweries of a beer called ale produce over 80,000 barrels. In 1826, from the tax on malt alone, the government collected £4,500,333.

NOTES:

1 East India Company. Founded in 1600 by a group of London merchants, the Company was granted a monopoly of all trade between the Cape of Good Hope and the Straits of Magellan. Driven out of the East Indies by the Dutch, it acquired vast wealth, power and territory in India. Between 1784 and 1858 the government took over control of what became the Indian Empire. The monoply of the tea trade was ended by Earl Grey in 1833.

2 Friedrich von Schlegel (1772-1829), German writer and critic. A pioneer of the Romantic movement, he studied Oriental languages in Paris and published an important work on Sanskrit and Indo-Germanic linguistics.

3 Sir Charles Wilkins (c1749-1836), English scholar. His *Grammar of the Sanskrit Language* was published in 1808.

4 Majewski- Skorochod (1764-1835), Polish scholar and Orientalist.

5 James Ward (1769-1858), English painter.

6 Tippoo Sahib (1749-99), Sultan of Mysore. Brilliantly successful in wars against the British in the 1780s, he was killed defending his capital, Seringapatam.

7 The Bank of England was designed by Sir John Soane (1753-1837) with a windowless façade and was built between 1788 and 1833.

8 Sir Thomas Gresham (1519-79), English financier, philanthropist and diplomat. The Exchange was modelled on the Exchange in Antwerp, where Gresham had served as ambassador. He founded Gresham College and eight alms houses in London.

9 Nathan Meyer Rothschilde (1777-1836), German financier. The son of Meyer Amshel, the founder of the international banking firm, Nathan established a branch in London in 1798. He received news of the defeat of Napoleon at Waterloo before anyone else in Britain and, in that one day, made a profit of over £1,000,000.

10 Edward Lloyd (d c1730), English-coffee house keeper. From 1688-1726 his coffee-house in Lombard Street was frequented by merchants and shipowners for whom he printed *Lloyd's News*. This became *Lloyd's List*.

11 In 1817 Longmans paid the Irish poet Thomas Moore (1779-1852) 3,000 guineas for the copywright on *Lalla Rookha*.

12 Washington Irving (1783-1859), American diplomat, historian and satirical essayist. The son of an Orcadian father and English mother, he was the first American-born writer to be recognised by the Brirish establishment. He is remembered as the creator of Rip van Winkle and biographer of Columbus.

13 Professor John Wilson, pseudonym Christopher North (1785-1854), Scottish critic and essayist. In 1817, with John Galt and John Gibson Lockhart, he launched *Blackwood's Magazine*, the Tory response to the Whig *Edinburgh Revue*.

14 John Galt (1779-1839), Scottish novelist and Canadian pioneer. All his novels show keen observation of rural life at a time of change; his masterpiece is *The Annals of the Parish*. He was an advocate of emigration and founded the town of Guelph in Ontario.

15 John Gibson Lockhart (1794-1854), Scottish novelist, biographer and critic. Writing for *Blackwood's*, he was a savage critic of other writers. His biogra-

phies of Burns and Napoleon are outstanding but he is best known as the biographer of his father-in-law, Sir Walter Scott.

16 Maria Edgeworth (1767-1849), Irish author and educationist. With her father, she wrote several books on education. As a novelist she wrote both for adults and children.

17 *Rozrywki dla Dziec* (The Recreation of Children) was written by Klementyna Hoffmanowa (1774-1845) in 1824.

18 Friedrich König (1774-1833), German printer. Inventor of the steam press, his improved cylindrical press was patented in London and installed by *The Times* in 1814.

19 Burlington Arcade was built during the Regency 'at the request of Lord George Cavendish of Burlington House, to prevent persons passing-by from throwing rubbish into his garden.'

Chapter Eleven

Charity institutions. Magdalen Asylum. The Foundling Hospital. Hospitals. Dispensaries Medical education. Doctors. Bedlam.

England is famous among all nations for its charity institutions. There is no distress, trouble or disability which is not the concern of some charity. In the capital there are 45 schools where up to 4,000 children are not only brought up but also provided for. There are seventeen schools for orphans and abandoned children and 234 parish schools maintained by means of voluntary contributions. They provide education and support for up to 12,000 children of both sexes. There are 22 hospitals for the sick, for cripples and for poor women in childbirth. There are 107 alms-houses which give shelter and provide care for the aged and the weary and eighteen institutions ready to take in the infirm at any time. The few institutions founded by the government are antiquated; the private foundations are far more numerous. Some function solely thanks to voluntary contributions which are so generous that the inmates do not experience any deprivation.

It is to the credit of the English nation that humanitarian feelings are so wide-spread. These institutions have various names – hospitals, homes, shelters and friendly societies – and are of interest for various reasons. Since I cannot describe all of them, I shall mention here only those with which the natives choose to impress foreigners. One of these is the Magdalen Asylum. The aims of institutions of this name are well known; the London one is the biggest. Some of the first ladies in the country are in charge of it. Within its grounds there is a church which is open to the public on Sundays and is visited due to its reputation for piety and the beautiful singing which can be heard from an enclosed gallery. The humiliated women are hidden from the eyes of the public but their singing is often interrupted by their sobbing. Where a woman's dignity is as highly valued as it is in England and critics are as harsh, one cannot imagine a more terrible misfortune than this sort of situation, which separates these women from their families, relatives and acquaintances. The church's own hymn and psalm books can be found in the pews. The sermons are appropriate for a place where Christian charity spares the sensibility of those doing penance. The most eloquent preachers are chosen. On the wall over the communion table, which takes the place of an altar, there is a text from the Scriptures: 'Joy shall be in heaven over one sinner that repenteth, more than over ninety and nine just persons which need no repentance.' Thus, from the year 1758, the year the asylum was founded, up to 5,000 unfortunate beings have sought and found shelter in it. Many of them were reconciled with their families and relatives and orphans have been provided with support and an honest way of earning a living. The asylum owes its establishment to the efforts of Doctor Dodd, a preacher famous in his time.

Another charity institution in London, a place of corruption and consequent misery, is the Foundling Hospital. Its aim is the same as that of the Hospital of the Infant Jesus in Warsaw. The children are given a proper upbringing and are then often employed by craftsmen and merchants as servants or maids or, should the boy's institute be overfull, they are sent to the navy. Everything is decided by the administrators. Some children are taken back by their own parents who had been forced, either by shame or poverty, to abandon them at first. Others may be adopted by childless couples who take them as their own. In this respect they are public property. A child leaving the institution is given new clothes and £10 and remains under the surveillance of guardians from the institution. Many members of the public go to the church at this hospital and worshiping there inspires them to practice charity. According to a common English custom a collection takes place at the door and it is not unusual for gold to shine among the silver. Behind the altar there is a painting by a fine artist showing the Saviour drawing children close to Himself with the inscription: 'Suffer the little children to come unto me.' It is on the bedrock of religious belief that all these institutions stand. Every year, to raise money, a great oratorio is organised in the church, its theme taken from the Scriptures. The revenue it brings tends to be substantial. For several years Handel conducted his 'Messiah' there and the organ which commemorates him is in the church.

Among the hospitals for the diseased the most notable are St Thomas's and Guy's. The first was founded by King Edward VI and has a revenue of £30,000 to £40,000. The latter, with an almost equal income, is the foundation of a London bookseller named Guy.[1] Its very erection cost him £18,790 and the later furnishing and equipment the enormous sum of £219,499. It is another example of the generosity of merchants and the use of one's possessions for the benefit of mankind. In a chapel of the church there is a beautiful white marble relief showing the founder touching the body of a dead person with one hand and with the other pointing with compassion to the frail and sickly bodies of two cripples, ordering that they should be carried to the hospital. You will not find a more moving monument commemorating any magnate. Both hospitals are so vast that they can accommodate 400 sick people. The wards are meticulously tidy and at each bed there hangs a chart with the patient's name and the history of his disease. Medical consultations and medicines are free of charge. Those who are ill are cared for by women and nothing that might bring comfort or relief has been omitted. As he observes this dedicated care, a foreigner forgets that he is visiting a place of suffering. In one bed he will be happy to see a pale sick person showing signs of recovery. On another this joyful sight is overshadowed by the struggle for life or death, enlightened only by a ray of hope emanating from the doctor in attendance. For another patient all joy and hope have gone: one's heart bleeds at the sight of the lifeless, motionless eyes, withdrawn from the world and gazing only along the path of death.

Doctor Scott, the chief doctor in this hospital and my guide, drew my attention to some of the more peculiar disorders. There was a young man who had had his eye pushed out by a tumour that had formed in his head; it was a terrible sight! Another had his skull swollen by water which accumulated in his brain to such an extent that it caused his face to disappear under the top part of his head. Though pale and ill, he was not sad and conversed cheerfully with the doctor. But the cheerfulness was not genuine, it revealed some confusion, which may have been caused by pressure on the brain. However, I am afraid of disgusting my readers by this enumeration of diseases: one needs nerves that are either strong or numbed by routine to endure some of the sights or even the very description of them. So abhorrent and disgusting can man's body become! Only the Bible, placed in this room on an elevated lectern, seemed to throw a consoling ray over this house of man's deformity. It was read by those patients who were able to read and in the morning and in the evening it was read aloud to everyone. I was told that from their deathbeds the dying gaze with dimming eyes towards this holy book.

In Guy's Hospital there is a separate ward for people suffering from severe insanity. I saw up to twenty of them in a spacious room, chained either to benches or to a wall. They were placed at a certain distance from each other and, what was apparently rather unusual, since I doubt it was their normal attitude, they sat silent and motionless like a serious court of statues, as indifferent to past and present as if they were unconscious shadows of the dead, having drunk from the springs of Lethe. All of them had their eyes fixed on some distant point but one could say, as in the Scriptures: 'They have eyes to see and see not; they have ears to hear and hear not.' Only one woman broke the silence of the place with her chatter but she could merely speak without communicating; speech remained but mental powers had faded. Some faces showed signs of cheerfulness but their forced smiles turned into grimaces, for they did not come from a sound heart or a clear mind. Most of these dummies sat motionless and gloomy. Everyone there had outlived their true personalities and what I was looking at were merely the shadows of people.

Among the most significant hospitals offering help to the poorest class of people are St Luke's, St Bartholomew's and the London Hospital. Although there are a few other institutions, they are not enough to cope with the poverty existing in such a vast city. They may help and save individuals, but who will help the families and orphans if their father, who had maintained the family, has been crippled or is temporarily unable to work? These cases need more effective assistance than hospitals can provide. In order to aid such people men's and women's charity associations have been formed and they have taken on the task of visiting poor-houses and searching for the poorest. These are given necessary aid from the common fund, though precautions are taken not to nurture idleness by aiding those unworthy of assistance.

In various large houses in the capital dispensaries have been es-

St Bartholomew's Hospital. Founded in 1102 by Henry I's jester, it was re-established in 1546 by Henry VIII. His statue over the Smithfield entrance is flanked by figures representing sickness and lameness. Rebuilt in the mid-eighteenth century by Gibbs, the grand staircase was decorated, at his own expense, by Hogarth.

tablished where the poor sick receive medical advice and free medicines. They are not taken away from the tasks they can still fulfil. Fifty thousand of the sick receive this kind of help. The supplier of medicines is the pharmacist who, at a public auction, promises to charge the lowest prices. The poor-fund is raised from annual contributions, which constitute the fixed revenue, and from single donations. The most prominent people in the country are proud to belong to such an association. Indeed, what can be more honourable for a man than compassion for his neighbour and all humanity? It is through this alone that one becomes human. No one who has failed to support the association's fund with an annual contribution may remain a member.

The hospitals have a function as training schools for future physicians. Some of them have theatres in which lectures in anatomy and other medical subjects are held. Each doctor or surgeon belonging to a hospital has a few young assistants who observe and treat the sick under his guidance. They are not paid for this; on the contrary, they themselves have to pay their teachers. A surgeon's apprentice pays £50 a year and £30 for a half year. The certificate he receives from the hospital helps him to become a licentiate or obtain a degree as a doctor. Experience in hospitals constitutes the main, though not the only, preparation of a physician for his future occupation. They do not teach much theory at their universities and Oxford and Cambridge are not famous for medical science. Thus England educates many practical physicians and surgeons but few doctors. Neither is their medical literature broad. Brown's system[2] is more popular in other countries than in England. However, one cannot deny the method is practiced; indeed, the English climate seems to dictate the use of strong and stimulating rather than soothing medicines. In the opinion of experienced physicians, medicines used in England contain more ingredients than elsewhere; and the amount of opium prescribed annually exceeds its consumption in five years in Germany. The real school for physicians, combining theory and practice, is in Edinburgh,[3] and for a physician to be educated there is an advantage. Young Englishmen, who are dedicated to medicine, go there to study.

Many believe that what contributes to the success of the English physicians is the severity of the climate, which causes the diseases to last

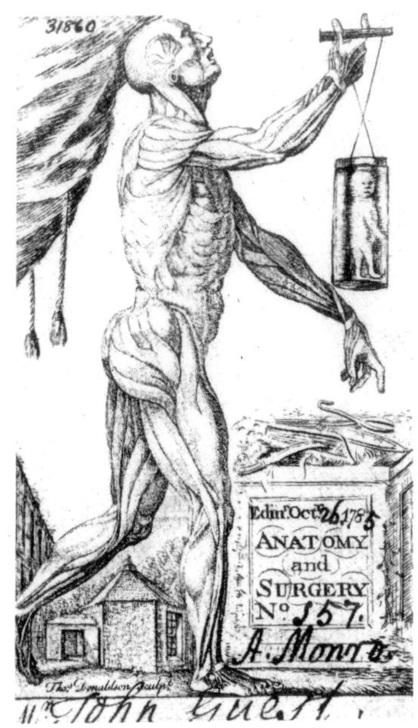

Edinburgh University Class Card. During the eighteenth century, when three generations of Monros occupied the chair of Anatomy, the Medical School of Edinburgh became famous throughout Europe and North America. Most of the senior doctors in the London hospitals had been trained there and Lach-Szyrma, while studying for a Doctorate in Philosophy, had attended classes in Anatomy.

longer without seriously endangering those who are ill. In hot countries, where diseases progresses faster, a physician is deprived of a chance to test his theories. This is the reason why many of their physicians specialise in treating one disease and achieve excellent results. Doctor Scott, from whom I have experienced so much courtesy in that he not only facilitated my entry to the hospitals but was also my guide around them, is particularly famous for treating liver diseases. During his eight-year stay in the Indies, where the English suffer from this disease most frequently, he had been so successful in his practice that he earned £200,000 and, like everyone who has made a fortune in India, when he came back to London, although he was not much over forty, he ceased to practice his profession. He dedicated himself to charity work and literature, especially Indian literature, in which he is said to be well read. In his studies during his stay in India he is said to have benefited from his acquaintance with the culture of the Brahmins.

Although the medical profession in England is very lucrative, the number of physicians in relation to the population is not high. This is due to the high cost of acquiring education. Only the wealthy can afford to pay all the fees for lectures, clinical practice in hospitals and examinations. A single licentiate exam, which takes place at the College of Physicians, costs £50. Just how many pulses does a young physician have to feel, how many prescriptions does he have to write for the costs he had incurred to be recovered! Consequently, a doctor's fee is considerable; a visit will cost not less than a guinea and, if given advice, four guineas. The more famous charge up to £10. Thus, due to their high fees, the help of expert physicians is available only to the wealthy; economic considerations force the middle class to follow Hippocrates' advice: 'Avoid physicians!' or, in case of pressing need, seek the advice of a pharmacist. Though he will not charge anything for this, since it is forbidden by law, he will make up for it in the price of the powders and mixtures prescribed. Everyone else must be satisfied with common medicines and secret mixtures called nostrums, which are heavily advertised in the papers and on street corners. These medicines sold in bulk circulate not only in England; whole cargoes of them sell well in all European countries in various forms: powders, oils, creams, balms – wherever naivety seeks to be misled. If it were not for the charitable spirit of the English nation, thanks to which so many hospitals were built where the needy may find the help of reasonable physicians, all the lower classes, who are as ignorant as the common people usually are, would have fallen prey to greedy charlatans.

On the 29th of November 1823, in the month when due to dull weather the English are most severely splenetic and are thus more disposed to commit suicide, I visited Bedlam. As is well known, Bedlam is a lunatic asylum in London. It is a refuge for those who are over sensitive to the suffering of other people, who react too violently when irritated, who worry too much or think too much. To retain balance people must avoid extreme reactions to experience. Bedlam is an enormous building, 580 feet long, with an inner dome and behind it a vast garden where patients can walk. Its porch has a portico resting on three Corinthian-style columns. On it the heraldic insignia of the three united kingdoms, a lion, a thistle and a harp are combined, as though to indicate that all Britons have an equal right to this building. We went into its tremendous vestibule and the iron door was opened for us. In the entrance hall our attention was caught by two marble figures. Furious Insanity represented the dangerous lunatics and gloomy Melancholy those driven mad by over-sensitivity, most frequently by love. It would be hard to relate all of the inmates to these images, for the causes of madness are legion. Often the soul and the body are at war and destroy each other. These illnesses are not always caused by one's own failings, sometimes they are transmitted as a sad legacy from parents to children. A lunatic asylum is not totally different from the world of the sane. Most of the inmates come from the common people and sit, passive and unthinking, gazing at whatever lies in front of them. A visitor feels compassion for these forgotten people but not curiosity. One's entire attention is directed to a higher sphere, where imperial dignitaries, reformers, politicians, heroes, prophets, kings and gods circulate. They are the ones pointed out to visitors by the superintendents of asylums, the men who record their histories. Ambition, conceit and fanaticism often persist in the highest social spheres and it is this height which can make people lose their mental balance. It would be hard to categorise all the mad in Bedlam, so I will describe only those whom I saw.

First, we entered the women's quarters. We were greeted by a woman who was permanently in labour pains. Having taken a closer look at me and Dr Scott, she greeted us as her sons. She was no ordinary mother but believed herself to be the widow of a late English king. Unexpectedly, we found ourselves joined by ties of brotherhood to royal blood. Another woman approached us who wanted to be a man; not just any man, but Christ. Addressing us with his words: 'I am the resurrection and the life; he that believeth in me, though he were dead, yet shall he live.' She asked whether we believed. She was then interrupted by another who was convinced that she had been condemned to eternal fire for her wrongdoings. She walked from one person to another, weeping and moaning. She was middle aged but very weak, dry and swarthy, as if blackened by soot: such was the effect that the nagging thought of eternal fire had had on her complexion. Oh, the incomprehensible and terrible influence of imagination! The

Christ-woman followed her and remonstrated with her about her unbelief, promising her redemption if she changed. In my opinion one should separate the redeemer and the unbeliever.

Behind the cheerful gang which pushed towards us, all talking nonsense at the same time, sat a woman who had murdered her own child, convinced that it would be an offering acceptable to God. She was sitting looking straight ahead, calm and indifferent to anything that happened around her. The insane who commit crimes are generally cheerless and taciturn. As we were observing the countenance of this offender, the superintendent, who was the recorder of the institution, promised to show us an even more interesting person. He stopped by an elderly, stocky and almost obese female and said: 'She is the famous Margaret Nicholson.' Knowing nothing about her, I asked him who she was. He replied she was the woman who had stabbed with a dagger and dangerously wounded King George III as he was descending from his carriage to go to the theatre in 1784. The king, who was of a kindly nature, said: 'Take her away, she must be insane.' The king's words were taken seriously and she was placed in Bedlam, where she grew old. Whether she was in fact insane the chronicles of Bedlam do not say. She too was sullen and taciturn. She was having dinner at the time and only at the sight of a bowl of soup, which stood in front of her, did she become more cheerful.

On our way back we met a woman in the corridor with a serious expression on her face. Walking pompously, she was casting a defiant look at the other women around her. Presumptuous conceit had brought her to this insanity. As she approached the superintendent she complained about the cruelty of keeping her in prison, like a slave. She said she was from an important family, had friends who were wealthy and threatened him with revenge. This poor creature did not comprehend that a lunatic asylum was not a prison or, at least, not a prison for the princess she believed herself to be. It is a particular feature of lunatics and the main obstacle to their recovery, that most of them do not know, nor can they grasp where they are. The speech of the princess was incoherent and affected and she spoke at a great rate. All lunatics speak fast and one can see that no time is spent on thought. In the way she held her head, in the expression on her face and in her every movement there was arrogance. There was another woman like her whose insanity resulted from an obsession with the elegance of her dress. She walked around rigged out in a Turkish turban and a wide and diaphanous coat, glancing around to see whether the other women were admiring her. There was also a coquette who laughed out loud when she saw us and ran off to hide, looking to see whether we were following her. Once she saw we were not, she came out and chattered fluently in both French and English, offering to follow us wherever we would go and to be persistent, loyal and loving. There was also a poetess, sitting like the Muse. This god-like creature was ready to sing for anyone who would listen. These creatures were harmless and were allowed to wander wherever they pleased and even to gratify their favourite fancies. The dangerous ones were kept behind iron bars, with their hands and legs chained, and some had their hands bound to prevent them from harming themselves and others.

From there we went to the men's quarters which do not differ much from those for women. Upon entering we encountered a few of the unfortunates mooning about in the corridor. Having noticed us, they came towards us immediately, greeted us by shaking hands, entered into conversation and asked a thousand questions, for lunatics can be very talkative and curious. It sent shivers down my spine to be surrounded by so many. Nothing awakens more mistrust and abhorrence towards a man than the loss of the gift of reason. Without it there is no security in relationships between people. I asked the superintendent whether they would always surround him in this manner. He replied that this was usual, both with him and with visitors whom they saw as their friends; only a few of them avoid people. I noticed they were not afraid of the superintendent. He asked each of them how he was, some of them he called by their names and to some more prominent persons (for, as has already been said, even here not everyone is equal) he offered snuff. Everybody seemed to like it tremendously and, once the snuffbox was empty, he calmed them by promising that he would bring some more the next day.

While the women's dwellings were a place of kindness, light, dressiness and smiles, this was a place of strength and seriousness. The male English lunatics have been observed never to smile, nor can I remember seeing any one of them laugh. Somebody called this 'the reason for their insanity'. Voltaire characterises them in the following way:

> Chez les Anglais, sombres et durs esprits,
> Toute folie est noire atrabilaire;
> Chez les Français, elle est vive et légère.

The first person whom we encountered in the empty corridor was a young man marching along in a military fashion. The superintendent warned us to let him pass, for he was always ready to fight; apart from that he was harmless. His sole illusion was that he believed himself to be General Wolfe.

We entered a room where we found some of the insane sitting at a table and having dinner. At the top of the table there sat no less a person than Julius Caesar. Where else would you expect such a great man to sit? In profile his face was Roman and resembled the portraits of Caesar on ancient medals. Unfortunately, he knew a lot about medals and gazed too often in the mirror. By what thin threads is human reason held together!

We were then taken to see the criminal insane who sat behind iron bars. In his insanity one of them had killed two of his own brothers. It was at this point that I asked the superintendent whether it was safe to walk among the ones who were not behind bars. He replied that caution is always advisable but much depends on the manner of approaching them; even if one of them showed obstinate resistance it would be easy to confuse him with resoluteness, for lunatics are very fearful. Obviously, cowardice is a matter of moral weakness. He told us the story of the terrible experience of the famous Dr Monro[4] in Bedlam. He was the senior doctor for the institution and the lunatics plotted to kill him. One day, when he came on an ordinary visit, they seized him but, having done so, they were in total confusion as to how to do away with him, since none of them had thought about this in advance. Suddenly one of them, probably the hungriest at that moment, suggested they should throw the doctor into the huge pot that was used for making soup. Everyone liked this idea. They were just about to throw him in when the doctor said: 'All right my friends, have me thrown in, but just let me undress myself, for I will spoil your soup with my shoes and clothes on.' These words confused the lunatics so much that they hesitated till one of them said: 'The doctor is right, let him first take off his shoes and get undressed.' They all repeated these words. Then the doctor started to undress and presumably took his time. But the shouting of so many lunatics could be heard throughout the entire building. It reached the superintendent who called the attendants and came to the rescue of the doctor before the lunatics turned him into broth.

We entered another room where we met a young man who was not more than thirty years old. On a table lay books and papers and on a shelf there were some volumes. I looked at the titles of the books which were French, English, German and Greek and all of scientific content. A flute and musical scores lay on a neatly made bed. All this did not look like the dwelling of a lunatic. My astonishment increased when I saw a copy of Homer, with accompanying notes, lying on the table and the young man expressed himself freely in three languages: German, French and English. Clearly, he was not at all the person I had thought him to be at first, since his reasoning seemed not only sane but exceptional. In my surprise, I could not refrain from asking what had brought him there. In reply, he only folded his arms firmly, indicating that he would like to talk but preferred to remain silent. Later I learnt that he was a student from Heidelberg who had served in the army and planned to free Napoleon from deportation to the Island of St Helena. His plan was discovered and he himself imprisoned but, since he was not yet an adult, he was freed. Having nothing to live on, he committed another offence by forging paper money, a crime punishable by death. However, once again there must have been some reason for his escaping punishment; he was judged to be insane and was committed to Bedlam. There is no doubt he was one of the many who were saved by Bedlam from Newgate and the gallows. *Relata refero.*

After passing a raving madman who pulled at his chains, ground his teeth and frothed at the mouth in a manner terrible to behold, we entered a cell in which lay a healthy man lying on his bed, convinced that he was dying. As we entered he shook hands, for he was bidding the world good-bye. As a faithful subject and a lover he was singing a song, in which King George and his lover's name were frequently mentioned. This death was not in itself such a horrible sight but the strain on his chest of his screams were enough to have caused his death!

I am not going to mention many more of the unfortunate sufferers whose madness was revealed in so many different ways. On our way out we stopped to look at a plaster statue, I forget of whom. Suddenly we heard a voice coming from behind us: 'Be gone: you worship idols, not the true God!' We looked back and saw a thirteen-year-old boy, whom we had previously seen jumping and playing happily with his ball. He had given us no reason to feel pity for him until we touched the real core of his madness. I would never have thought it possible that the greatest gift of the Creator, the ability to distinguish the true from the false, could be destroyed so early.

As we were still recovering from the shock the superintendent showed us to a lonely chamber where we found a man, of about fifty years of age, who was sewing shoes. This man was a shoemaker only to us; in his own eyes he was a prophet who prophesied to the Israelites the longed-for coming of the Messiah. I shall repeat here a conversation he had with the superintendent who knew best how to talk with this sort of person.

Superintendent (after a few words of indifferent talk and having sat next to him on a stool): I doubt you could be a prophet.

Lunatic: No, I am not. (He put the awl aside, as if showing that more important matters were at stake.)

Superintendent: The other day you pretended to be one, did you not?

Lunatic: I am not a prophet for the unbelievers but for the believers.

Superintendent: So the Messiah has not yet come?

Lunatic: No, but he shall come, revealed not by the mouth but from the mouth (the lunatics are often very subtle).

Superintendent: How do you know this?

Lunatic: It has been revealed to me by a double-edged sword from heaven.

Superintendent: Where is this sword? Let us see it.
Lunatic: It is in my heart, it is invisible.
Superintendent: So, you do not consider yourself and us Christians, Sir? We have been baptised, have we not?
Lunatic: Our baptism was one of the body, the world needs the baptism of the soul.

The shoemaker-prophet wrote a book about the coming of his Messiah. In the conversation he had a ready answer for every question, only his presumptions were false. He was harmless, for religious lunatics are harmless but so persistent as to be incurable. He had long hair and his countenance was mild and unremarkable.

The total number of lunatics in Bedlam at that time was over five hundred. Women most often take leave of their senses due to love. However, in their insanity they commit fewer murders than men: compared to forty-five male offenders the number of women was twenty-four.

After we had left the walls of this sad institution, Doctor Scott asked me: 'How do you feel, Sir?' 'Not particularly well' – I had to reply – 'and it cannot be otherwise, having emerged from contemplating the ruins of so many men's reason.' All ruins have something sad about them, but the ruins of man's reason are the saddest. Once destroyed, its delicate structure is hard to restore. There are some immemorial laws a man should not break if he does not want Providence to turn its back on him. Excessive reasoning leads to fallacies and illusions, wherever there is excess: human arrogance is hoisted with its own petard and prepares its own fall. So numerous are the resulting falls that we had seen only a few in Bedlam. Let lofty pride seek a lesson in humility here and persistent conceit a lesson in modesty. It would do no harm to bring the malleable minds of the young to this place. Hearing the histories of some of these people, they would watch their own behaviour more carefully and not allow some *idées fixes* to take root so easily. They would comprehend their destiny better. The impression one gets there is so profound that it would be enough to visit a lunatic asylum once. One should not need a second visit.

NOTES:

1 Thomas Guy (1644-1724), English bookseller, printer and philanthropist. He made his fortune importing Bibles from the Netherlands and printing Bibles for Oxford University. He financed the building of three wards at St Thomas's Hospital before founding Guy's Hospital and several almshouses in London.

2 Dr John Brown (1735-88), Scottish physician and assistant to Professor William Cullen. He divided diseases into the sthenic, caused by over-excitement, and asthenic and treated the former with debilitating medicines and the latter with stimulants. He condemned the practice of blood letting and challenged Cullen's theories of medicine.

3 The Faculty of Medicine at Edinburgh University was founded in 1726 by Alexander Monro (1697-1767) and other Scots who had been inspired by the teaching of clinical medicine by Boerhaave at Leiden. It rapidly became world famous. While studying for a doctorate in Philosophy from 1820-22, Lach-Szyrma had also matriculated as a medical student.

4 Alexander Monro (1733-1812). A Scottish physician, he followed his father as Professor of Medicine at Edinburgh Universiry. He wrote on the nervous system, the brain, the ear and the eye and on the physiology of fishes.

Chapter Twelve

Law. The Lawyers. Schools of Law. Lord Eldon. The Temple. The Knights Templar. Knights Made of Stone. Temple Bar.

Nothing contributes more to strengthening the happiness of a nation than a well-wrought system of laws and their strict execution. Though not a lawyer myself, I frequently expressed my sincere desire to learn more about English legislation and sought advice from experts in that domain as to which books I should read in order to acquire a general knowledge in this field. But whenever I put that question the answer was accompanied by a reservation about the imperfection of works written so far on this matter. Everybody seemed to be of the opinion that in order to acquaint oneself with English legislation one should consider Blackstone's book as the main source of information and, in order to learn about its history and spirit, one should turn to Miller's writings on the constitution. There was also agreement that Lyttelton[1] and Coke[2], who had written on that subject earlier, had expressed some interesting ideas but that their works lacked any order. When it came to foreign writers, the succinct book by Mr de Lolme was lauded. The widely recognised writings on English criminal law by Mr Cottu were not then well known. Of the works by the German writers, Phillips, Mittermaier and Biener, they know nothing at all. One reason for this is the German tongue which is not as widely studied in England as is French; the other of the discrepancies which exist between English and German legislation. For, while in the latter everything is based on theory, in the former it is practice that determines the law and the English lawyers cannot bear to express legal theories even in their writings. Such a concept may astound many readers since England boasts numerous men excelling in this profession. It is the case however, for the very spirit and quality of the laws rids them of any theory. As far as their origins are concerned the laws fall into two categories: common law, which was collected during the reigns of Alfred the Great and Edward the Confessor and, being rooted in custom, is not subject to deliberation, and statute laws, which are Acts of Parliament and, since already deliberated, render any further deliberation pointless. It is only in countries where there are no laws whatsoever or the existing laws are not precise that theory is required. In countries like England lawyers pay exclusive attention to the letter of the law and its strict observance. It has the final say and makes any theory ineffective. For this reason Bentham[3] was praised for the constitutions he wrote for other nations. His much respected book on legislation could serve for many foreign nations as the basis of useful parliamentary acts but it had no effect on English legislation. Whereas abroad it was translated into all the European languages and praised by academic circles for the soundness of its principles, in England it was deemed to be merely a nice system of laws, containing nothing novel for the Englishman. Esteemed elsewhere as an oracle and properly valued by foreign monarchs, in his own country, where the phenomena he described existed, Bentham is barely regarded as an eminent writer. When juxtaposed with other lawyers, he is often compared to a theoretician who knows the theory of medicine but does not practice it, whereas others through practice itself are believed to have surpassed his theory. In England practice is preferred above all, not only in medicine but also in law. The theory of law, Roman law and laws of other nations are studied out of mere curiosity rather than genuine need and no lawyer refers to them. Indeed, they ignore them as in many cases contrary to the spirit of English legislation. This arises from various judgments made in the past and is not based on systematic rules.

Blackstone's significance consists in the fact that he was the first to have emphasised the importance of the structure of English law and to have introduced some order into its codification. But he also contributed to establishing the connection between English legislation and those philosophical principles which are more sensible than Hobbes's[4] self-contradictory tenets. The principles in question are not in any sense new since they were taken from the common books of natural law and aptly applied to statute law. This sufficed to prove that what in the case of other nations is theory must, in the case of the English, turn out to be practice. Bentham himself, the most outstanding English theoretician of law, could not abandon practice when laying down utility as the principle. He derived and developed an entire system of legislation from this principle. This was not directly influenced by any other system and is still a motley collection of various elements from different places and centuries. It is the labyrinth of Daedalus[5] from which the most proficient lawyers cannot find the way out and if one of them essayed to visit all its corners, he would die before finding the key to it. Their laws are derived from such disparate sources that they encompass rules from well nigh all legal systems, and are, therefore, of some considerable philosophical importance.

The impossibility of comprehending the whole structure of laws leads to lawyers choosing a particular field to which they devote themselves and in which they become superlative masters. And since there is a multitude of local laws, a lawyer unrivalled in one county may be of little use in another with whose laws he is not acquainted. If there is an intricate case, especially when it must be settled according to the local Acts, an assembly of lawyers, like a case conference of doctors, is convened for greater certainty. Each case is usually preceded by special pleading; arguments aiming for victory rather than truth. Should this fail they go, as they put it, to law. Whichever party prevails the lawyers make sure of their remuneration from clients, not even waiting for further developments. Should clients fail to pay, the law forbids lawyers to take them to court so as to prevent a situation in which a lawyer prosecuted his own client. In order to avoid such contradictions they abide by an ancient rule of prudence:

> Dum aegrotus visitatur,
> Dum processus ventilatur,
> Cura te accipere!
> Nam aegroto restituto,
> Et processu absoluto,
> Nemo curat solvere.

Most of the trials in England are held orally and not, as is the case in Germany, in writing. This is not surprising taking into consideration the number of possible writers and the room required to store such a quantity of court records. Therefore, a lawyer is considered to be accomplished when his legal knowledge is combined with eloquence, a gift particularly necessary to obtain a favourable verdict in cases tried by jury. Hence, in order to acquire appropriate powers of persuasion the lawyers appearing in these trials prefer studying philosophical works and poetry to poring over the Pandects[6] or arranging diffuse sources of national laws into a systematic whole. The best example set for the English lawyer is Cicero. Like the famous Roman, the lawyer attains eminence by combining the merits of a lawmaker, orator, philosopher and citizen. For such people law is a way to the Bench and the highest ranks of state. Thus Lord Eldon,[7] who used to be a poor legal trainee, became Lord Chancellor. In the national assembly such merits are displayed by Mackintosh,[8] Brougham,[9] and Scarlett [10] and, in the past, used to be shown by Canning,[11] Erskine,[12] Pitt,[13] Fox,[14] Curran[15] and Burke.[16] For centuries legal knowledge has been fused with eloquence and, as was the case with the Athenians and Romans, legal eloquence has enriched literature. It is best seen in state trials which, by giving rise to so many laws, have contributed to consolidating the country's constitution.

I decided to write this introduction after my visits to the institutes of law in London. They are called the Inns of Court and the four major ones include the Inner Temple, the Middle Temple, Lincoln's Inn and Gray's Inn. Within, the adherents of Themis,[17] who will in time replace their renowned predecessors and contemporaries, are subjected to a dubious course of education. I say dubious for these institutes, even if once sound schools of law, must have altered dramatically. Excluding Oxford and Cambridge whose law departments are not highly rated, these are the only eminent schools of law in the country. Yet no lectures are delivered, no examinations held or marks given by which recognition by the public could be achieved. There are no procedures there by means of which, in Poland and everywhere else, the young become accustomed to work and prepare for their professional duties. Since time immemorial those who hope that one day they will distinguish themselves in the temple of Astrea have to be admitted into one of the said institutes and board there. From boarding, however, they can be exempted provided that they pay the institute annually £130 sterling. This peculiar requirement is imposed for a period of five years and students have to pay it each time they appear for regular sessions. The money collected is spent by the company of lawyers on delicious and sumptuous feasts. This habit of eating up to the bar has been frequently ridiculed but no one abandons it and everyone slavishly fits into the pattern. The practices of the past have to be continued in the present.

The members of those institutes, which could more appropriately be called fraternities, for they resemble guilds rather than schools of law, are benchers, barristers or trainees. Should the latter wish to benefit from their sojourn at the institute, they should arrive equipped with some previously acquired knowledge. In the past this could be obtained in several preparatory schools but these no longer exist. Five years after being admitted a student is permitted to take an examination which is not reputed to be exceptionally difficult. If he gains a majority of votes, which again is not hard to achieve, he becomes a barrister, after which he may accept cases and stand at the bar on his own. The benchers are the elders. They are obliged to administer the institution and from among them a treasurer is chosen who records the income and expenditures of the assembly.

Apart from barristers there is yet another group of lawyers who are called attorneys. They act as notaries, for which post they undergo a traineeship in a proper office which lasts for several years. They draw up documents and prepare evidence for barristers before trials. Their profession, though not as honourable, is certainly equally profitable. This comes as no surprise in a country where, by virtue of the profusion of manorial, mercantile and inheritance relationships, each agreement must be legally clarified. The number of attorneys is greater than that of lawyers – in the year 1822 there were 1,800 of them in the capital and 2,400 in the provinces.

In spite of such a ridiculous organisation of schools of law, the law as a science is not neglected but depends upon the efforts and aptitude of students. Familiarity with the law is pleasantly apparent in every action of daily life. It is not only the lawyer who needs it on account of his vocation but also the wealthy who hope to have a seat in Parliament one day. It seems to me, however, that there is no better way of acquiring it than through practice. That is why the young are entrusted to the care of expert lawyers who supervise their work and development. I once happened to visit a lawyer at Lincoln's Inn who had engaged several trainees and charged each of them £300 a year for the mere right to work under his supervision. The youth is also taught law by attending trials and listening to eloquent lawyers, by reading legal works and descriptions of cases, as well as by discussing legal matters. For this purpose societies for reading and discussing moral and legal subjects are formed. Having taken into account the cost of board, lodging, apparel and traineeship one becomes conscious of the fact that only the affluent can afford to pursue such an expensive career, which to some brings fame but to others mere chagrin. Great mistakes may be made only once in a lifetime but their consequences are dire.

The school reputed to be the most significant is Lincoln's Inn. It is a huge edifice erected in the form of a quadrangle enclosing a garden. It houses students' and lawyers' accommodation, the latter frequently including offices for business purposes. It also includes a courtroom where the Lord Chancellor sometimes presides. At the time of my visit such a trial was proceeding and it was the first time that I had seen Lord Eldon. He was sitting in the judge's chair, wearing a long red gown and a wig, and his face was stern and grave like that of a statue. In front of him, on a long table spread with a green cloth, were two considerable silver maces and two lawyers were arguing their cases at the bar. Lord Eldon is said to be the most able lawyer in the whole kingdom. He appeared to be approximately seventy years of age. He is tall, with an oval face and calm eyes and speaks in a quiet and slow fashion. I heard him admonish barristers who had wandered off the point, for the law tries to prohibit loss of time through vain discussions. A lawyer may not speak longer than three quarters of an hour. When time has elapsed the floor is denied him. A throng of people had gathered for trials there, as in Poland, are held in public. The courtroom was embellished with portraits of famous judges, among whom was Lord Erskine, to whom the jury owes additional clearly defined powers.

The society of lawyers at the Temple is governed by the same rules and members expelled from one institute for some misdeed cannot be admitted into another. When visiting the Temple I did not have a chance to see any of its lawyers who, by reason of the building in which they dwell, are referred to as the Templars. I deliberately avoided the possibility of meeting one, for members of this group are exceptionally busy and engrossed in their affairs. The very compass in the courtyard, which bears the inscription 'Go about your business,' seems to warn visitors not to detain the residents of the Temple for too long. The economical use of time is so important in England that it is not acceptable to keep a merchant, a doctor or a lawyer more than five minutes without compensating him for the delay. Time is measured in gold and the more important one is the more money one receives for one's time.

There is an old saying in England: 'to drink like a Templar'. No one knows to which residents of the Temple it should be attributed – the former or the current ones. For it should be noted that the Temple, before becoming the property of the lawyers, had been owned by the famous order of Knights Templar and, if virtues are inherited, no one should wonder if the practice of draining goblets has passed from the Knights of the Sword to the Knights of the Quill.

Within the precincts of the Temple there is a church where the remains of the distinguished lawyers, Plowden,[18] Selden[19] and Thurlow[20] are buried. Particularly interesting for a visitor is its round extension, which is said to have been modelled on the Holy Sepulchre in Jerusalem. It was built in 1185 and is, therefore, one of the oldest buildings in London. Inside there are nine full-length knights carved from stone and lying in the very middle of the church. Judging by the crosses on their armour they must have been Templars. They are behind an iron grille.

Standing in front of their images, on the spot renowned for so many memorable events, I began to picture the whole history of the Templars: the order's modest origins and rapid ascent to power, the sudden fall, as if caused by a thunderbolt, and the well-nigh complete oblivion of their name. The Order of the Knights Templar was established in the year 1118. Its purpose was the protection of pilgrims travelling to the Holy Land and the defence of the Holy Sepulchre against the assaults of the infidel. They were called Templars from the

Temple Church. The Knights Templar were in England from 1130. They built their New Church in 1160 when they moved from Holborn to the Strand. Its circular nave was modelled on the rotunda of the Church of the Holy Sepulchre in Jerusalem.

Temple in the vicinity of which they lived and for which they were to be a shield. Above all, they constituted a military order. Consisting originally of Hugo de Paens, Gottfried Uldemar and seven other knights, the order was to become both rich and numerous. As St Bernard of Clairvaux, their first legislator and historian writes: 'Living under vows of poverty and obedience, simply clad, dusty and sun-burnt, they seemed immortal, like the faith which inspired them. Nothing could diminish their valour, no adversity could discourage them. Dangers added glory to their victories and they went into battle armed by their faith and the strength of their armour. Every step was a step forward and every blow was that of a man confident of victory. They trusted in God and their arms and sought nothing but victory or glorious death.' The order was led by the Grand Master who was elected from among its members. He enjoyed the status of a prince and was on a par with European monarchs for, by a papal bull, the order was subject neither to church nor secular jurisdiction. They possessed enormous estates and their power was spread over many countries where they attracted numerous followers and adherents. Their presence in England dates back to the reign of Stephen when, from the Temple, they spread their preceptories over the entire kingdom.

Their obedience to the Grand Master was absolute and he was occasionally called the Father. 'Many a time,' writes Kazimierz Brodziski, 'they would risk their lives to protect the Grand Master, who invariably fought like an ordinary Templar and was no different from them but for the additional courage he showed. If the Grand Master's valour led to the death of one of the knights, the warrior would recommend himself to God with the words: 'Thanks be to thee, Providence, for delivering our Father, our Grand Master!' The Templars were at their most active during the crusades and, for two centuries, made the greatest contribution to the preservation of European supremacy in the East. The military principles imparted by their founder guaranteed their pre-eminence among other knights. There was a curb on their gallantry which, though not being dishonourable, prevented the reckless audacity which on occasions endangered the result of a battle and condemned many a man to pointless death. However, by virtue of an oath which they had to swear, none of them could shrink from facing their enemies. The whole order was divided into knights bearing arms and lay brothers acting as their servants. They were later joined by clergymen acting as priests and scribes.

The growing power of the order inspired envy and the envious began to seek for evidence of vice.[21] Ultimately there was no depravity, crime or heresy of which they had not been accused. Their tragic fate is well known. The Grand Master of the Order, James de Molay, along with several of his comrades in arms, were treacherously lured from Palestine, held for a long time in captivity in France, his motherland, and finally burnt alive on the square where the statue of Henry IV now stands. This happened on the 18th of March 1313 during the reigns of King Philip the Fair and Pope Clement V. From the fiery stake the Grand Master, the innocent victim of their revenge, is reputed to have foretold that God's judgement would descend on them within a year. According to the chronicles the prophesy was fulfilled – the Pope and the King died within the year. Nevertheless, it did not save the order from being abolished. It survived longest in Germany where, as late as six years after the tragic events in Paris, the Templars were still being mentioned in Goerlitz. After the abolition of the order many of its members joined the Knights of the Order of St John of Jerusalem, the Knights Hospitaller, which went through different vicissitudes, lost its original character and finally metamorphosed into the Order of the Knights of Malta, so named after their residence there. The last Grand Prior of the Templars in England was Thomas More and in spite of his fierce defence of the order he did not manage to clear it from accusations and avert its abolition. However, not a single knight lost his life as happened in France nor were any tortured into admission of crimes. Altogether there were 250 Templars in England, Ireland and Scotland at that time. They were denounced primarily for arrogance. This is quite understandable considering their customary knightly independence and pride.

When I was looking at the sepulchral effigies of these once doughty comrades in arms, now slumbering after their battles, it seemed that in spite of much damage I was able to recognise basinets and caps on the heads of some, chain mail jackets and iron greaves.

Temple Bar. Guarding the western approach to the City, Temple Bar was rebuilt by Wren after the Fire. The statues on the west side are of Charles I and Charles II and of Elizabeth and James I on the east.

Each of them had a sword at his side, the symbol of his knighthood, and each was girt with a broad woollen girdle, the token of chastity. All this was covered with a wide cloak made of wool and adorned with a red cross. Their shields also bore a cross, the symbol of the Crusaders. But time had obliterated all trace of inscriptions by which their names or deeds might have been identified. They were shielded by the tall fluted pillars of the Gothic vaults and the spirit of past centuries seemed to be whispering a common epitaph for them all:

> And on his brest a bloudie Crosse he bore,
> The deare remembrance of his dying Lord,
> For whose sweete sake that glorious badge he wore,
> And dead as living ever him ador'd:
> Upon his shield the like was also scor'd,
> For soveraine hope, which in his helpe he had:
> Right faithfull true he was in deede and word,
> But of his cheere did seeme too solemne sad;
> Yet nothing did he dread, but ever was ydrad.

Returning from a place so memorable in history I happened to go through Temple Bar. It is a gate erected in the middle of the city and now the only one in London. On his way to the City the king knocks at it with a hammer, asking for permission to enter. He is received there by the mayor of London, accompanied by councillors and sheriffs. The mayor then precedes the king on a horse and with a bare head. The City has the privilege of not admitting the military without the prior consent of the mayor. In the past it was on this gate or at Tyburn that the heads of the executed were displayed.

NOTES:

1 Sir Thomas Lyttelton (1415-81), English jurist whose *Tenures* was the first authoritative account of landholding. Written in French, it was translated into English in 1500 and later commented upon by Coke.

2 Sir Edward Coke (1552-1634). An English jurist and politician, he became the leading champion of national liberties against encroachments by chusch or state. His *Institutes* were the first textbooks on early common law.

3 Jeremy Bentham (1748-1832), English jurist, philosopher and social reformer. A utilitarian, in his *Introduction to the Principles of Morals and Legislation* he argued that the objective of all conduct and legislation should be the greatest happiness of the greatest number. He was a founder of University College London, the first university in England to be open to non-conformists and atheists.

4 Thomas Hobbes (1588-1679), English political philosopher. He tutored the exiled Charles II in mathematics. His *Leviathan* expressed his belief that in a state of nature man's life would be 'solitary, poor, nasty, brutish and short' and that the power of an absolute sovereign was required to protect him from himself. His atheism offended the royalist party and his support of absolute monarchy the parliamentarians.

5 A mythical Greek sculptor, Daedelus was believed to be the father of Icarus and the architect of the labyrinth in Crete.

6 *The Pandects* were a sixth-century digest of Roman law.

7 John Scott MP, 1st Earl of Eldon (1751-1838), English lawyer and politician. An opponent of reform and religious liberty, he is remembered for his judgment in the Leeds Grammar School case of 1805. He ruled that the introduction of modern subjects like French and German into the curriculum would be illegal in a school endowed to teach the grammatical reading of the learned langauges.

8 Sir James Mackintosh MP (1765-1832), Scottish lawyer and writer. Secretary to the Friends of the People and an opponent of Burke, in 1815 he published *On the State of France*, a recantation of his earlier views.

9 Henry Peter Brougham MP, 1st Baron Brougham and Vaux (1778-1868), Scottish jurist and politician. One of the founders of the *Edinburgh Revue* and London University, he played a major part in the abolition of the slave trade, the Reform Act of 1832 and in the reform of the legal system. The brougham carriage was named after him.

10 James Scarlett MP, 1st Baron Abinger (1769-1844), English lawyer, attorney general and chief baron of the Exchequer.

11 George Canning MP (1770-1827), English statesman. A leading reformer in a reactionary Tory party, he supported the abolition of the slave trade, Roman Catholic emancipation, the freeing of trade and a liberal foreign policy.

12 Thomas Erskine MP (1756-1823). Scottish jurist, he was famed for his defence of political radicals and sympathy with the ideals of the French revolutionaries.

13 William Pitt MP (1759-1806), English statesman. Prime Minister at the age of 24, he held office for 17 years. An early supporter of parliamentary reform,

his government passed the India and Canada Acts but became increasingly reactionary. He played a Churchillian role in the wars against France.

14 Charles James Fox MP (1749-1806). An English liberal statesman and orator, he was the leading opponent of the government's coercive measures against the American colonists and Britain's participation in the wars against France. During his brief premiership after the death of Pitt in 1806, he tried to end the war and to make the slave trade illegal.

15 John Philpot Curran MP (1750-1817), Irish orator, lawyer and statesman. Though a staunch Protestant, he sympathised wih his Catholic fellow countrymen and opposed the Union of 1800.

16 Edmund Burke MP (1739-97), Irish statesman and philosopher. A leading reformer and supporter of the American colonists. Although he sympathised with the ideals of the French revolutionaries their excesses led to his early disillusionment. His *Reflections on the French Revolution* was widely read and encouraged the rulers of European states to resist the revolutionary armies.

17 Themis was the Greek goddess of Justice and assistant to Zeus. Their daughter Astrea is usually represented holding the scales of Justice.

18 Edward Plowden MP (1518-85), English Catholic lawye, treasurer of the Middle Temple from 1561-71 and author of *The Commentaries*. These were notably accurate reports of cases in which important principles were involved.

19 John Selden MP (1584-1654), English jurist, historian and antiquarian. An opponent of absolute monarchy, he helped to draw up the Petition of Right and was twice imprisoned. He represented Oxford University in the Long Parliament and was a moderate, opposed to the disestablishment of the Episcopal Church and the execution of Charles I.

20 Edward Thurlow, 1st Baron (1731-1806), English politician and lawyer. A supporter of George III's American policy, he was briefly Lord Chancellor and presided at the trial of Warren Hastings. Reputedly arrogant and vulgar, Fox said of him that 'no one was so wise as Thurlow looked.'

21 By the thirteenth century the Templars had become international bankers to whom Philip the Fair was heavily indebted. Having expelled the Jewish community and the Italian bankers from France, he welcomed an excuse to abolish the Order and confiscate its wealth.

Chapter Thirteen

London Police. The Thames. An Overstated Number of Criminals. Kinds of Offence. The List of Misdemeanours in the Last Seven Years.

In such a populous capital as London, the police[1] maintaining order and public safety surely deserve the attention of a foreigner. In the country they are responsible to the sheriffs, high constables and Justices of the Peace. The first of these are appointed by the King and the others chosen by the counties themselves. In London, where the city appoints the sheriffs, the police are responsible to the mayor and council. This consists of the aldermen who hand over the execution of their orders to marshals and constables. These are not distinguishable by their dress but they carry wooden truncheons which have the royal coat of arms at one end. Moreover, they carry a hidden six-inch long tipstaff which they show when they want to arrest somebody who then becomes a prisoner in the name of the King. Detaining prisoners as well as supervising and guarding over prisons remains with the civil authority. It is only in the gravest situations when there is the threat of rebellion that they make use of the army. The Mutiny Act has to be read by the civil authority before violent measures can be resorted to.

In order to improve policing the whole capital is divided into a number of parishes, in each of which one police officer lives. These officers are paid £600 a year and they are appointed from among the lawyers so that, knowing the law, they can fulfil their tasks more skilfully. Apart from such an officer each parish, according to its population, chooses and pays a number of constables and night watchmen. The constables are supposed to be the householders, but everyone prefers to pay for a deputy to serve in his place rather than undertake an obligation that is often unpleasant and in time of disturbance dangerous. The night watchmen belong to the lowest and poorest social class. They are commonly poor navvies or porters with big families who, having spent the whole day working, still have to earn at night. It has been calculated that within the boundaries of the city up to 3,000 people watch over the safety of the inhabitants. If there is a fire the night watchmen give the alarm by maintaining a constant rattle in the streets and they do the same when they catch a thief or a vagabond. The police spread their activities from ten to fifteen English miles around the city and send night patrols out to guard the major roads. These patrols have contributed to putting an end to the robberies that used to happen so often. It is not easy to eradicate them in a city where, according to the law, every house is a citizen's castle and, thus, a safe hiding place for a criminal. A part of the capital, St Giles, is infamous as a hideout for gangs of thieves. I was told that there used to be a tavern where such was the honesty of the company that spoons, knives and forks had to be chained to the tables to prevent the guests from taking them away.

The Thames police are also well organised. With so many ships on the river disembarking and loading their cargoes, carefully planned robberies were often carried out by the crews. Mr Colquhoun,[2] to whose insistence London owes the formation of a police force on the

West India Docks. The Docks covered an area of over 50 acres on Poplar Marsh. This became known as the Isle of Dogs to which the royal kennels were moved when the Court resided in Greenwich Palace. Before the formation of the River Police by Patrick Colquhoun, the valuable cargoes stored in the warehouses attracted armies of professional thieves who co-operated with ships' crews to steal goods of high value and small bulk.

Thames, claims in one of his publications that 11,000 people, well versed in their trade, pursued this disgraceful way of life and that the value of the stolen items amounted to £500,000 a year. Although one could criticise this writer for his excessive fondness of round numbers, it would be most unrealistic to think that robberies did not take place there. In 1798, when he was writing, 13,444 vessels called at the port annually, some carrying valuables which, because of their small volume and weight, could easily be stolen amid the uproar of the crowd, especially with the connivance of some of the crew. The measures undertaken could not eradicate these riverside robberies but they significantly reduced them. The people occupying themselves in this way, as well as the receivers of stolen goods are, sooner or later, brought to justice.

Generally, I have to add here that travellers exaggerate the number of crimes committed in the capital of England. If someone took their reports on trust he would wonder how, in such a den of iniquity, anyone could live. We cannot deny that the number of crimes is great; that the English dictionary is far richer in words relating to theft and fraud than all other known dictionaries in the world; that of all the people getting up in the morning in London up to 20,000 do not know what they will live on throughout the day. Nevertheless, taking into account a population of nearly half a million and the exposure to public view of so many valuable goods, one has to wonder why there are not even more robberies with violence. With so much temptation it is difficult to be virtuous and it is easier to be virtuous when there is nothing to tempt you. A poor country will always have fewer thieves to punish than a rich one and, where there is little to steal, the laws can be more lenient. This forbearance is natural: severe penalties for only minor misdemeanours would be unnecessarily provocative but, where a breach of the peace is threatened, severity is justifiable.

To what extent these reports by foreigners deviate from the truth can also be proven by the fact that, in such a vast centre of commerce and diverse activities as one finds in London, thousands of people go about their businesses not only by day but also at night, going everywhere around the city without being molested or robbed. I know from my own experience that the inhabitants do not feel the slightest anxiety about going out in the city late at night. When invited to Mr B's house in Hackney, a good half mile from my apartment, I frequently came home after eleven at night and, although I had to cross a big open field, no highwayman barred my way or frisked my pockets. Thus, the threatened dangers seem to me to be bogeymen to frighten children rather than reality. However in this case, just as in any other, it would do no harm to be careful. It is not wise to look for unnecessary trouble and danger can be easily avoided. You should be sure to know the way to your destination so that you do not have to ask anyone for directions and do not risk acquiring an overly attentive guide who might lead you into a trap. Once this happened to me but, when I realised his intentions as he was leading me into still darker back streets, I took to my heels without further ado. It was the first time I had ever run away but what better could I have done when faced by certain danger? Above all you should not fear robbers: they lie in wait only for the timid and do not attack people who walk firmly and confidently. You have to be sober, stay away from suspicious company and avoid brawls, squabbles and arguments. It is safest to stick to main roads. Even though it involves taking a roundabout way, beware of side streets. On the main streets there are no hideouts and, should need arise, it is easier to find help where people walk all through the night. Most important is individual courage and prudence. Someone who does not expose himself to danger and knows how to behave in any situation can be certain that not a hair of his head will be touched.

The main reason for the number of criminals to seem so huge is that crimes are punished regardless of birth, status and wealth and none can be concealed from the public. In the first case this is because of the openness of the courts of law and in the second because of the custom of publishing whole cases, from beginning to end, in the papers. The harshness of these laws, which punish delinquency with death, a penalty that in other countries would be deemed inhumane, contributes to the increasing list of notorious felons, who would not be considered as such if they lived elsewhere. The steps that have been taken in recent years and institutions which have been established in order to diminish crime will be discussed at length later. They make us hope that criminal activity will diminish with time.

However, although it is easy to avoid obvious robbers, thieves and ruffians, it is much more difficult to avoid the concealed ones who, under the mask of honesty, lure the careless and the credulous. London has been aptly compared to a great beehive to which the righteous and the villainous are equally attracted. The aforementioned Mr Colquhoun lists in his work eighteen different classes of swindlers who, like venomous vermin, infest the capital, living by looting honest but foolish people. Indeed, the deceivers benefit from such people everywhere, but nowhere is the harvest as rich and as skilfully collected as in London. I shall describe a few so that the reader may see the image of this capital from its bad side as well as from the good.

There are pawnshops which accept costly household goods, commodities and tools and are licensed by the government. Their owners often have close links with thieves and on the pretence that they had been pawned they store stolen goods. They are called shapers. Fraudsters who pretend to be hucksters buy goods in the city, supposedly with the intention of selling them in the provinces, but they too have links with thieves, coiners and smugglers, from whom they buy things dirt-cheap and peddle them around the country. Another group of swindlers are those who, having obtained a government permit, sell the articles at auctions to the highest bidder. Their shops are in crowded streets and at the entrance there is usually a man called a barker who invites passers-by to come in. At these auctions new and old items are sold but they are of poor workmanship or counterfeits. Pretenders (puffers) are employed to raise the bidding above their value and, on the first bid by a stranger, who may not have wished to buy but was only having a joke, they knock down the sale and the buyer discovers the deceit too late. In addition to the inflated price of the article he has to pay the tax. Then there are quacks who sell bonds which have to be cleared by a certain date. They lie in wait for the wealthy and prodigal youths who never have enough money to spend on games, ostentation and costly amusements. Loitering around the houses of the wealthy are Jews who, under the pretence of buying antiques, old china and silver, prompt the servants to steal. It is known that up to 1,500 of these tricksters roam around the city. These frauds are sometimes carried out on such a huge scale and the snares are set so skilfully that the sagacity of even the most cautious is defeated.

To defraud tradesmen there are swindlers who associate together. One, pretending to be a merchant, rents a house and establishes an office where he appears to be pursuing his trading business, aided by two fellow swindlers pretending to be clerks and a few others acting as servants. They find some smart looking servants, dress them as ladies and have them driven to the counting house or the shop in carriages. In the presence of other people they order goods which are then delivered to their apartments. In this way they manage to throw dust in the eyes of both the public and tradesmen. These let them take the products from their stores on credit. By immediately pawning them they are able to pay back, fully or partially, the debts they contracted elsewhere and with such settlements gain credit and may be recommended to other tradesmen. These swindlers sometimes make out bills of exchange but, having made out so many that it has become dangerous to risk any more, they disappear from the sight of their creditors, taking what they can.

By the nature of their organisation the police are inefficient at pursuing frauds. A host, on leasing his house to a stranger, only cares that the rent should be paid and the terms and conditions of the agreement kept. In addition, the stranger travels the country without a passport. Having spent four years moving from place to place, I have never been asked where I came from, where I was heading or what my name was. I could have changed my name, status and title in each place and be known as a different character. It is sufficient for a foreigner to register in the Aliens' Office on arrival and departure. So it is easy to grasp how profitable for the thieves, swindlers and villains such lax policing is. It seems as though the unnecessary harshness of the criminal laws demands a lenient police system to enforce them. This is why the extraordinary number of complaints filed against robbers, thieves, swindlers and other rogues so rarely come to a successful prosecution.

There are other thieves whose origins are unknown who play

the role of celebrities. They rent beautiful rooms, dress themselves according to the latest fashion and write confidential letters addressed to themselves which suggest that they are friends of or related to some of the finest families in the country. They do all this in order to gain credit from tradesmen and moneylenders and in the end, having made their pile, they run off with their loot to start their frauds somewhere else under a different name. Apart from these and similar crooks living, as it is said, by their wits, there are also regular scoundrels. These ensnare the inexperienced, roam around the shops and public places and crowd up to the newly arrived carriages and carts loaded with merchandise, seemingly out of curiosity but actually to steal. They are inexhaustible in approach and change their manoeuvres according to the situation.

Even the members of the fair sex commit fraudulent acts. There are women who dress themselves very elegantly, attend fancy-dress balls and masquerades and by extraordinary effrontery force themselves into the finest salons of St James. Quite some time ago one neatly dressed female swindler dared to come to the Court on the King's birthday and, with an assumed spouse who was dressed as a clergyman, she stole property worth £1,700. This respectable couple acted so skilfully that nobody harboured the slightest suspicion or caught them red-handed. There are establishments which lend the most fashionable clothes to such swindlers on condition that they later have a share in the gains from the robbery.

Major robberies are carefully planned by professional burglars. Outside the houses that have attracted the thieves' attention reconnaissance is conducted. There are people on the watch and servants are drawn into the plot and, as it is they who secure all the ways in and out of the house, committing the robbery is a trifle. Sometimes cabmen are in collusion with the thieves; they arrive at the exact moment of the robbery and, in order to avoid the keen eye of the police, they drive the robbers and their loot to their hiding places. The inhabitants are only too aware of the dangers to which their property can be exposed and for this reason their houses resemble fortified strongholds, or so one might imagine. In front of each house there are iron rails; sharp on top so that it is difficult to get over them

– these are palisades. Behind them there is a deep ditch separating the house from the street – a moat. Over the moat there are stairs leading to the house – a drawbridge. The doors are closed night and day, or, should we borrow a stronghold metaphor, barricaded. The thieves rarely break them open with battering rams, which would be dangerous; instead they steal in by wile.

That is more than enough about the swindlers. One could write about cardsharpers, gangs of thieves, pickpockets and suchlike rogues but I would not like to saturate the image of the capital with descriptions of people of this sort. Paris is no better than London in this respect; rogueries there, though planned, are less well concealed. Every huge capital will be the same because crime always increases with the growth of population. As Cowper[3] rightly said, 'God made the country and man made the town.' He wanted to suggest that the country will always be the home of simplicity and honesty and those towns are a mixture of hypocrisy and vice.

The reasons for this criminal activity are various. The main ones are drunkenness, immorality and idleness. Among the culprits are frequently dismissed servants, boys and journeymen who, if still ignorant of their craft, are unable to earn their living. There are also Jews who, not only in Poland, cannot be converted from their false religious beliefs. A curse seems to hang over this despised nation. Misdemeanours are also encouraged by the great ease with which stolen goods can be disposed of. It has been estimated that there are up to 3,000 receivers' houses in London and that the value of the items received is £700,000. The annual reports of these burglaries and frauds filed in Parliament show neither a significant decrease nor increase in crime if we take into consideration the growing population of the country. Each year is different. The number of various crimes in the course of seven years, from 1820 to 1826, is as follows. This list will give an impression of the sorts of punishments meeted out in England:

Cases brought to court	Total 95,611	
Of which	Men 60,304	Women 15,307
Sentenced to death	7,656	

Robert Adam's design for an Edinburgh town house. On a more modest scale, thousands of houses of similar plan – described by Lach-Szyrma as 'fortified houses' - were built in the squares and terraces of Georgian London

Sentence carried out	588
Transported for life	1,000
Transported for shorter term	12,027
Imprisoned, flogged and hard labour	42,488
Flogged and fined	1,832
Found guilty	65,005
Not guilty	18,505
No appearance in court	12,103
Total	95,611

As far as criminals condemned to death are concerned, barely one in fifteen or twenty is executed. So even though the letter or the theory of the law is very strict in England it is in practice significantly softened by the enlightenment of the judges, the humanity of the jury and the graciousness of the King.

There have been several attempts to make the organisation of the police more efficient but none of these has been effective. It is generally believed that the successful policing of any country, to quote Mr Leigh, depends on 'rational and humane laws... in an effective and enlightened magistracy... and in the judicious and proper selection of those officers of justice in whose hands, as conservators of the peace, executive duties are legally placed. But above all, on the moral habits and opinions of the people... The institutions of the country being sound, its laws well administered and justice executed against offenders, no greater safeguard can be obtained without sacrificing all those rights which society was instituted to preserve.'

NOTES:

1 The organisation of the London police, in which there was no co-ordination between parishes, probably dates back to the Anglo-Saxon period. Sir Robert Peel's reforms of 1829 created a unified force of trained, disciplined and adequately paid constables. Their efficiency drove many professional criminals into the provinces but it was ten years before similarly co-ordinated forces were established outside London.

2 Patrick Colquhoun (1731-1800), Scottish tobacco merchant and reformer. Lord Provost of Glasgow and founder of the Glasgow Chamber of Commerce, he moved to London in 1789 and became a police commissioner. His *Police of the Metropolis* was published in 1795.

3 William Cowper (1731-1800), English 'Nature' poet associated with the Evangelical movement.

Chapter Fourteen

Prisons. Houses of Correction. Newgate. The Society for Improving Prisoners. Beggars. The Destitute. Workhouses. Schools in Prisons.

We have contemplated the misdeeds and trespasses resorted to by the London rabble so it would be in order now to consider some of the means applied to restrain criminals. It is time we spoke about prisons and houses of correction.

It was less than half a century ago that throughout Europe such places were in a most miserable condition. Since they had been designed to provide accommodation for pariahs of the human kind, no one was concerned about them. To have acquired a reputation for caring for rogues, thieves and miscreant would have been unacceptable. This mistaken attitude had existed before the birth of Howard,[1] whose humanity will make him immortal. Having relinquished the ubiquitous callousness and deep-rooted prejudices of his contemporaries, he was the first to show that a man, though in disgrace, condemned and not rid of his old vices, does not cease to be a man. He merely forfeits our respect but, like a demented lunatic, does deserve our pity.

The House of Correction. John Howard's report on conditions in English prisons led, in 1774, to the creation of prisons where inmates could do useful work for which, on discharge, they received a small payment.

Before Howard's appearance prisons were hideous caverns in which vermin, foul air, and the dearth of food and bedding precipitated the death of inmates even before sentence had been passed. As in some cauldron containing various ingredients, criminals were housed with the innocent, those condemned to death with the ones accused of minor offences, inveterate scoundrels with debtors and persons whose misdeeds resulted from ignorance or sheer chance. All of them were crowded together, irrespective of their age, the nature of the offence or even sex. Moral perversion as well as maladies of the flesh would spread among them and the anguish caused by breathing air permeated by blasphemy and curses transformed the most blameless into villains. When visiting a gaol in Paris Howard did not manage to find a single prisoner who would undertake to lead him through the gloomy and musty dungeons of the Bastille. Having left it, he could no longer wear the clothes in which he had visited it on account of the hellish odour which they had absorbed. Even vinegar, which he had usually inhaled in order to invigorate himself, lost its natural power in such filthy places. After the death of this philanthropist who in Cherson, far away from his home, was afflicted with plague and fell victim to his solicitude for the welfare of human kind, Nield[2] and Buxton[3] followed in his footsteps. To the latter England and Scotland owe the inspection of their prisons and proposals for their improvement. In a work on prison penalties, *On Prison Discipline*, he depicted the full gruesomeness of the prisoner's plight:

> Let us follow the prisoner from the moment of his detention. With his hands tied he is led to the gaol through a mob, sometimes in the company of a few people, wretches like himself, exposed to the scorn of an uncharitable pack and perhaps to the pity of those who used to hold him in high esteem. As soon as he has crossed the threshold of the prison, he is fettered with manacles – from that moment he becomes a fellow inmate, though possibly unjustly for no sentence has yet been pronounced – of malefactors of every nature. At night he is confined to a cubbyhole where conceivably a few robbers or renowned thieves have their pallets and along with them he lies on a mangled palliasse, in grimy rags, amidst various

> kinds of vermin. On one side there may be a grim murderer, on the other an eminent swindler. Near him may be a person suffering from a malignant fever or a repulsive plague. He is barred from breathing the fresh air and taking the exercise requisite for his health. A great many have deserted the families whom they can no longer support. Penury and privation harass him from all sides; he is tormented by hunger, has nothing to cover himself with and shivers in the bitter cold. As a consequence of his poverty, he has to consort with degenerates, tolerate their humours, suffer their blasphemies and jest in order to be left in peace. In time he may become accustomed to their company and ways, accepts their criminal concepts and out of necessity and despair he too becomes a villain. His health deteriorates, and his morals fare no better. The purest virtue could not remain innocent in such a company. Moreover, his sentence can be delayed – he is a suspect, appearances speak against him and he cannot clear himself.
>
> When at long last the moment of his acquittal comes he is released from prison penniless, without the possibility of returning to his birthplace. Should, however, he be proved guilty, the severity of the sentence and the increased rigour of prison discipline will lead him, unreflecting and unrepentant, to take his own life.

Such conditions in prisons could certainly not contribute in any way to preventing crime. I quoted the above excerpt from *On Prison Discipline* for, even though it contains some frightful details, it is the result of the plans for reform submitted by Howard, Buxton and other friends of humanity that a standard of prisons in England has been achieved which may serve as an example to be followed. Other countries have already made use of them. As a result of the calamities which have overwhelmed our country in the past it has fallen behind in introducing reforms in this area. It also seems that there was less urgency to implement those changes in Poland either because of the peaceful character of the nation and the leniency of domestic laws or, ultimately, that in a country which is less affluent and has a smaller population there is less crime. Today, however, when a reforming government is directing its attention to prisons and an enlightened representative was sent abroad to visit gaols and any related institutions, I believe I must describe several things which struck me on my journey. These illustrated the principles upon which English prisons are established, for when it comes to their general system and structure I shall have some more weighty advice to give.

There are several large prisons in London which I do not intend to enumerate, as interested travellers can find them listed in the available guidebooks. One of the most important is the House of Correction at Coldbath Fields, founded according to Howard's proposal. From 2,000 to 3,000 prisoners are committed to it annually. Each is allotted some work so that, having a useful occupation, there is no time left for wrongdoing. Such methods render the financing of prisons easy and inexpensive, for inmates maintain themselves from what they earn. Their earnings, however, are not handed to them but amassed in one pool. Personal shares are then recorded in a book.

Another similar house of correction is the one called the Penitentiary. It was planned to study the effect of dividing malefactors according to the nature and gravity of their crimes as well as the effect of giving them suitable instruction. It is situated on the Thames, at an open, healthy location outside the city. The colossal edifice is spread over an area of 25 acres. Its shape is peculiar: it comprises seven separate wings which at the corners abut on one another and form a hexagonal courtyard, in which the house of the warden of the prison stands. Without leaving it he can observe what is happening in each cell, for all of them give onto the courtyard. Cells are of equal dimensions, measuring twelve feet in length and seven feet in breadth. Each contains a bed, a mattress, a thick quilt resembling a saddlecloth, a bolster and a sheet. In winter they are heated and aired, the windows being barred with iron gratings. The erection of such an immense edifice cost up to £500,000. In the original plan it was supposed to house 400 male and the same number of female inmates, but it can accommodate up to 300 more. And since the purpose of this institution was to reduce the number of wrongdoers, meticulous attention is given to the progress of improvement, which, if sincere, contributes to reducing the sentence of a prisoner and his early release as a worthy citizen. There are separate areas for men and women. The cells and occupations of women are supervised by a female warden and, according to regulations, the governor himself is not admitted there when not accompanied by her. This circumstance ought to be mentioned, as so far there have been no examples of women being entrusted with the supervision of gaols. Under this regime the comportment of many prisoners becomes exemplary, calm and seemly in spite of the fact that most had been hardened criminals. The leniency with which they are treated and genuine care for their welfare makes them indebted to their wardens, especially since shortening their sentences is dependent solely upon the same wardens. Here too the convicts support themselves by their own work, and the industrious and the orderly earn enough to accumulate a sum which is handed to them as their property upon release. Therefore they are not left, as was the case formerly, without means to live by, and penury and privation do not plunge them into vice. The inmates are not permitted to see their relatives and friends – the governor himself cannot allow them to do so without the prior consent of a committee, which

The Penitentiary from Vauxhall Bridge. Rennie's toll bridge was one of three built during the Regency to deal with London's rapidly growing population. At the cost of £458,080 the Penitentiary was designed as a model prison to house convicts waiting for deportation to Australia. Single cells, workshops, an exercise yard, religious instruction, a school and medical care were provided for from 400 to 800 prisoners. Built on marshy ground, it had to be evacuated in 1822 when an outbreak of scurvy and typhus affected over half the prisoners and killed 31. It was demolished in 1893 and replaced by the Tate Gallery.

grants permissions only to those whose good conduct has been confirmed by the governor, the chaplain and the foreman who oversees the work. The visits must take place in the warden's presence and visitors are not permitted to bring anything for the prisoners. Members of the committee managing the gaol are appointed by the Privy Council and no stranger is admitted without a clear order from the Home Secretary. Having no connection with him I did not visit it – I only visited Newgate.

Newgate is one of the ancient London prisons whose horrendous condition is reputed to have contributed most to the determination to reform English prisons. The picture drawn above by Mr Buxton could be related in its entirety to the gaol under consideration. Convicts lived there without any differentiation as to the nature of the crime: debtors, robbers, thieves, the healthy and the ill mingled together. Today matters are different. In particular, in the cell block for women, there have been considerable alterations which can be attributed to the benevolent efforts of Mrs Fry.[4] I was fortunate enough to have visited it twice in the company of Mrs Fry herself. The appearance of the Newgate prison reflects its function. It is built of huge ashlar blocks, the walls are pierced here and there with small narrow grated windows and in the casings there are figures whose meaning I could not comprehend. There are no sentries in front of it or anything suggesting that it is a prison. We knocked at the door, whereupon a handsomely clad and mild-mannered man appeared who became even more courteous when he noticed Mrs Fry. It was the warden of the prison himself. Having notified him of the reason for her arrival and recommended us as foreigners interested in prison reform, Mrs Fry asked him to show us around the men's cells and went with a female warden to those of the women. Wherever we looked there was hustle and bustle as prisoners performed different tasks. Here too work was deemed an effective means of improvement and a check upon fierce passions. It was work, as numerous wardens would repeat, that most successfully eradicated criminal propensities and taught criminals to prefer legally acquired profits to those obtained by illegal and dangerous means. Finally, it provided the hapless with an honest way of maintaining themselves. It is not acceptable to employ prisoners for work in public places – it was considered to be a mistake to make an exhibition of a man in front of a rabble and to disgrace him, for such a person is more susceptible to evil. Even within the prison there are no fetters jangling derisively around inmates' ankles. The walls of the gaol are strong enough to prevent escape and even putting guards at the gate is deemed unnecessary. In one room we found three convicts who were to be executed the following day. It was only here that no work was being done – the world did not need them any more. They sat by the flickering fire, holding the Holy Scripture in their hands and awaiting the chaplain who was to prepare them for death. In a nation as religious as the English, the utmost care is taken that a sinner does not die without prior reflection and the possibility of repentance.

From there we were led by the warden to the chapel. We walked through a courtyard paved with broad ashlar stones and kept spotlessly clean. There were similar courtyards in which prisoners were permitted to saunter and enjoy fresh air. In the chapel we encountered Mrs Fry accompanied by a few of her friends and opposite them were female inmates, sitting in pews arranged and ascending like stairs. As we entered, she beckoned us to take seats and, from the Bible lying in front of her, read a chapter from the New Testament which was relevant to their situation. Her reading was so mild and pleasant that the very sound of her voice was reassuring. The prisoners were listening to her with the most assiduous attention and seemed to value not only the gravity of her words but also the magnificence of her dedication to their well-being. Only one of them was somewhat absent-minded. Having finished the reading, Mrs Fry gave them a few words of advice inspired by her feeling for humanity. Later she talked to everybody, as she knew all of them and called them by their names. She asked the warden about their needs and the tasks completed that week. She did not address the absent-minded one; having turned to us after leaving she merely mentioned that she had been recently admitted to the prison. They believe that the recently admitted inmates are the worst behaved; in time they become less wayward. And that is all I have to say about these frequently lauded prison sermons given by Mrs Fry. In addition, prisoners are supplied with moral and religious books to be read in their leisure time, and particularly on Sundays when all labour is suspended and the prisoner, unaccustomed to reading though he may be, might occupy his time with books.

How far such procedures can contribute to curbing crime and transforming degenerate members of society is suggested in the report which Mrs Fry made at the beginning of her efforts to improve conditions in prisons. Submitted to the Committee on London Prisons in 1818, after only one month's experience, it was couched in typically lucid terms:

> It is true that our regulations were sometimes ignored but such occasions were extremely rare, generally speaking order was kept. I would almost be tempted to venture a claim that we can do with prisoners whatever we wish. One of them confessed that it would be more dreadful for her to be brought before me than before the court, even though we apply only clement methods. I have not yet punished a single person and I have no intention of doing so. Yet it would be difficult to find a private house better organised, in which order was more strictly preserved than in the prison, so regularly do convicts follow directions given by me or any other member of our society. As far as the work carried out by them is concerned, there are 20,000 products of many different sorts. Nothing has gone astray so far apart from three items for which, however, we do not want to hold the prisoners responsible. They produce from 60 to 100 pairs of stockings a month as well as some yarn. The clear profit from that per person is eighteen pence a week. It is used to improve their food and clothing. Thus, they themselves can perhaps collect around £4 a month, which, if we consider an additional £8 paid out of our own pocket, suffices for a decent and proper livelihood. The benefits accruing from religion, as we have learnt, are invaluable: we read to them from the Holy Scripture twice a week. There are women who can read, others have learnt only a little and the consequences of that are startling. I think that not all of them comprehend the Scriptures with equal facility; for many the Christian faith and the moral principles underlying it were equally unknown. Whenever I wanted to read it to them I observed with the utmost

satisfaction how ardently they gathered round me. It seemed as though it was in this way that I gave them the greatest pleasure.

The most difficult task was organising hard labour in prisons. Some time ago treadmills, a set of steps of sorts, were introduced, to which miscreants and vagrants were condemned. This labour is said to be exceedingly tedious and enfeebling, especially when prisoners are forced to move the treadmill around, without adequate rests, from five o'clock in the morning to seven at night. In some gaols this may amount to 13,000 steps. Mrs Fry endeavoured to exempt women from this fatiguing punishment but whether she succeeded I do not know. It was still going on shortly before my departure. All things considered, I am of the opinion that some form of occupation is advantageous to inmates, not only to reduce the burden on society but also for the sake of their health which requires exercise, provided it is moderate and does not exceed their strength.

In order to advance more effective reforms in prisons and to improve prisoners' lives, a society comprising citizens concerned for the welfare of humanity was established in England. Its female members are obliged to supervise women convicts. How far-reaching and unexpected the consequences of the efforts of this society were is evident from reports on the state of prisons which are submitted and published annually. The society did not restrict the scope of its activities solely to Britain; on the contrary, it encouraged the foundation of similar prisons in other countries. As well as the exchange of information with regard to plans, organisation or specific cases, it set up a common fund to deal with the needs of prisoners. Societies related to that in London were created in Bavaria, Wurttemberg, Denmark, Sweden and the Netherlands. In the year 1825 the Amsterdam society included 4,390 members. It was also introduced in Russia, where the department of prisons for men was under the supervision of Prince Golicyn and that of prisons for women under the supervision of the Duchess Meshcherskaya. Would societies of a similar nature and of benefit to the country not bring honour to Poland? Would it not be useful if such societies assisted in the development of similar institutions in our country? The nexus of those associations is London.

Journeys made recently by several Quakers through Germany were in response to the organisation of prisons and the establishment of similar societies. Societies created for so laudable a cause ought to be supported, for they are the greatest blessing to humanity. A man, however charitable, must die and with him dies his charity. A society, however, is immortal – it continues to exist through its new members and may carefully and systematically develop an effective plan of improvements. By mutual encouragement and support it strengthens noble endeavours. The advances stemming from such a source are neither mere caprice nor a reckless pursuit of novelties but the fruit of sound reflection and experience. They do not originate from selfishness or vanity but from ardent dedication to the wellbeing of the country and its people.

The major obstacle in the path of eradicating crime was deemed to be the poverty of a large portion of the population. It was calculated that in London itself twelve people out of every hundred are poor, without any means to live and left to the mercy of society. So substantial a number cannot benefit society, particularly in a wealthy country where the cunning can find such a multitude of opportunities to get richer illegally. However, no obnoxious cripples, ragged beggars or any other obvious tokens of poverty can be seen in the streets. It is said to have staggered even the monarchs entering London who, upon seeing crowds of interesting and handsomely clad people, are reputed to have asked: 'And where are the beggars?' And truly, so much is written about them that England might appear to be a land of destitution. Surely, where the opulent are there must also be the poor, but begging as we imagine it with all its horrors is the creation of writers. The huge amount of money spent in England on the poor (poor-rate) prevents vagrancy and privation, for the poor and their families are provided for without the need to leave home. It should also be borne in mind that poverty is a relative concept: in England a person believes himself to be destitute if he cannot afford wheaten bread and meat for dinner or, at the least, a mutton head, which is deemed to be the nourishment of the poor.

Beggars proper are scarce, for in England begging is forbidden. Those who earn their livelihood in this way usually assume some occupation in order to evade the watchful eye of the police and hide their intentions under a disguise. Some sweep busy streets on inclement days; others sell matches and flints for lighting fires so as to arouse pity with such petty articles of trade; others sing ballads, play some instruments or attract the attention of a charitable audience by means of the many tricks which the human mind can concoct. These paupers are not importunate: they do not follow passers-by with persistence; they do not make abhorrent motions or fill the air with shrill cries and moaning. It is through their meek demeanour and modest looks rather than voice and gestures that they indicate their need for alms. As long as they remain within these bounds the police have no power over them; immediately when they cross them they are detained and put in gaol like vagabonds. Those from the provinces are sent back to their birthplaces where they must be maintained at the expense of the parish. How important it must be for the parishioners to have only worthy and orderly members among them! How much they must be concerned for the education of their youth so as to avoid the obnoxious burden of keeping idlers!

The rules against begging in the metropolis have made it a fine art and have led to the proliferation of beggars. The loafers assume a style of life which they believe to be the easiest one. With skill and astuteness it may become an exceedingly profitable profession. So they resort to varied expedients: they assign to each other streets in which to beg, they change clothes two or three times a day so as not to be recognised and, so disguised, they repair to charities where they receive money two or three times, sometimes at the expense of others. Children are frequently used for begging so that the poverty of these little creatures can evoke more sympathy from merciful people. Being sent to the city, they are ordered to collect a specific sum of money. Children are also purchased from their needy parents or engaged in exchange for remuneration of from six to nine pence a day and sometimes more. The more squalid a child's appearance the more money is paid for him or her. From the report of a certain Englishman, who in 1815 undertook to count all beggars, it became apparent that, out of 14,164 tramps, 7,288 were children and one third of the adult beggars were Irish. According to Mr Martin's[5] calculations, the funds required to provide board, clothing and accommodation for vagrants would amount annually to £977,126. But this would be insignificant when compared with the sums out of which the public were swindled by cunning, a sum at least twice as high. On average, each beggar receives from three to five shillings a day. A blind mendicant is remembered who, in order to attract attention, would allow a dog to lead him in the streets and thus earned 30 shillings (60 Polish zloty) daily and occasionally even more. A certain Negro accumulated £1,500 from begging and afterwards went to America.

The district of the city called St Giles, renowned for its nests of thieves and crooks, is also famous for its clubs of beggars. Two houses were discovered in which not less than 200 tramps gathered in the evenings. A book was kept in which their names were recorded and only beggars themselves or persons introduced by them could be admitted. In this distinguished club vagrants treated themselves to food and drink, read papers and discussed politics. It is intriguing to wonder to what conclusions this pack, having neither an honest occupation nor a place of their own in which to live, could have come to as regards to the security of society. Each of them is said to have spent in the club up to two and six pence, in addition to six pence for a bed. An experienced beggar, as they will tell you, visits approximately 40 streets a day and he deems it a bad day if he has failed to collect eight shillings.

What has been said thus far pertains only to those mendicants who are not of necessity in need but rather have a propensity for vagrancy and vice. There are however others who are necessitous through no fault of their own, who have been plunged into penury and destitution by chance, by too large a family or by the shortage of employment which is not infrequent in an industrial country. Widespread unemployment occurred during the rule of Elizabeth, when a special post of overseer was established, whose duties included providing the needy with work. Since the time of her rule the number of the impoverished has risen steadily every year, as if bearing testimony to the fact that work which occupies a man may not automatically earn him a living wage. When the demand for goods is low a worker, drudging day and night, may not be able to satisfy his basic needs. The situation is that the poor are not provided with employment but with money. This generosity, though accepted with bitterness by some, did not contribute to diminishing the number of its beneficiaries; on the contrary, it increased their number. This process has been intensified from the time that, in workplaces, human hands began to be replaced by machines. These, as is well known, gave rise to the dangerous riots in Liverpool and Manchester.[6] The tax levied on behalf of the penurious (poor-rate), which has been increased each year for the last three centuries, totalled in the year 1826 £6,966,150 and, next to the enormous national debt, is the second most onerous and unavoidable burden on the country. It is financed entirely by England and the principality of Wales; such a calamity did not befall Scotland and Ireland, for matters related to the destitute are regulated in a different manner there.[7] The only hope of removing it rests upon the savings institutions whose number has been increasing steadily. The disadvantages of this tax are multifarious and pernicious: it is generally considered to undermine the industry and damage the prosperity and even the morals of a worker. Accustomed to regarding it as a secure benefit in times of privation, he does not attempt to avert poverty through work and thrift. This tax is unjust in its very nature, for in order for it to be a virtue, charity should be voluntary. It is even more unjust on account of the fact that it does not affect the whole population equally, for some parishes, primarily in industrial cities, know nothing of it and rural ones are forced to carry an excessive burden. Hence, it could be inferred that industry conduces more to the restriction of poverty than agriculture. The equal division of this tax among people would also protect them from legal expenses and the vexation associated with police procedures. Workers would also move around the country whereas now there are too many in some areas and too few in others. Furthermore, the tax is contrary to morality, for it teaches some to live in idleness, notwithstanding the fact that they are a burden on the working community. Others are discouraged from seeking work, knowing that some of their hard-earned money will disappear as tax. It would have been abolished a long time ago had it not been for fear of the riots which might result from abruptly depriving so large a group of people of the means to live, a group is the more likely to start rioting because it has so little to lose. Fear of a greater evil sustains the lesser one, although the latter is potentially equally dangerous. The financial expectations of skilled craftsmen are very high. There are already far more craftsmen than peasants, for the number of the latter is 896,000 and that of the former amounts to 1,130,000. There would be even more craftsmen had not the machines, which replaced 2,000,000 (according to estimates prepared ten years ago), diminished their incomes. In Ireland, where workshops are scarce and people mainly live by the land; poverty is severe.

Different steps have been undertaken to reduce poverty and thus begging and crime. The introduction of savings institutions for workers and workhouses of various kinds were regarded as the most efficient measure for this purpose. In some workhouses prisoners are admitted and employed immediately after being released; in others anyone who does not want to lead an idle life and is unable to find employment is admitted. Such a workhouse at St. Martin-in-the-Fields is worthy of praise. Up to 800 people, when in need, can find there a suitable livelihood and protection from hardship. Of a similar kind is the Refuge for the Destitute. It is intended mainly for those who, after having served their sentence, enjoyed its remittal or been granted a royal pardon, are released penniless and, having dishonoured their names cannot find a place of their own. Thus humanity delivers from doom people who, regardless of the high price they have paid, continue to be pursued by vice. Where the seed of virtue is still alive it suffices to extend a comforting and compassionate hand and virtue will flourish again. This charitable institution has existed since 1806 and there are several similar ones in London. To each is attached a transitional institute to which those who have been admitted have to pay seven shillings a week, though this may be paid by a society for the improvement of prisons and the restriction of begging. These institutions can occasionally be so overcrowded that inmates have to wait in prisons until a place becomes vacant. It is also there that the destitute are admitted who are to be returned to their birthplaces as soon as the necessary money is sent from their parishes. This shelter is a great help to them, for they are not exposed to the company of the London rabble, which would surely have a damaging effect. Into these institutions are also sent people who committed some crime but whom compassionate people want to shield from the full stringency of the law. In order to avoid excessive congestion, especially as regards persons whose reform is difficult or sometimes impracticable, inmates are not admitted indiscriminately, the young are preferred to the old. When I was visiting this poorhouse the group of people between the ages of fifteen and twenty-two years was the largest. Inmates of the transitional institute as well as residents in the permanent one are subject to the same severely enforced discipline, whose observance is believed to be a major step towards improvement. Young men and boys are trained there in such crafts as shoemaking, tailoring, weaving or other skills which may secure them an honest livelihood; women and girls are taught spinning, sewing, laundering, making blankets and various types of needlework. Each room is supervised by a training master. Rooms used by women are superintended by a female steward. The dwelling of the guardian of the house is situated so as to facilitate communication with all other rooms. Through windows and apertures he can see and hear what is taking place as well as giving orders. In spite of the most rigid discipline they do not apply corporal punishment. The impudent and the wayward are not permitted to sit at the common table, they dine separately. A board is hung in the hall with an account of the transgression for which they are being punished; in the worst cases inmates are put on bread and water or locked up in a dark chamber. Those who cannot be reformed are expelled so as to protect the others from corruption. The guardian keeps a watchful eye upon the conduct and the progress of each person; he maintains a journal in which, under various headings, are recorded his orders, their execution, former admonitions, the inmate's replies and the state of his morals. An extract from the journal is hung in the dining hall on the following day. Each Sunday a sermon appropriate to the educational level and the situation of the people is delivered in the chapel. A catechism for study was compiled which comprises questions and answers taken from the Old and the New Testaments in the original biblical wording, without the admixture of religious dogmas which might offend prisoners of different denominations. In the first weeks after admission no one is permitted to leave the precincts of the house; it is only later, after some progress has been made, that a person is granted this privilege. The improvement of an inmate is assessed on the basis of his desire to prolong his sojourn in the institute. At this stage he would be released. The wish not to stay there any more is regarded as evidence that the reforming process has not been completed. It is generally assumed that one out of every six people cannot be cured of his weaknesses. But were it every second person, would it not still be worth every effort?

Usually such charitable institutions are headed by a prince of the blood. The chairman of the Refuge for the Destitute was at the time of my visit the Duke of York and the long list of its patrons includes members of some of the most distinguished families in the country. Thus it was England that first set an example of how to combat evil. Her example, which did so much good, is worth following everywhere. A concept whose efficacy and utility have been confirmed by experience is not a chimera or illusion. The endeavour to uproot evil and inculcate order has resulted from the proper enlightenment of people, for the testimonies of miscreants before courts have shown that many resorted to crime solely owing to lack of education and ignorance of moral principles. Schools have been founded in prisons and even on ships used to transport convicts overseas. During their voyage they learn to read and count and in their new country they start their lives as orderly and honest members of society. And this is how civil awareness (for all such institutions in England were created thanks to private initiatives and funding) contributes to the achievement of man's finest aim, the restoration to society of those previously rejected. It is the greatest triumph that the nobility of human nature can secure.

NOTES:

1 John Howard (1726-90), English prison reformer. His own experience as a prisoner of war in Brest in 1756 and the conditions in the Bedford prison which he visited when High Sheriff of Bedfordshire inspired a life dedicated to reform. His *The State of Prisons in England and Wales with an Account of Foreign Prisons* was published in 1777 and *An Account of the Principal Lazarettos in Europe* in 1780. He died of typhus contracted when visiring a prison in the Crimea. The Howard League for Prison Reform was founded in 1866.

2 John Nield (1744-1814), Scottish philanthropist.

3 Sir Thomas Fowell Buxton MP (1786-1845). An English brewer and social reformer, he worked for the reform of criminal law and prison conditions and succeeded Wilberforce as leader of the anti-slavery movement.

4 Elizabeth Fry (1780-1845) English prison reformer. The daughter of John Guerney, a rich Quaker banker, she devoted her life to prison and asylum reform, at home and abroad, after a visit to Newgate in 1813. In London she founded hostels for the destitute and other charitable institutions.

5 Richard Martin MP (1754-1834), Irish lawyer and humanitarian. Dubbed 'Humanity Martin' by his friend George IV, he sponsored the first legislation which made cruelty to animals illegal. This led to the foundation of the Society for the Prevention of Cruelty to Animals.

6 Bread prices had soared during the French wars and were kept artificially high by the Corn Laws, passed in 1815 by a parliament dominated by landowners. Hunger marchers, the Blanketeers, were dispersed with violence by the army in 1817 and peaceful advocates of parliamentary reform killed at Peterloo in 1819. The Luddites, unemployed workers in the textile industries, destroyed the machines which were mechanising production in the industrial north.

7 The Elizabethan Poor Law raised money for the support of the poor by a compulsory assesment of parishioners. In Scotland the Poor Fund was made up by a voluntary collection at church services, fines imposed by the kirk session for misdemeanours, the hire of the mort cloth and an assessment, when necessary, of the heritors, who were the landowners, and the major tenant farmers.

Chapter Fifteen

The Tower. The Bloody Tower. The Traitors' Gate. The Church. The White Tower. The Spanish Armoury. The Horse Armoury. The Treasury. The Beauchamp Tower. The Animals. The Fees. The Guard.

As I did not want to miss any of London's attractions I visited the Tower, a place which bears the traces of a jail, for sometimes it was used as a jail and sometimes as the residence of kings. Today it is a fortress. It is surrounded by a moat and high walls upon which the canons are fired at every ceremony that is important to the nation. As a whole the Tower looks like a mixture of keeps, towers, pinnacles, turrets and irregular buildings in the centre of which stands the White Tower. It is not known when it was built[1]: some people connect it with the times of Julius Caesar, others with those of William the Conqueror. Throughout the centuries this invincible isle was invaded

The Tower of London. One of three towers built by William I to dominate London, the curtain wall was added by Henry III and the Traitor's Gate by Edward I. From the twelfth century wild animals, the gifts of foreign monarchs, were kept in one of the inner courts. It was used as a royal palace until the reign of Elizabeth.

by Romans, Saxons, Danes, and Normans and the attackers always chose London as their base.

My head was full of the events that happened there, many of which are horrifying. When I looked at the gloomy, windowless walls, when the drawbridge clanked under my feet and I was about to enter the fortress through the heavy iron vaulted gates, the history of this eerie place sent a shiver down my spine. Everything forced you to think about the brutality and crimes of the feudal period and of the blood shed over the centuries. Immediately in front of us was the Bloody Tower. In its walls was the small barred window which let a little light into the room in which Richard III, a monster of a man as Shakespeare called him, imprisoned his two nephews. Although their guardian, he gave orders for them to be strangled in the night. In Shakespeare's play two of the three murderers ordered to do this, having fulfilled the king's commands, expressed their secret grief.

> '"O thus" – quoth Dighton – "lay the gentle babes"
> "Thus, thus" – quoth Forrest – "girdling one another
> Within their alabaster innocent arms.
> Their lips were four red roses on a stalk,
> Which in their summer beauty kiss'd each other.
> A book of prayers on their pillow lay;
> Which once" – quoth Forrest – "almost chang'd my mind;
> But, oh, the devil"– there the villain stopp'd.
> When Dighton thus told on: "We smothered
> The most replenished sweet work of nature,
> That, from the prime creation, e'er she fram'd."'

For a long time nobody knew what had happened to them, for fear silenced any questioners. It was two hundred years before their bodies were found under the stairs of the Bloody Tower. Charles II ordered that they should be laid to rest in royal tombs and honoured with a memorial.

We were walking past the Thames's side wall when the halberdier who had welcomed us at the gate pointed to a low niche in which an iron door was placed. This was the Traitors' Gate through which the enemies of the state had entered the Tower. Amongst those who suffered such fate were Fisher,[2] the Bishop of Rochester, decapitated in 1535; Lord Rochford[3] in 1537; Thomas Cromwell,[4] a friend of Henry VIII, in 1540; Seymour[5] the Duke of Somerset in 1552; Dudley[6] the Duke of Northumberland in 1553; Scott[7] the Duke of Monmouth in 1685. On almost every page of the history of those years one can read about some courtier or minister or magnate sent to the Tower, sentenced and decapitated on Tower Hill. The history of England is the bloodiest of all. The last to be decapitated were the Scottish lords who in 1745 fought for Charles Stuart, the Pretender. Since that time only the country and not the throne has been disturbed.

The White Tower which stands in the centre was of no interest to us. A collection of naval weapons placed there cannot possibly interest anybody; it did not interest me. This Tower is reputed to be the most perfect remaining example of Old Saxon architecture.[8] It has three stories, the walls are eleven feet thick and there is a cistern on the roof which is used to catch rain in case the guards should be in need of water. Such tanks now exist in every fortress in England; it would be interesting to know whether such a way of supplying water was known to our ancestors. Whenever I visited old castles, no matter how high they stood above the surrounding countryside, I only found deep natural wells dug into the ground. Maybe our predecessors could not count on rain, which is less frequent in our country than in England. Also it is harder to dig wells here than it is for us because all their fortresses are built on rock. To one of the rooms in this Tower, the Modelling Room, there was no admittance. Detailed models of English fortresses, including Gibraltar, are reported to be placed there.

Opposite to the White Tower stands the Armoury, built half of stone, half of brick. Its facade, supported by Doric columns, is wonderful. In the entrance are displayed enormous cannons and other weapons that were used in the past. The stairs lead to the first floor where, in a 345 feet-long room, modern weapons of all kinds are arranged in an orderly manner. On the walls hang swords and guns, most beautifully polished and arranged in the shapes of shields, stars, suns, wreaths, snakes, and Medusa's heads. There were pistols and rifles arranged in such a way that they formed a pipe organ but the human race is happiest when it does not play on such an organ. It is reported that there are weapons here for 200,000 people. When visiting this Armoury the Emperor Alexander, on the sight of such enormous supplies of weapons, is reported to have said: 'It does not look as if the war had ended; rather that preparations to start a war were being made.' Weapons for 500,000 soldiers were supplied from this Armoury during the wars against Napoleon.

Continuing the sightseeing tour in an orderly manner, we were led to the Spanish Armoury. There we looked at the relics of the invincible Spanish Armada which were sent by Phillip II to conquer England and was totally destroyed by Drake, assisted by the winds. Fluttering over piles of instruments of death, spears, rifles, halberds, swords and axes, is the ensign of the Armada. The guides do not miss the opportunity to point out the thumbscrews and the machine for twisting limbs out of their joints. With these instruments of torture the Spaniards had hoped to extract information from the guardians of England's treasures. Although English technology was far advanced at the time, they had nothing so fully mechanised as these machines. Another exhibit is the axe with which the unfortunate Anne Boleyn,[9] wife of Henry VIII, was decapitated on her husband's order. The blade which had dripped with blood was blunted by rust; the handle was eaten by worms. She was accused of treason but actually killed to make a place for another whom the king married the day after the execution. For six years Henry negotiated with the Pope about a divorce from her but not managing to get one legally he decided to get rid of her illegally. This also gave him the pretext to break away from the Catholic Church. Anne Boleyn was the mother of Elizabeth. Cruelty was hereditary in Henry's family and Elizabeth, his daughter, sentenced to death Mary Stuart and even her own favourite, the Earl of Essex. Also kept here is Henry's staff in which two pistols are hidden. The King used to walk around the city with it, checking the behaviour of the police.[10]

There is a third armoury called the Horse Armoury. In it are displayed naturalistic figures of English monarchs on horseback, dressed in their own armour and with their personal features carefully depicted. They are arranged chronologically, starting with William the Conqueror and going up to George II. However there is little art in them and they look like horrible monsters, blank and in poor taste, not worth looking at unless by children or the rabble. Henry VIII, if he resembled the image, must have been an enormous person, and even more so John of Gaunt, Duke of Lancaster and son of Edward III. His suit of armour is seven feet high and his sword and spear are in proportion. To please national pride the armour of French cuirassiers brought from the battle of Waterloo have been placed in this gallery.

As we did not want to miss anything we visited the Jewel Office. It is a dark, vaulted room in which are placed the signs of the king's power, the crown jewels and the regalia which were used during coronations. These are the golden orb with its cross, the sword of state, the golden spurs and brassards and the golden eagle in which the oil for the anointing of the king is kept. They also keep there the silver baptismal font, in which the princes of royal blood are baptised, and the two crowns of the present king. One of these was used during his coronation and the second, smaller one, was used when he was Regent. Whenever he came to Parliament it was laid next to him as a sign that he had the right to it but not yet to wear it. All this was shown to us by candlelight from behind strong, iron bars and from a considerable distance. An old woman was the gryphon guarding these treasures.

The next thing we were shown was a little window in a tower called the Beauchamp Tower. Here Jane Grey was imprisoned and from the window she must have looked with a breaking heart as her husband's body, drenched in blood, was taken from the scaffold and carried to the graveyard. Not long after him, nine days actually, she laid her head on the same executioner's block. Jane Grey is reputed to have been of exemplary beauty, virtue and intelligence. The judge who sentenced her to death became insane and in his madness he shouted 'Get out of my sight Jane!' Remorse drove him into the grave a few days later.

The last thing for us to see were the lions, tigers, crocodiles and other animals and reptiles. For some inexplicable reason, they are kept in this place which is so full of historical memories. As if for a joke the lions have been given human names: Miss Charlotte, Miss Nanny and Miss Jenny. Some of them were born and grew up here which is supposed to make them the wildest and the most inaccessible of all animals. Each of them, as the custom requires in England, has a separate room in which she sleeps and a second in which she receives visitors. Visiting them is considered to be in bad taste which seems to suggest that this is not a proper place for them to be. Thus we did not feel like visiting them. Where so many important thoughts and memories from the past come to one's mind such a visit would be inappropriate.

One cannot overlook the not inconsiderable expense of such a visit. A visitor pays one shilling for the animals in the Tower; two shillings for the Treasury; one shilling for signing the visitors book and at least two shillings for the halberdier when one leaves. All this costs at least sixteen Polish zlotys, for which the donor will hardly be thanked with a 'God bless you!' If one wished to be generous, and who would not, it is not enough to double that sum. This is a great deal to pay in order to satisfy ones curiosity, particularly for the foreigner who, with so many things to see, must pay for everything. Thus it is reasonable to visit only those things which are important and cannot be seen elsewhere. Travelling in England is usually extremely expensive and anyone who is not financially secure will gain little or nothing from his travels, especially if he stays for only a few months. A period of several years is hardly enough to learn about the number of things manufactured, the complexity of industry and trade and about the organisation of the government.

Having signed our names in the visitors' book, for which each of us paid a shilling, we bid the halberdiers goodbye. I do not remember how much we paid them but it cannot have been a small sum for one Frenchman who joined our company, probably *un bel esprit*, maybe some Pichol or Blanqui, when paying for himself quoted La Fontaine, with the cheerfulness characteristic for his nation:

> O temps! O moeurs! j'ai beau crier,
> Tout le monde se fait payer.

The governor of the Tower is called the Constable; he lives there and during coronations he watches over the crown jewels. He has a small military company under his command whose uniforms are totally old-fashioned, a long crimson coat, stockings, bootees with buckles and a small flat hat. These soldiers lead a life of blissful comfort. Undisturbed by drill and similar military activities, they all have rosy cheeks and substantial figures. Thus the Londoners call them His Majesty's Beefeaters. They carry long halberds and two of them accompany each group of visitors. Maybe this escort is needed but it looks strange and ridiculous.

As peculiar as the escort is the old custom of collecting the keys and opening the Tower. Every morning a sergeant, along with six soldiers, goes to the Constable's house to collect the keys. Then, together with these soldiers, he goes to the gate where, in the French language and in a situation which has nothing to do with the French, he calls to the guards standing there: 'Prenez les clefs du roi Georges!' The guards take them and open the gate. In the evening, with the same ceremony, the keys are taken back to the Constable who usually awaits them together with the officers of the guards. When the soldiers come he calls: 'Qui va là?' He receives the answer: 'Les clefs!' after which he says: 'Passez les clefs!' The sergeant comes and hands them over saying, in English: 'God save King George!' The soldiers add 'Amen!' and still under arms they go to rest.

NOTES:

1 The White Tower is one of the oldest Romanesque buildings in England. It was built between 1086 and 1097 on a Roman site.

2 John Fisher (1469-1535). An English prelate and humanist, as Chancellor of Cambridge University he advocated the New Learning and the internal reform of the Church. He refused to recognise Henry VIII's claim to be head of the Church of England.

3 Lord Rochford. Brother of Anne Boleyn; he and four others were accused of being her partners in adultery.

4 Thomas Cromwell (1485-1540). Chief agent of Cardinal Wolsey and Henry VIII in the dissolution of the monasteries, he was the author of the Act of Supremacy. He was created Earl of Essex in 1540 but the disastrously unsuccessful marriage to Anne of Cleves led to his attainder and death.

5 Edward Seymour, 1st Duke of Somerset (c1506-52), English soldier and statesman and the brother of Jane Seymour. He commanded the English troops during the Rough Wooing of 1543 when Henry VIII tried to force a marriage between Mary, Queen of Scots and his son Edward, who was Seymour's nephew. He became Lord Protector during the minority of Edward VI and furthered the Reformation by introducing the First Book of Common Prayer. He was deposed for 'over ambition' by his rival, the Earl of Warwick

6 John Dudley, Duke of Northumberland (1502-53), English soldier and statesman. He was created Earl of Warwick and joint Regent, with Somerset, for Edward VI. He married his son Lord Guildford to Lady Jane Grey and proclaimed her queen in 1553.

7 James Scott, Duke of Monmouth (1649-83). The son of Charles II and Lucy Walters, he took the name Scott when he married Anne Scott, Countess of Buccleuch in her own right. Commander in Chief of the army and his father's favourite, he claimed to be the legitimate Protestant heir to the throne. He was defeated by the forces of his Roman Catholic uncle, James II, at the Battle of Sedgemoor.

8 Lach-Szyrma frequently confuses Anglo-Saxon, Romanesque and Gothic architecture.

9 Anne Boleyn (c1504-36). Anne's second child was a still-born son. To make way for Anne Seymour, mother of Edward VI, she was accused of adultery and executed four months later. Henry's prolonged negotiations failed to obtain a divorce from Catherine of Aragon, whose only surviving child, Mary, came to the throne in 1553.

10 Pistols are believed to have been invented in Pistoia, in Tuscany, by Caminello Vitelli in the 1540s. They were not in general use till the seventeenth century. Their butts were at right-angles to the barrels and would not have been easy to hide in a staff.

Chapter Sixteen

The British Museum. Curiosities of Primitive Nations. Diamonds. Crystals. Aerolites. Fossilised Human Skeleton. British Natural History. The Gallery of Antiquities. Mummies. Egyptian Monuments. Elgin Marbles. Manuscripts. Magna Carta.

The only institution in London which does not charge you for entry is the British Museum. It houses a collection of curiosities of art, science and nature whose size is appropriate for such a wealthy nation. It was founded in the year 1753 by Hans Sloane,[1] who endowed the government with his collection of books and other curiosities. For this, which was worth £50,000, he received £20,000. The collection was later increased by purchases and by donations from the king and other private individuals. It is now so enormous that it would be hard to find something of this sort anywhere else. Both the British and foreigners visit it in great numbers and it is customary for visitors to sign their names in a book. The numbers give some idea of the nation's growing curiosity and, perhaps, education. I chose the figures from a sequence if six years, from 1820-1825. They are as follows:

Year:	1820	1821	1822	1823	1824	1825
People:	62,543	91,151	98,801	89,825	112,840	127,643

The building which houses this collection used to belong to Lord Montague.[2] Its architect was Puget,[3] a Frenchman. It is modelled on the Paris hôtels, the homes of the old French nobility, and it may be the only relic of Gallic housing in the capital. In a vast square with an Ionic colonnade lie pillars of ancient temples, tombstones with inscriptions, and damaged statues from Greece, Italy and Egypt, all brought over at great expense. It is sad to see them isolated from the temples of which they were once a part. Statues of gods once worshiped in those temples and tombstones taken from the catacombs lose their meaning in the modern capital of a strange country. They are the debris of a great and once grand past. Some of the inscriptions cast a light on the history of nations. It takes more time than a traveller may have at his disposal to understand or guess their meaning. The ordinary catalogue of exhibits on sale at the entrance gives hardly any information. More detailed information can be found in the descriptions of the particular parts of the collection e.g., the description of the marbles, vases and medals by Combe and the classified catalogue of books and manuscripts by Ellis, Plant, Nares, and Hyscough. I shall mention only the items that caught my eye at first glance.

The major part of the building is taken up by the library. The public has no access to it which is reasonable since the mere exterior of books is meaningless. There is a room for reading where there is access to any book in the collection. It is enough for the reader to write the title of the work, with his signature, on a piece of paper. However, there are some limitations as to who is allowed in; one needs a letter of introduction from a citizen which is handed to the librarian. At the time when I was there it was Doctor Needhen, a German and the author of a German grammar for the English. Having been

Montagu House. The British Museum was founded in 1753 to display the thousands of antiquities, books and natural history specimens donated to the nation, Montagu House was bought in 1759 to house these. From 1804 wings were added to display the rapidly growing collections and Robert Smirke was invited to design a new building. It was 1845 before his portico was completed and Montagu House demolished.

personally recommended to him, I made use of permission to read whenever time allowed me to do so. There were not as many readers as in the Royal Library in Paris for the English avoid overt intellectual work. One is not allowed to take any books home.

From the lower rooms to the first floor one walks up a flight of magnificent marble stairs. Up above, on the ceiling, there is a beautiful fresco of Phaeton setting out into the sky on his newly acquired sun-chariot. The fresco is by Lafosse,[4] a Frenchman whose works are much admired by the experts for the vividness of their colours. One of them, in the cupola of Les Invalides in Paris, is considered a great curiosity. The landscapes on the walls and various architectural decorations are by Jacques Rousseau,[5] who excelled in perspective. From there one proceeds to the rooms filled with the curiosities of nature. In the cupboards, behind glass, lie rare stones, minerals and shells. Against the walls and pleasantly arranged are animals, birds and reptiles. Each object has a label attached to it, giving both its common and its scientific name.

At the entrance to the first room decorative and useful tools of savage nations catch the visitor's attention. It is full of weird clothing, household tools and arms revealing the primitive stage of art and industry. I saw wooden armour and garments and many of the hats had heads of birds and animals carved on them. There were wooden birds filled with stones and used as rattles, waterproof clothes for fishermen made from whale interiors, bread made of the roots of Cassava (*Iatrofa manihot*), screens made from eagle feathers and hats of various shapes and colours, some decorated with representations of whale hunting. These samples of primitive art were brought from Nootka-on-Alaska. Clothing from northwest America also revealed the savage state of its inhabitants, it was made from cypress bast (*Cypressus thuyoides*). The Otahitans, in turn, make it from the bark of Paper Mulberry (*Broussonetia*) and paint it in different colours; at war they use feather armour. Feathers are also used by the inhabitants of the Sandwich Islands and their entire country probably looks like the country of Papageno and Papagena. Fishing hooks are made of the bones and teeth of predator sharks. The women of the Sandwich Islands wear tortoise shell bracelets, sometimes made of boar tusks and chains from little shells and the seeds of fruits. Obviously, as anywhere else, the elegant world likes to dress up and anything serves as adornment if it is fashionable. They make their mirrors from black slate stone, which they polish smooth and decorate their elegant clothing with rattling husky fruit and chattering teeth so as to produce the greatest possible noise while dancing. The women of fashion on the Friendly Islands dance in clothes plaited from coconut palm bast and aprons made from little birds' bones and tibias. We also saw fifes played by the inhabitants of these islands with their nostrils, a multitude of arms, spears, arrows, bows, quivers and maces, some of these with various figures of animals carved on them. There was a wooden drum and a saw made of shark teeth used for sawing up captive enemies, for the cruelty of savages is inexhaustible.

The rooms dedicated to the realm of minerals are also full of curiosities. They have been organised decoratively with little reference to their geological origins. First came the flammable artefacts: fossil resin (bitumen), liquid paraffin, coal and finally diamonds. They were displayed with samples of the rocks in which they were found in India. These are slightly rounded and have from eight to twelve facets. In their natural state they are covered in soil which is washed off by river water. The brightness and the sheen are obtained through polishing. The usual colour of a raw diamond is pale grey, sometimes verging on yellow. Some are of the colour of a lemon, the rare ones are blue and green; the ones of a homogenous colour and free of any marks are considered the most beautiful. This precious stone exceeds all other known solid bodies in hardness and the hardest steel cannot make a scratch on it. For it is the dense condensation of its particles that causes the light rays to bend and be reflected so intensely. For this reason they have always been polished so as to be given the biggest possible number of facets. After polishing some diamonds are as transparent as the clearest water and have practically no colour. Most of them are found in Brazil but these are neither the biggest nor the most beautiful ones. The biggest diamond ever found in its mines weighed 108 karats. The lucky slave who found it was granted freedom and a life salary of £50. The Asian diamonds are considered the most beautiful and they are mined for in Vizapur, the Deccan and Golkonda and also on the Island of Borneo. The least valued are the European ones. They are found in between rocks and in rivers. The biggest diamonds known so far are: the Koh-i-Noor, weighing 279 karats, two in France, of which one, called the Regent Diamond, was worn by Napoleon on the hilt of his sword at great celebrations and the fourth can be found in Russia. It was bought by Catherine II. It weighs 109 karats and is the size of a pigeon's egg. In the Museum I saw accurate models of their shapes and sizes.

After the diamonds there are numerous intriguing crystals of various shapes and colours. Due to the properties they share with diamonds, they have been of interest to many swindlers: they were known as Gibraltar and Bristol Diamonds. One can never tire of looking at the variety of colours in rock crystal; topaz, amethyst, cairngorm or emerald. Like diamonds, none is absolutely clear; all contain impurities. Outstandingly beautiful are the opals: they owe their sheen to an invisible crushed surface that bends and reflects the light which falls onto them in different ways. One of them was brought from Mexico and was called the sun opal. One of this kind when immersed in water becomes transparent and hence is called the eye of the world (*oculus mundi*). There were pieces of jasper from the vicinity of Cairo called Egyptian jasper. They were all round and their shape was ascribed to the process of primary condensation and not to the action of river water. A piece of platinum brought from Brazil had been mixed with grains of gold and there were some most beautiful types of striped jasper which is found mostly in Siberia. British gold and silver has survived in the shape of plates, chains, and pellets. Silver is the most malleable of metals. The purest and most important gold is brought from Bengal, Sumatra and Guinea. The latter region gave the name to one of England's golden coins, the guinea. There was also a lot of native copper, iron, lead and zinc exhibited. These are important due to their wide use but, as they are commonly known, they do not awake much interest from the visitor. Surprisingly, amongst an abundance of ores whose country of origin is given, I did not find a single Polish one. To have seen a piece of my motherland would have made me happy. But we visit foreign countries often remaining ignorant about our own. So far there has not been any mineralogist among us who could describe the geological structure of our land in such detail as to awake the interest of foreigners.

Behind the minerals there is a large collection of aerolites, stones that fall from the sky, i.e. meteoric stones, since they were believed to have been formed from meteors. Some of these were enormous. Among them was a piece of a stone which had fallen on 27 June 1807 near Smolensk.

Worth one's attention is the gallery of Natural History. With their numerous trade relations and bases in all parts of the world the English were able to enlarge this collection. Still, it is poorer than the Jardin des Plantes in Paris. What is positive about Paris is the many living animals. Here everything is lifeless; sometimes just a single bone or a skeleton. The exhibition includes the bottom jaw of a Siberian Elephant, believed to be a mammoth, an extinct species, and the enormous bones of a North American animal called 'Mastodon ohioticus', also believed to be a mammoth and a creature eagerly sought by the explorers.

What particularly caught the visitors' attention was an entirely fossilised human skeleton excavated near Guadalupe in a limestone mountain. Judging by the shape of the bones it is believed to be female. Its head has come off, one of the sides has been partially damaged, the other one entirely. Its left hand rests on the hip. The skeleton is wholly immersed in limestone and has almost turned into lime itself. It is in lime of this kind that fossils are most rapidly formed. Most of the fossils found in it are small trees, plants and insects but, so far, no man had been found in this state. Thus the skeleton mentioned above is a real stone guest, not an imaginary one as in *Don Juan*.

What deserves special attention, for I have not seen anything like it before and it may be an example worth copying, is the way in which exhibits in the natural history section of the Museum are arranged. A visitor from any of the seven counties of England can find a section displaying its soul, minerals, animals and birds. To clarify information about native birds each of them is displayed with the eggs it lays, its nest and a dissection of its various parts, the neck, the throat, the wings, and the breast. All the animals which could not be preserved by drying, pressing or stuffing, like the fish and reptiles, were preserved in spirits.

Having visited the Natural History section one proceeds to the Gallery of Antiquities, where numerous statues, busts, vases and reliefs are gathered. This part is of great importance to lovers of antiquity and artists, especially historical artists, for whom it is a source of models of the human figure. The painter Haydon,[6] whom I have mentioned before, found models for his historical paintings here. The foundation of this gallery was based on the collections made by Charles Townley,[7] Sir William Hamilton[8] and the Earl of Elgin.[9] Hamilton was a legate at the court of Naples and Elgin at the Ottoman Porte. For the first, Rome was his source of monuments, for the latter, Greece. However, there are quite a few Egyptian antiquities taken by the English army from the French in 1801, after the seizure of Alexandria. The King gave them all to the Museum.

I would gladly give more information about the objects collected in this gallery if I did not feel that it would be beyond my skill or that of any other writer. One cannot judge a museum of this kind without visiting it. However, since I do not wish to leave the reader uninformed and fear the accusation that I am confusing the arduous with the impossible, I will describe as much about them as I can.

Among the reliefs one depicted a woman immersed in deep grief; she is sitting with her head resting on her right hand, surrounded by people who seem to share her sadness. It is said to be an image of Penelope missing Odysseus. Another relief depicts a boat with two human figures apparently sailing on the Nile. This can be guessed from the surrounding objects: two hippopotamuses, two alligators and some plants from the 'Nimphaea lotus' species. In the distance there are some buildings with three ibises on the roof. These birds were worshipped by the Egyptians, for they devoured snakes and locusts.

A relief of great beauty depicts the apotheosis of Homer. The father of poetry is sitting on a throne on Mount Parnassus, the glorious home of the Muses. In front of him stand people probably bringing their offerings. In the distance one can see Apollo surrounded by the Muses, and on the very top of Mount Parnassus stands Jupiter who seems to allow this worship of Homer. This beautiful antique sculpture was found in Bovillae, ten kilometres from Rome and for a long time lay in the Colonna Palace, from which it was bought by the Museum in the year 1819. There is a Greek tomb with an image of a knight on horseback and a woman breast-feeding a snake. This coils around a tree on which the sign of victory is hung. The inscription on the tomb gives the names of those who died in the battle and the tomb is their cenotaph. Beside this stood some humble clay cinerary urns which were used by the Romans for burying the earthly remains of the poorest people. An inscription on one of them reads Anniolena and Servilla Irene. On another, in the Etruscan style, there was a relief depicting the duel of the brothers Eteocles and Polyneices, the women in the background being the Furies, inciting the brothers to violence. A delightful candelabrum was decorated with the emblems of Apollo: a griffin, a raven and a tripod.

There are numerous sarcophagi with images of wedding and burial rites, celebrations connected with Bacchus, satyrs, fauns, cupids and various human figures. One of them showed nine Muses with all their emblems. The sarcophagi (literally: carnivores) are a kind of coffin where the bodies of those who had not been cremated were laid. The stone for this purpose was taken from the quarries near the town of Assos in Moesia. It was light, sponge-like and, according to Pliny, had a specific characteristic: it destroyed the body which had been laid in it within forty days. Later this name came to be used for any coffin.

What fascinates one most among the Egyptian monuments are the enormous coffins covered in hieroglyphs on the inside and the outside. Their shape is not that of our coffins but rather like cases, oblong and deep. They hold mummies. One of them was decorated with coloured glass beads, another one entirely covered with paintings, its face gilded, and with a child mummy at its side. This coffin was brought from the catacombs in Saqqara, two miles outside Cairo.

For my younger readers I must add that mummies are human bodies which were embalmed by the Egyptians in order to try to prevent them from decaying. They look black as if they were blackened with smoke and are dry, hard and fragile like tree bark. They are rarely seen in one piece for they are subject to accidents and may be destroyed during the long journey from Egypt. They smell, which suggests that some strong, aromatic and fragrant herbs were used for the anointment. Before the anointment of a dead person could start, the internal organs would be removed and a special tool would be used for taking out the brain through the nostrils. The body would be placed in saltpetre, where it would be kept for 70 days. It would then be oiled on the inside and on the outside, wrapped thickly in cotton clothes and oils would be poured on it once again. As a result, all mummies look like swaddled children. One cannot see the body apart from the face, which is often so well preserved that the eyes are intact. The clothes in which the mummies were wrapped before placing them in their coffins were gilded and decorated with precious stones. One of those I saw in the Museum had an ibis, the sacred bird, at its side in the coffin. Some had inscriptions on the papyrus plant laid on their chest. The biggest of the Egyptian sarcophagi was made of black granite and it was wholly covered in hieroglyphs. It has been brought from Cairo, where it had been used by the Turks as a cistern named the Well of Lovers.

There was also a collection of Egyptian vessels known as the Canopic jars. Like the Greeks, the Egyptians used to decorate them with their gods. Thus on one lid there might be Osiris, the god representing the sun, the Nile or the fertility of nature; on another Isis, nature itself, the mother and the nourisher of all things. Others depicted wolves, hawks, falcons, monkeys and sphinxes. Most impressive is the statue of Isis. It is as tall as a man but has the form of a woman sitting on the ground with her hands on her knees. In her left hand she is holding an ear of corn, either to indicate that she was the first to teach people how to sow wheat, or that she receives offerings from them during the annual celebrations in her praise. She is the Ceres of the Egyptians. In front of her stood the head of her son Horus, who was worshipped by the Egyptians in place of the Greek Apollo.

Among all the Egyptian gods, the statue which amazes visitors most with its size and beauty is that of Memnon, which came from the ruins of the temple in Thebes. It had been discovered and brought to the British Museum by the famous traveller Belzoni.[10] It is an enormous bust of Egyptian granite. Parts of the left breast have been damaged and it has a Nubian headgear and a short, wedge-shaped beard. Its countenance is confident, radiating tranquillity and gentleness and with a delicate smile which gives the impression that it was kind-heartedly mocking the explorer's attempt to solve the mystery of its eternal existence. His elder brother had apparently been even more mysterious, since the moment he was touched by the rays of the rising sun, he was said to have given off harmonious tones. Suspecting that the sounds were of magical origin, Cambyses ordered the upper part of the statue to be crushed. The remains still lie in the ruins of the temple. Pausanias[11] reported that in his day the crushed trunk and its enormous base had not ceased to emit the former tones. Having heard this beautiful music, Strabo[12] accounted for it either by the use of a particular kind of stone or by the deceitfulness of the Egyptian priests. Pausanias believed the statue had musical tools hidden inside. Their strings tightened due to dampness in the night, and the moment they were exposed to the warmth of the sun they expanded, giving out tones resembling music. Other ancient writers express different opinions but, judging by the number of accounts that have survived, it is unlikely that the statue did not exist. At such a distance in time, however, it is difficult to know what really happened.

For enthusiastic antiquarians it is fascinating to see the stone brought from Rosetta.[13] There are three inscriptions on it: in the supposedly secret hieroglyphs, in modern Egyptian writing and in the Greek language. I do not know whether they were known to the researcher Champollion[14] but they could contribute to his claim about the hieroglyphs, which have so far been considered a mystery and in his opinion are only letters. The inscriptions praise the merits of Ptolemy V; their engraving was commissioned by the high priests during the general assembly in Memphis at which he formally became the king.

In order to have the right impression of both the Elgin Marbles, which have been mentioned before, and the details described here, it is essential to visit the Museum. The Marbles show various events from Greek history and mythology. It is worth looking at Theseus in the figure of Hercules, resting on a rock, and covered with a lion skin. Although damaged, due to the perfection of anatomical measurements and the skill of the chisel it is still considered one of the most prominent works of sculpture. It has been brought from Athens, where it had decorated the eastern wall of the temple of Minerva. Also placed there is the statue of Iris, which has been taken from the same wall of the Parthenon. The daughter of the Ocean and the messenger of Juno is depicted running with her cloak inflated with air and fluttering behind her. She appears to be carrying the message of the birth of Minerva to the confines of the world.

I have found no monuments connected to the history of our country. I saw only one relief depicting various kinds or arms of the old Dacians and Sarmatians. I am not describing it here, for it would be neither accurate nor interesting enough. Investigators of the old Sarmatian tactics and art of fighting could satisfy their curiosity in the Museum, where the relief can be found in room 10 number 45, unless the present order is changed.

Some of the monuments go back to distant antiquity: this is proved by their inscriptions, which are written boustrophedon, i.e. back and forth, like ploughing oxen. It is enjoyable to find the history of man and the rays of education reaching out so far. There are many rare and interesting manuscripts: many were written on parchment in the Saxon language, many on palm leaves. Of great significance are the manuscript of Homer's *Iliad*, two original copies of a larger series of Greek orators, two very beautiful copies of the *Gospel* from the tenth and twelfth centuries and Ptolemy's *Geography*. One can find no less than 43 volumes of Icelandic literature and 41 concerning the history of Ireland. There are innumerable letters of famous people, which could allow a detailed reconstruction of their lives and of the history of the times they lived and acted in. A Polish historian would also be able to find useful materials among them, especially in the manuscripts from the Elizabethan period, when Działyski[15] was a Polish delegate to England. He could supplement additional information just from the 7,000 volumes of newspapers which have been stored in chronological order from 1603 to this day. Interesting are Elizabeth's to the Earl of Essex, her favourite, which read no differently from the letter ordering his execution. Though the words in the letters are flattering, the signatures are stylised and formal. As Lavater[16] would have put it: they show no heart. There are also letters addressed to her by the unfortunate Mary Queen of Scots: one of them which was written as she was crossing the English border and was full of kind and tender words for the author had no evil foreboding. They are mostly written in French, since Mary, who had spent time at the French court from her childhood, knew the language better than her mother tongue. This would not have helped her to win people's hearts in her homeland. Presented as a special exhibit is the original, visibly revised, speech by William the Conqueror, who tried to convince the English he had come there out of love for the English nation, to make it happy.

One can also see the manuscript of Pope's *Essay on Man* with numerous corrections. The entire poem was written on scraps of paper of all colours and shapes, on envelopes, on visiting-cards, on newspaper edges: a reasonable man could not have pushed it to a further extent without provoking an accusation of avarice. It was justifiable for contemporaries to call him 'the paper sparing Pope'. He stitched various scraps and fastened them together. The life and the works of this poet are known to my compatriots from the elegant translations by Niemcewicz and Kamiski. This is also where the manuscript of the famous Rousseau[17] is stored. It bears the title: *Rousseau juge de Jean-Jacques*. From its very introduction one can tell this man had always been trying to escape some imaginary misfortune, and in some way it always followed him. Since this work has not been published, I shall quote an excerpt from the foreword, which is as follows:

> 'Qui que vous soyez, que le ciel a fait l'arbitre de cet écrit, quelque usage que vous ayez résolu d'en faire et quelque opinion que vous ayez de l'auteur, cet auteur infortuné (vous) conjure par vos entrailles humaines et par les angoisses, qu'il a souffert en l'écrivant, de n'en disposer qu'après l'avoir lu tout entier. Songez, que cette grâce, que vous demande un coeur brisé de douleur est un devoir d'équité, que le ciel vous impose. Barbarus hic ego sum, quia non intelligor ulli.'

On a table, behind glass, lies the original manuscript of Magna Carta, the shield of English freedom. For a long time it was believed to have been lost. Good fortune saved it from the scissors of a tailor, who was just about to cut it in pieces. Next to it lies a beautiful facsimile illustrated by Mr. Payne, whose illustrated publications of the classics are well known. It is worth noting that among the 36 barons who signed the Charter only three were able to write, the rest made a cross. What enormous progress in education has taken place since 1215 (the year Magna Carta was granted) to this day, when the simplest subject has the ability to read and write and probably has a clearer picture of everything than the first magnates in the country had had in those days.

The number of objects listed so far gives an idea of the vastness of the museum edifice which is capable of housing so many curiosities. However, it is not big enough, so a new and spacious building is being erected and one of its wings has just been finished. One part of it is to house the enormous collection of books left by George III and the other a gallery of paintings. The building is in the Ionic style. Its architect is Smirke.[18]

NOTES:

1 Sir Hans Sloane (1690-1783), naturalist and doctor, physician to George III. He founded the Chelsea Physic Garden and was the author of *The Natural History of Jamaica*. His library consisted of 50,000 volumes and 3,560 manuscripts.

2 Montagu House was the seventeenth-century home of the Earls and Dukes of Manchester. It was demolished in 1847 on the completion of Smirke's design for the Museum which was built round it.

3 Pierre Puget (1622-94), French architect, a contemporary of Mansard.

4 Charles de la Fosse (1640-1716). A French painter and professor at the Royal Academy in Paris, he studied in Venice and was influenced by Veronese. The paintings in the dome of Les Invalides are amongst his few surviving works.

5 Jean-Simon Rousseau de la Rottiere (1747-92), French decorative painter, much of whose work was in Versailles.

6 Benjamin Robert Haydon (1786-1840). English historical painter, his 'Mock Election' was bought by George IV but, constantly in debt, he shot himself.

7 The Towneley Collection of Greek and Roman sculptures, bronzes and terracottas was bought in 1805. A wing was added to the Museum to house it.

8 Sir William Hamilton (1730-1803), Scottish diplomat and antiquarian and the husband of Nelson's mistress, Emma. While British ambassador in Naples, he took an active part in the excavation of Herculaneum and Pompei. He sold one of his collections to the British Museum in 1772.

9 Thomas Bruce, 7th Earl of Elgin (1768-1841), Scottish diplomat and conoisseur. Believing them to be in danger of destruction, he had some of the sculptures on the Parthenon moved to Britain. They were bought by the British Museum in 1816.

10 Giovanni Battista Belzoni (1778-1823). Italian explorer, antiquity hunter and tomb robber, he held an exhibition in London in 1819 and published his *Narrative of the Operation and Recent Discoveries within the Pyramids, Temples, Tombs and Excavations in Egypt and Nubia* in 1820.

11 Pausanias (c 2 AD), Greek geographer and historian. Widely travelled, his *Itinerary of Greece* was intended to be used as a guide book.

12 Strabo (c 60 BC-20 AD), Greek geographer and Stoic. Only fragments of his 47-volume *Historical Studies* have survived but his 17-volume *Geographia* is almost complete. Much of it based on personal observation is of great value.

13 After the defeat of France at the Battle of the Nile in 1801, the Rosetta Stone was one of the many artefacts found by the French scholars who had been brought to Egypt by Napoleon which were surrendered to Britain. The texts are in classical Greek, the language of the rulers, demotic, the language written by native Egyptians in the c 2 BC and hieroglyphs, the written language used by the priests.

14 Jean-François Champollion (1790-1833). A French linguist, he studied Oriental languages as a young man and his knowledge of Coptic and classical Greek enabled him to decipher the hieroglyphs on the Rosetta Stone.

15 Pawel Dzalynski (d. 1641), Polish diplomat at the court of Elizabeth.

16 See Chapter 3, note 10.

17 Jean-Jacques Rousseau (1712-78), French philosopher and educationist.

Rousseau, juge de Jean-Jacques was published in Paris in 1782. A justification of his actions, it is less well known than *The Social Contract* or *The Confessions*.

18 Sir Robert Smirke (1781-1867), English architect. His design for the building which gradually replaced Montagu House was caried out between 1823 and 1867. He was architect to the Board of Works, designed Covent Garden Theatre, the Post Office and the College of Physicians.

Chapter Seventeen

Dramatic Literature. Theatres. Drury Lane. Kean. The Actress Stevens. Braham. Particulars Appertaining to Theatre. Covent Garden. Opera. Nowosielski. Smaller Theatres. Admission Fees.

Some nations of distinctive character have also produced excellent dramatic works. This is true of the English, the French and the Germans. In the past the Greeks were renowned. The Romans were too engrossed in conquest to be theatrically creative; as was true in other fields of art, craft and science, they were mere disciples of the Greeks. The Italians who currently build upon their ruins, are, as regards their drama, the same relative to the Romans as Rome used to be to Athens. They may have resurrected science and dramatic literature in Europe during the time of the Medicis and Leo X but political anarchy has impaired their intellect; what is left to them is solely

Drury Lane. The Theatre was opened in 1794 to house an audience of 4,000. Burnt down in 1809, it was rebuilt, with raked seats in the pit, by Benjamin Wyatt. Candles and a drunken audience made theatres particularly vulnerable to fire.

the vividness of gesture and the gift of singing. Slavonic peoples, as can be inferred from their present condition, do not yet merit any mention in this respect. So far their social situation has prevented them from achieving in the field of science. They are however making great strides towards maturity. The establishment of order and fraternity among them should lead to the development of a distinctive national character and literature. Their theatre, which has so far been dependent upon foreign examples, will find its own native field.

At the present time dramatic art in Europe can be divided between four nations: the Germans dominate drama, the Italians opera, the French comedy and the English tragedy. And truly, in no other respect does the English theatre deserve more attention. Drury Lane and Covent Garden, which vie with one another for precedence, are the two major theatres in London staging tragedies. On my first visit to Drury Lane, Shakespeare's *Richard III* was being performed. Kean,[1] who is the most proficient actor on the English stage, was to play the part of Richard.

We came half an hour before the start of the play, for one cannot come too early when Kean is to act. In front of the theatre there was already a throng of people through whom it was barely possible to make one's way. We were almost carried into the box office. Within the theatre it was already crowded and more and more were still arriving. The theatre was lit by gas. A most beautiful crystal mirror was hung below the ceiling and a smaller one next to the boxes. Thus everything was lit up and it was as bright as day.

To hear Shakespeare in his own tongue and before his own compatriots in so great a theatre is a moving experience. It seemed to us that we were to behold the greatest spectacle in the world. Mesmerised, I let my eyes rove once or twice over the ground floor and boxes where there was already a crowd of about 3,600 people of both sexes, the number the theatre can hold. The audience seemed to be growing with every minute and, especially on the ground floor, increasingly resembled a teeming ant heap. Women and men were mixed together, which resulted in an enormous medley not to be encountered in any other theatre. The boxes were arranged in three tiers running around the interior: they were not divided from one another, as is the case in Poland, but were open and furnished with raked benches. The benches, as well as the boxes themselves, were upholstered with a crimson cloth whose colour flattered the ladies who displayed themselves superbly, especially in the first row of boxes where only formally attired persons are admitted. Men attend plays clad in black tailcoats, stockings and boots with white scarves round their necks, for colourful and motley garments are deemed vulgar in London. This row of boxes appeared to be occupied by people of a superior status or at least by those who had sufficient means to afford elegant apparel. Less refinement could be described in other boxes where the company is reputed to be mixed, sometimes more so than would be desirable. As in other theatres, the gallery is the favoured place for the commoners. By virtue of their position it is to them that the highest authority is endowed in England and the qualities of common sense and good taste, which in other theatres are attached to the ground floor, in London are moved to the gallery. It is there that the mob, which has been accurately described as a hundred-headed and hundred-tongued monster, hovers above the entire congregation, whistles, hisses, howls and boos. Occasionally dirty jests, loud laughter and national songs can be heard. The rest of the audience can do nothing but tolerate the mob's caprices and listen to the judgements passed. The ground floor has to show the utmost humility unless it wants to risk being pelted with orange peel, apples and potatoes. In English theatres it is the gallery that sets the tone; the boxes and the ground floor remain silent. I was told that this high tribunal had become more polite towards the spectators sitting below and the storm and hail of its wrath is wreaked solely upon the orchestra and actors if, in its opinion, they have offended. Everything must suit its omnipotent will. If actors appearing on stage for the first time want to avoid being booed and hissed, they must acknowledge this Areopagus[2] which judges from the benches of a one-shilling gallery. Contempt expressed towards it is an unpardonable offence, for which even the best actors have to pay. This once happened to Kean when playing a guest role in one of the provincial towns. Infuriated by cries from the gallery he dared to address it with words from *Richard III*:

'Unmanner'd dogs! Stand ye when I command.' Thereafter, he had to make a very rapid escape from the town.

As I was thus occupied considering the design of the theatre, demands for music became audible from the gallery. Upon this the orchestra, which was neither large nor musical but perhaps adequate for a tragedy, began to play. The Muse of music does not grace English theatres with her presence. The quality of orchestras is just passable in London but not in Edinburgh where, instead of an overture, they keep performing melodies from their folk music. But it was not long before the gallery grew tired of the orchestra's playing and the cry 'God save the King' resounded. The orchestra was forced to obey and began to play this favourite national anthem, whereupon the boxes, the ground floor and everybody else doffed their hats, ladies and gentlemen rose from their seats, and began to sing the lyrics to the accompaniment of the solemn melody. The whole theatre was transformed into a church. Party loyalties disappeared as everyone united to pay tribute to the highest authority, bringing to mind the power of the following words from the English constitution: 'The King sins not, the King dies not.'

Finally, a bell rang and the curtain rose. Once again the calls 'Hat off!' could be heard from different comers for, till that moment, the whole audience, save for the time of singing the national anthem, had been sitting with their hats on. For the most part, John Bull is not courteous in the theatre: he sprawls upon a bench, paying no heed to whether his neighbours have enough room or not and is mindful solely of his own comfort. Sometimes he stands in order to see better and does not feel any compunction about blocking another person's view. He does not give up his seat to a lady, no matter how tired she may be after standing the whole evening, and it is with the utmost reluctance that he doffs his hat. When he finally does so, it is not out of civility or respect but due to those who have forced him not to hinder their enjoyment of the performance. His obstinacy frequently gives rise to squabbles. These gradually intensify, so that after being asked he is threatened and finally violence is resorted to. The hat of a man who refuses to remove it is taken off or knocked off with a staff. Such incidents, apart from setting a bad example, are also unpleasant for the audience, especially as not a single evening can pass without them.

On such occasions one has genuine pity for the actors, for it is apparent that they wish to continue but if they attempt to do so one can only see their lips moving inaudibly. Usually they have to wait until the row and din subside and that may take some time. Even if people are quietened there is never complete silence, for the room resounds with chattering, coughing, sneezing and other liberties which these free people sometimes take too eagerly, drowning out the words of any actor, no matter how powerful his lungs may be. These noises occasion the frequent call: 'Silence!' which only adds to the general uproar. How different from French theatres where the silence is overwhelming and where, at the slightest murmur, the audience immediately calls 'A la porte!' Those, in London who desire to hear the words of a play come early to the theatre in order to occupy seats near the orchestra and bring a book in which they can read the passages which have been made inaudible. Many people know the plays being staged by heart, particularly the ones by Shakespeare, and are therefore able to guess a given passage of the play from the actor's gestures and facial expressions. On our first evening, not anticipating those inconveniences, we were barely able to comprehend half of the ideas expressed in the play and the rest we had to infer from the relationship of events and the natural and emphatic acting, which rendered everything easier to understand.

Presently, after one preparatory scene, the avidly awaited Kean appeared as Richard. The theatre resounded with unrestrained clapping and stamping (for this is how they express applause) which lasted for several minutes, subsiding and rising by turns. The English Roscius[3] thanked the audience by holding his hand to his heart and making a slight bow with his head while waiting for the welcome to die down before commencing the famous monologue of Richard. He was unequalled in it, for the role of Richard is his main role. He is of short stature and hence seems destined to play a character who is said to have been lame, hunchbacked and born so crippled and ugly that, according to words put into his mouth by Shakespeare, 'That dogs bark at me as I halt by them.' But in so ghastly a body dwelt an even more horrid soul. By going in his acting through all levels of Richard's character, through cunning, betrayal, murders and finally reflection, Kean nears the borders of acceptability, but in so adroit a manner that he never goes beyond it. He expresses Shakespeare's ideas rather than his words; whenever he is at a loss for words he conveys their meaning with gestures and facial expression. His supreme talent kept other actors at such a distance that the stage seemed to be exclusively for him. This was quite compatible with the role he was playing, for he acted as the king and presented a real figure of a king surrounded by a swarm of obsequious courtiers. Having seen him as Richard someone aptly observed that his words pierce like daggers and his glances make one shudder as from the glare of an evil spirit. He is a peerless mime and can alter his facial expressions with great swiftness, which makes him a perfect actor in plays by Shakespeare, in which each character allows for so much variety. Moreover, his acting is distinguished by the utmost simplicity. Rather than acting to an audience he seemed to be interacting with the other characters in the play. Frequently ignoring the commonly accepted rules about positioning himself, he seemed to forget about the spectators as he walked to and fro, up and down the stage, sometimes without turning to the audience at all. For this he would be castigated by those accustomed to rigid principles in the theatre but the English neither permit nor impose upon their actors any restricting rules. The liberties taken by Kean seemed peculiar to me, but he used them so appropriately that he never abused them; without them his acting would not have been half as genuine and brilliant. At significant moments he would stand, so as to make his features visible in profile, a stance similar to that of a Greek statue. He himself, not being of particularly attractive appearance, used this as the most suitable one to express strong sentiments and – if I may put it so – silent speech. He is unrivalled in this practice and sometimes resorts to it for a period which spectators other than the English could find too lengthy to be tolerated.

But this originates in the nature of Shakespeare's plays, which contain so many pauses, so many silent moments between thoughts that they require silence in order to be comprehended. They cannot, therefore, be declaimed like French tragedies. Thus Kean's speech reflected Shakespeare's thought. It was typified by certain melodiousness typical of the English language, which from the stage was adopted by all good readers. But his articulation was never monotonous – words came slowly or as rapidly as a stream, as prudence or passion dictated. Important words were uttered as slowly and with such emphasis as if they were being weighed like gold on a pair of scales. His skill as an actor is married in his case with a rare power of intellect. This was already evident in his youth when, after joining the navy in a moment of folly, and rapidly growing tired of it, he simulated deafness in order to escape the predicament. He did this so well that during the two-month voyage neither the doctor nor the ship's crew noticed that his deafness was not genuine and he was sent back to London as unfit for service. The suppleness of his limbs is exceptional. He acquired this in his youth while being trained by a ballet dancer and perfected it to such an extent that in the theatre he was employed, if required, as a harlequin, a monkey, multifarious other animals and even for the transformation of Aaron's staff into a serpent. He makes good use of this suppleness in *Richard III*, for he could often make his extremities tremble so convulsively that his clothes and calves shuddered with anger and with his hand he was able to beat his breast as though he had talons instead of fingers and wished thus to mutilate himself. His gait was interrupted and violent, his voice hoarse and barely human and, especially as he was leaving the stage in anger, resembling that of a furious cat. The scene of Richard's slumbers on Bosworth Field was terrifying – the shadows of slain victims passing before his eyes and the harbinger of certain doom wakening him before the battle. The monologue is wonderful but frequently disconnected so everything is contingent upon good acting. Kean succeeded in it but also showed how highly proficient an actor appearing in Shakespeare's plays must be. In other plays the actor finds everything ready so that he does not have to add anything. In Shakespeare's works the opposite is the case. How true it is and how little declamation they suffer will be obvious from the example of the following passage in the penultimate scene of the tragedy.

Waiting for reinforcements for the army to fight against his foe, the Earl of Richmond, later King Henry VII, Richard asks the oncoming messenger:

King	What sayes Lord Stanley, will he bring his power?
Messenger	My Lord, he doth deny to come
King	Off with his sonne George's head
Norfolk	My Lord, the Enemy is past the Marsh:
	After the battaile, let George Stanley dye
King	A thousand hearts are great within my bosom.
	Advance our Standards, set upon our Foes,
	Our Ancient word of Courage, faire St George
	Inspire us with the spleens of fiery Dragons:
	Upon them! Victorie sits on our helpes.

Alarum, excursions. Enter Catesby.

Catesby	Rescue my Lord of Norfolke,
	Rescue, Rescue:
	The King enacts more wonders then a man,
	Daring an opposite to every danger:
	His horse is slaine, and all on foot he fights,
	Seeking for Richmond in the throat of death:
	Rescue faire Lord, or else the day is lost.

Alarums. Enter Richard.

King	A Horse, a Horse, my Kingdome for a Horse .
Catesby	Withdraw my Lord, I'll helpe you to a Horse.
King	Slave, I have set my life upon a cast,
	And I will stand the hazard of the Dye:
	I thinke there be sixe Richmonds in the field,
	Five have I slaine today, in stead of him.
	A Horse, a Horse, my Kingdome for a Horse.

Alarum, Enter Richard and Richmond, they fight, Richard is slaine.

Having uttered it he expired, but before that he had been trying to pull the sword from his breast for no less than five minutes, while at the same time struggling with mortal pain. Women were swooning in the boxes; even spectators with strong nerves averted their eyes, so much anguish the struggle occasioned. Finally, he straightened up from his huddled position, emitted a profound groan and fell to the ground as if crushed by the hand of death. All heroes on the English stage pass away in this manner and with a final groan. One might wonder why they fall so directly on their backs as though they were really lifeless and such a fall cost them nothing. Save for the pity which they inspire by bruising themselves to produce the illusion, I can see nothing improper in dying on stage instead of backstage, as in the French theatre. Particularly since as they perform with such elegance that Iphigenia herself could not have fallen in a more agreeable manner at the steps of a sacrificial altar. It is a different matter to watch the demise of a person emaciated after an illness and different still when one considers the death of one in perfect health and clad, moreover, in the robes of sentiment and poetry. Were one to follow closely the stringent rules of the French school, the art of painting would not depict the important events of history which are so frequently represented. For what is art is not reality; it can therefore find its place everywhere without causing offence. How far critics should interfere with what is commonly enjoyed, particularly as regards public spectacles, where everyone tends to appreciate only what he himself finds enjoyable, will not be discussed here. There is no doubt, however, that on the English stage it is poetic fantasies that, by assuming the faithful form of reality, win most acclaim. Actors, conforming to the taste of spectators, imitate grinding teeth, convulsive shudders, astonishment and the groans of the dying. Dramatic writers often enable them to do this by filling their plays with adventures of a most horrid nature and presenting upon stage lunatics, gory feuds, funerals, phantoms, graveyards and coffins – in a word, everything which intensifies the sense of tragic catastrophe.

The acting of Kean surpasses everything that I have ever seen in the theatre. I saw Talma's[4] performance in Paris but Kean amazed me more. He is more original than Talma, though less refined. This can be attributed partly to the plays and partly to an audience which revels in strong and emphatic acting. One could say that before him no actor had done justice to Shakespeare's genius. In the history of English theatre he can be ranked third to Garrick[5] and Kemble.[6] An actor like Talma would not be appreciated in England and an actor like Keane would not be appreciated in France. They are both endowed with genius but all genius is national and only a national audience does them justice. It would be hard to imagine Talma in connection with plays other than those which are referred to as classical and Kean with plays other than Romantic ones. The acting of each of them assumes the spirit of the work being staged, hence that of Talma is grave and composed and that of Kean volatile like the volatility of human life and the impulses of passion. Each is a master of his art. Talma evinced more social sophistication and Kean greater natural power. Talma had that power but it was suppressed by the rigidity of French plays, which does not affect Kean. But the voice determines the echo and Talma achieved everything that could be achieved in French tragedies; The French themselves, recognising flaws in their own theatre, give precedence to English actors in tragedy. In his letters from England Pichot puts it in the following fashion:

> Tragedy is better staged in England than in France where it nearly puts one to sleep. In Paris the experience is literary, in London truly dramatic. Works by French dramatists are formed in accordance with rules and by virtue of that take priority over the English ones: social decorousness imposes restraints upon writers and actors. Neither feeling nor passion is acceptable; they are subjugated to ceremony and ceremony stifles dramatic liveliness. The reverse holds true for England where, restricted by no rules, the writer and actor yield to the impulse of their genius. The writer takes no heed of rhymes, metres or whether he writes prose or poetry nor, as long as the public is entertained, is he interested in the unity of time or place. Whereas a Frenchman concentrates events of a day into three hours, an Englishman is capable of concentrating twenty-four years into three hours and no one considers it an irredeemable sin that Shakespeare marries Othello in Venice and within three hours transforms him into his wife's slayer on the island of Cyprus. Were he to be tried for this, he would not comprehend such poverty of imagination.

The superiority accorded to the English as regards tragedy is due to the French when it comes to comedy. No English comedian has surpassed Molière. Since the days of Sheridan and Cumberland[7] none of the writers has been able to remain in the repertory. At the present moment the romances by Walter Scott are being dramatised and they are becoming popular owing to an actor called Terry.[8] Nationalism appears on stage and its representatives are John Bull, Paddy and Sandy, each with his peculiar bad habits, superstitions and miscellaneous quirks made more amusing by the provincial dialects spoken by each of them.

On a different occasion I saw Kean in the role of Hamlet. His performance was masterly, even though his figure was too poor for the prince of Denmark. Among other actors I saw many good but no excellent ones; arguably, such talent is rare everywhere. Miss Stevens, the renowned singer, played the role of Ophelia. She impressed the listeners immensely when, sprinkling her father's grave with flowers, she sang the following stanza:

> He is dead and gone, [lady],
> He is dead and gone;
> At his head a grass-green turf,
> At his heels a stone.
> White his shroud as the mountain snow.

The song had exceptional charm, partly in the manner of the singing, partly in Ophelia's lunacy, which aroused sympathy, and partly in the national character of the melody. This must have been an early folk song which had been incorporated into the play by Shakespeare. It was typified by inexpressible melancholy, softness and simplicity. These characteristics harmonised well with the mildness of Miss Stevens' character. She is known for her singing rather than her acting, in which she was unable to overcome her true self and always appeared the way she was in reality. A Frenchman would call her 'un bon enfant du théâtre'. I had the opportunity to hear Miss Stevens sing several times. Her singing is splendid in its own way but quite unlike that of the famous Catalani, for it is neither as full nor as strong. But in its femininity it gives greater pleasure than that derived from the Italian's singing.

Among male singers Braham[9] was renowned. His name is reputed to have been abbreviated from Abraham, for he is said to be a Jew and in England, as everywhere else, Jews are held in contempt. His voice is a pure tenor, broad but not strong. His concerts are frequented by many. I heard him sing in Edinburgh at a concert organised by Catalani. There was a time when he was a member of the dramatic company at Drury Lane.

The English theatre has certain interesting characteristics, of which some are contingent upon custom and others upon organisation. The ground floor is filled with immovable benches: there are no chairs, nor is there a place called chairs. There are also benches in the boxes. Boxes cannot be reserved for a season, but only for one evening and then with only a specific number of seats. Even so, one has to arrive before the end of the first act or send somebody to keep the seats, for after the first act anyone can come and take them. Remonstrating that the box has been paid for will be ineffectual, as the established principle is that no one has the right to prevent others from enjoying the entertainment if he does not occupy the reserved seat himself. The absence of such a law could lead to abuses, especially in a country as affluent as England, where many a person might be tempted to rent half of the theatre and leave it vacant. Even the royal box has to be reserved beforehand or occupied by someone from the court if it is not, like any other one, to be used by the public. After the first act the price of a seat is halved. It is then that the throng is thickest.

An actor performing on stage must be sure of his role and know it by heart, for there is no such thing as a prompt box. There are only two prompters standing backstage to help an actor should he be in trouble. For this reason actors are not as eager to linger in the middle of the stage, as is often the case in our theatres where they are attracted to the centre of the stage as though by some magnetic power. Here they saunter to and fro as though they were not on stage, which subtly conduces to the naturalness of their acting. When an actor has something important to say he turns directly towards the listeners and speaks with increased emphasis. After that applause usually ensues, he waits until it subsides, speaks on and earns applause again. This may, however, be interlaced with booing should his words not meet everyone's approval. More often than not, their acting resembles a conver-

Boswell at Drury Lane. Lach-Szyrma was shocked by the behaviour of London audiences. Rowlandson's cartoon of James Boswell imitating a cow suggests that rowdies in the pit had been acceptable for a long time.

sation between actors and spectators, with the difference that the former speak with words and the latter answer them with applause or booing. After the play has ended the actor, honoured by being summoned onto the stage, thanks with a bow and usually a short speech which he always begins with 'Ladies and Gentlemen!' When there is singing or dancing it is inevitable that the audience should call once or twice 'Encore!' Bearing in mind their slow and dragging declamation, plays tend to be prolonged so that a performance may last from seven until as late as midnight. This prolongation is well nigh typical of all meetings in England; they sit long at the table, long in Parliament and long in the theatre. It seems as though this intelligent nation wanted to exhaust everything to satiety.

The main play, which is usually a tragedy, is followed by a farce or ballet. Its purpose, like that of the satirical drama of the Greeks, is to enliven spectators after the sadness of tragedy. For a month after the coronation of George IV this ceremony was staged every evening with the smallest particulars, beginning with the king's departure from the palace, through the anointing in the abbey, until the sumptuous dinner given on that occasion for state dignitaries. It is said that in order to render this procession as faithfully as possible the management of the theatre purchased the clothes which persons participating in the ceremony had been wearing. A platform was erected over the ground floor for the herald. On this he sat on horseback and, in keeping with an old custom, challenged to a duel anyone who dared to question the king's knightly valour.

Equally large and beautiful is the theatre at Covent Garden, but at the time when I was in London it was not as much frequented as Drury Lane, where Kean had attracted vast audiences. Previously the former theatre had enjoyed more popularity when Garrick and after him Kemble and Mrs Siddons[10] had been playing on its stage. Mrs Siddons is reputed to have possessed extraordinary talent, great dignity and a pure and tender voice. She was called the tragic muse. To Kemble, who has died recently, the English theatre owed what the French theatre owed to Talma - exact correctness in the staging of plays and the consistency of attire, country and period. At the present time the two main actors employed in the theatre are Macready,[11] who in a way follows a path between Kemble's classicism and Kean's energy, and Young,[12] who does not evince much genius but is able to entertain with his speech and action. A Frenchman accustomed to his own theatre would like him best. Among the London actresses there are no distinguished ones. Nonetheless, Mrs West, Miss Foot and Miss Tree[13] are not without some talent. The latter has been playing the role of proud Elizabeth in Kenilworth superbly. Miss O'Neill might have become a worthy successor to Mrs Siddons but she was lucky enough to have espoused an opulent Irish lord. She was the first actress to have been thus honoured, for it was only recently that actors have begun to be held in greater respect. Before that they were deemed to be on a par with vagrants and in 1579 they were expelled from the city. A few years later ten of them were distinguished by being permitted to refer to themselves as His Majesty's servants; every year they were given ten ells of cloth and an appropriate amount of braid. The theatre was so notorious a place that ladies would not dare to be seen there unless masked. Deceased actors were denied internment in consecrated ground, as was recently the case with Talma in France. Since the days when Shakespeare and Garrick were buried next to kings,[14] the people have abandoned all prejudice against actors. Their private lives too should be honoured and, by comparison with those of French actors, can be lauded as examples to be followed. The phenomenon of 'le scandale des coulisses' is unknown.

The construction of theatres is such that separate entrances lead to the ground floor, the boxes and the gallery. The entrance to boxes, where polite society usually gathers, is conspicuous by its splendour. The outward appearance of boxes is puzzling. They contain spacious extensions and magnificent parlours adorned with pillars, statues and reliefs and remind one of the ornamentation of ancient edifices. Since they illustrate the national taste of the English, I shall describe here some of the decoration of the theatre at Covent Garden.

Its extensions and colonnade are similar to those of Minerva's temple in Athens. The pillars upon which the edifice rests are of the Doric order and the stairs leading to it are made of ashlar. From all sides they are ornamented with reliefs depicting the forms of entertainment to be found within. One can see there Aeschylus, the father of tragedy, Aristophanes and Menander, the authors of ancient and modern comedies and Thalia, standing with a crooked staff and holding a mask in her hand, encouraging them to pursue their art. Other reliefs represent Polyhymnia and Euterpe with their lyres, Clio with a horn, announcing the glory of action, followed by Terpsichore, the Muse of acting and mime, walking with light steps. Then come three nymphs, who are following Pegasus and are wearing fir garlands. Minerva is situated opposite Aeschylus, who seems to be awaiting a signal from her. Among them Bacchus is leaning against a young kid, symbolising the belief that the god of wine was the inventor of tragedy. Behind Minerva stands Melpomene represented as a masked and menacing figure with a sword in her hand. Further on there are two Furies chasing Orestes, who is beseeching Apollo, standing in his chariot, to save him. In the very middle stands the immortal Shakespeare surrounded by emblems of poetry. Before his eyes appear Caliban with a bunch of wood upon his back, Ferdinand producing his sword and Miranda, along with Prospero, in supplicating attitudes. The spirit of Ariel is hovering above them and enchanting them with the beauty of his singing, elsewhere we can see Hecate, the daughter of Tartarus and the mistress of magic, in a chariot being pulled by oxen, Lady Macbeth with a bloodstained dagger and Macbeth averting his eyes with horror from the slain Duncan. At some distance from Shakespeare there is Milton, broodingly raising his eyes towards Urania, and the mighty Samson lying tied at his feet. Behind him two youths are driving away Komus accompanied by three priestesses of Bacchus. The sculpture terminates in two tigers. Reliefs of a similar nature incorporating national elements could contribute to the decoration of the new theatre under construction in Warsaw.

The most fashionable spectacle frequented by high society is the Italian Opera. It commences an hour after other theatres and is therefore suitable for the upper classes, whose dinners begin late and last for many hours. Should one come too late for it, which happens more often than not for it is fashionable to come in time for the last act, one will not have missed much as singing and music can be comprehended even when only the last verse has been heard. This is not true of tragedy or comedy for, if one wishes to derive pleasure from them;

one must follow the action from the beginning to the end and keep in mind the whole context of the play. Since it is exclusively Italians and Italian singing that can be heard from the stage, John Bull, who above all things prefers his own national songs and the solemn 'Rule Britannia', derides the opera and those who visit it. It is solely the theatre of polite society and its finances are stretched to the limit: many a time its management announced bankruptcy. Its interior is magnificent and constructed in a similar manner, though on a larger scale, to La Scala in Milan and the Italian opera in Paris.

I must add here that its architect was Nowosielski[15] who, judging from the name, was either a Pole or of Polish descent. However, he must have been a famous architect if he was charged with the erection of so important an edifice. It was finished in 1790, when Nowosielski must have been at the peak of his fame. The whole theatre is in the shape of a horseshoe, a form later adopted for other theatres before a better understanding of the laws of acoustics suggested a more appropriate construction. And it is also interesting, ineffectual as it may have been, that in order to increase the power of sound the walls of the theatre, which are built of bricks, were covered with wood. The longest possible timbers were applied for that purpose so as not to impede the spreading of sound and for the same reason the whole orchestra was suspended above the ground.

In addition there are not less than ten smaller theatres in the metropolis. The best of them is situated at the Haymarket, in which performances take place only in the summer, when bigger theatres are closed. In others, melodramas, mimes, ballet, dancing upon a tightrope and equestrian spectacles are staged. In one of them water spectacles similar to those enjoyed by the Romans are organised. The decrepit French theatre, where comedies and operettas are put on, was revived in 1824 but, as Francophiles are scarce, it is difficult for it to support itself.

There is a peculiar and fairly new spectacle called *Matthews at Home*. The said Matthews[16] is an actor, but the kind of actor who can hold the stage by himself and appears upon it both as author and actor. By accurate observation of human quirks and habits and their witty presentation, he attracts a large audience for his performances every evening and entertains it for several hours in a most agreeable and well-nigh unrivalled fashion. In 1818, when he revealed his talent for the first time, he talked about events which befell him while travelling by stagecoach. In the following year he gave an account of various experiences collected during the journey from London to Paris. In 1820 he brought his cousins from a country parish to the capital and acquainted them with Londoners. In 1821 he described his feelings and observations from a trip through air, earth and water. I saw him in 1822 when, in a most amusing manner, he presented a description of events in his own life. In 1824 he is said to have recounted the details of his journey to America and in 1825 he presented secret notes from his journals. And thus, year by year he finds something new to amuse the public. It is not difficult in England with so many classes of people and so many eccentrics. A ticket for his performance costs not more and not less than seven shillings per person (fourteen Polish złoty). He gives his performances in London on no more than forty evenings but they are so popular that the theatre can barely accommodate the spectators. One can easily surmise how enormous his profits must be. But that is not the end of it: he travels to the provinces and going from town to town amuses some with his jests while in others he collects material for future shows.

Admission fees in theatres vary greatly: at Drury Lane and Covent Garden one pays three shillings and six pence for the ground floor, seven shillings for the boxes, two shillings for the high gallery and one shilling for the highest. In opera it is ten shillings and six pence for the ground floor, and five shillings for the gallery. In smaller theatres the fees are somewhat lower. This price is stable: when an attempt was made to raise it, the people in the metropolis were so indignant that, after several memorably wild riots, the management was forced to return to the previous price.

It is only in the winter season that plays are staged at Drury Lane and Covent Garden; in the summer actors depart for provincial cities to perform guest roles there. This provides them with a substantial income. Kean sometimes goes as far as America. It is not usual for actors to be employed on a regular basis in one theatre. More often they sign a contract with the management that offers most. Apart from a regular salary they obtain a certain number of benefit performances; Kean's benefit usually brings him £500. What a huge difference in comparison with Shakespeare's day, when the most successful performance would earn a mere £20! Of that, how little must Shakespeare himself have received? Peerless author though he may have been, he is reputed to have been the worst of actors. In the famous tragedy *Hamlet* he was only allotted the role of the Ghost.

NOTES:

1 Edmund Kean (1789-1833), English actor. Having been taught singing, dancing, elocution and fencing, he was on the stage before he was eight. His first major role was as Shylock in 1814.
2 Areopagus is a hill in Athens near the Acropolis on which a council of elders met. Under the kings of Athens it was entitled to judge and punish those accused of immorality or law breaking.
3 Quintus Roscius (c 136-62 BC), Roman comic actor and elocution tutor to his friend Cicero.
4 See Chapter I, note 7.
5 David Garrick (1717-79), English actor, manager and dramatist. Equally at home in tragedy, comedy and farce, he was the first actor to be buried in Westminster Abbey.
6 John Philip Kemble (1757-1823), English actor and manager. One of a family of actors which included Mrs Siddons, he was manager of Covent Garden at the time of the fire in 1808. His attempt to raise prices to pay for repairs to the theatre led to the Old Price Riots which stopped performances for 71 nights.
7 Richard Cumberland (1732-1811). His sentimental comedies have not survived. He was caricatured by Sheridan in his *The Critic* as Sir Fretful Plagiary.
8 Daniel Terry (1780-1829). English actor, he became an admirer and friend of Walter Scott.
9 John Braham (1774-1856), British tenor of German-Jewish origins. Reputed to be the greatest tenor of his day, he ruined himself financially by buying the Colosseum and building the St James's Theatre.
10 Sarah Siddons (1755-1831), English actress and eldest child of Roger Kemble (1721-1802). A member of his travelling company from her childhood, she became the greatest tragic actress of her generation.
11 William Charles Macready (1793-1873), English actor. He became famous in the 1830s for his productions of Shakespeare at Covent Garden.
12 Charles Mayne Young (1777-1856), English actor. He was reputed to be second only to Kean and was able to retire with a fortune in 1832.
13 Ellen Tree (1806-80). An English actress, she married the actor Charles Kean (1811-68), son of Edmund.
14 'Buried next to kings'. A mistake: Shakespeare was buried in Holy Trinity Church, Stratford upon Avon.
15 Michael Joseph Nowosielski (1750-95), Polish architect in London in 1782.
16 Charles Mathews (1776-1835). An English comedian, he made his theatrical debut in 1793 but did not develop his one-man entertainments till 1818. He had two successful tours in the USA.

Chapter Eighteen

Amusements. The Taverns. The Diorama. The Sculptor Chantrey. The Art of Sculpture.

Apart from theatre and concerts, there are other forms of entertainment which the people of London pursue. The most fashionable balls are held at Almack's,[1] where only select members of polite society gather and no one is admitted without a special recommendation from one of the patronesses of the ball and an appropriate entry made by her in the visitors' book. For horse lovers there is Tattersall's,[2] a place where transactions are reputed to be so delicate that a man might fear to be defrauded by his brother. Reference should also be made to boxing, for which schools have been established in England where the best methods are taught. Their outstanding alumni receive valuable prizes and those of long standing in boxing are awarded pensions.

Cockpit. Like boxing, wrestling and racing, cockfighting attracted audiences from all social classes.

Other gory entertainments which delight both the upper and the lower rabble and can frequently be read about in the papers are cock-fighting and the baiting of bulls by dogs. I would write about these if I did not know that such gratuitous and inhumane amusements, as they do no credit to the English people, would bring no pleasure or benefit to the reader. Nonetheless, I shall describe the English tavern, for it distinguishes the character of the people in a curious manner and nothing similar can be seen anywhere else.

The one to which I am referring has for dozens of years occupied a pre-eminent position among the London taverns; it is known as the Cider Cellar. My first impression was that the customers were minor merchants, skilled craftsmen, book-keepers and other self employed people. Some of them, I was told, came regularly every evening and had their own seats which would not be occupied by any other person. These were usually situated at tables in the quietest corners from which the whole company could be surveyed. I went there on a Friday when, for reasons incomprehensible to me, this gathering place is always at its merriest.

Within I found a considerable number of guests – they were smoking cigars, drinking strong beer (ale), punch, grog made of rum or French spirits, while the thrifty Scotch were preparing their national toddy. At the ring of a bell a servant immediately appeared, asking for orders. An Irish piper had been engaged to play on his pipes the tragic songs of his native country. These had been published by Moore[3] who had also written various new ones in the same mode. About ten o'clock, as more customers arrived, the player was instructed to stop and a chairman was elected. I was astounded at first, for I could not understand why one was needed. At length he was chosen from among several people, not without excuses and vacillation on their part. He was supposed to be what the Romans called the King of the Feast. He seated himself in a chair on a platform at the far end of the room and, having silenced the room with a sign from his gavel, expressed his gratitude to the voters, as if he were thanking them for a great honour. The singing followed, led by the chairman. Each singer chose the next and no one with any confidence in his voice declined. It is not customary in England to conceal one's talents. They all earned rounds of applause and sometimes rewards were given. As a relief, the songs were interspersed with comic recitations and passages extracted from comedies, including imitations of the voices of renowned actors and actresses. Among the guests was an actor who had everyone in stitches. In the style of Mathews he impersonated typical London characters – the deep and nasal voices of carters, the thin and delicate ones of dandies, the slow and slurred voices of the elderly and the shrill and squeaky ones of quarrelsome women; his imagination was inexhaustible. He performed with exceptional talent and, in order to make his performances more enjoyable, he interlaced speech with song. I was told that such entertainments often last far into the night. People famed for their education and genius occasionally seek respite and relaxation in such taverns. I gather that Mathews and Kean sometimes attend in order to learn more about multifarious characters and use these as models to develop their own talents. The portrait of the illustrious and erudite Porson,[4] who had sometimes presided over the evening's entertainment, hung above the chairman's seat. I observed that order, though in a tavern, hurts no one and is of enormous benefit to all. There was neither deafening commotion nor hellish din: everything was controlled by the chairman. He knew what to demand and no one dared defy him.

A new and exceptional kind of spectacle preoccupied the London audience in 1823. This was the diorama, a kind of panorama. The two are different in that the latter represents cities and their environs as seen horizontally from a chosen vantage point. The scene remains motionless and lifeless. The former combines perspective and colour with the chiaroscuro effect of air and climate. When displayed by a slide it appears to be a real view rather than a work of art. When I saw it the interior of the Gothic cathedral at Canterbury, which I have already described, was being presented. In the projection it seemed as if a thick cloud were drifting over this magnificent edifice, enveloping in dusk its lateral chapels, pillars and the entire vault; later it appeared as if the sun emerged from behind the cloud and shone through the delicate stained-glass windows. The light radiating from them, as if from precious stones, flooded the marble floor and the outlines of pillars and vaults became more distinct. Equally charming, though in a different manner, was the projection of the Swiss valley of Sarnen: one moment the sun illuminated the neighbouring mountains, ravines and the crystal sheet of the lake, the next it cast upon it the shadows of moving clouds, which, driven by the wind, passed over the water; and finally the brilliance of the sun disappeared altogether as in a storm and everything was shrouded in the gloom of night. As I was looking at the two views it seemed to me that, as though by means of supernatural power, I had been transported into the precincts of the cathedral I had already visited and into the most beautiful valley in the world in order to feast my eyes once again upon these views. It was solely by comparing what I had seen in reality with what art had represented that I was able to judge how many illusions the diorama can create. A similar invention called an eidophusikon had previously been exhibited in London. Loutherbourg,[5] its inventor, showed by artificial light a fine day, moonlight, a sunset, the Fire of London and a gale which originated as a light wind and intensified into a fierce hurricane with heavy rain, thunder and lightning. The diorama requires no artificial light; objects are presented in daylight which falls upon a transparent picture of the item to be displayed and, should the need arise, can be regulated or enlarged as one pleases. The part of the diorama where the audience is seated is dim: on entering one can barely see anything, then the picture gradually emerges. In order to magnify the illusion it is made mobile and revolves mechanically. It is as though the observer were floating along the stream and seeing objects on the bank of the river. So far only two views can be shown, one after the other, but with time the human brain will undoubtedly invent a machine which can do more. People who now travel far and wide and, at great expense, visit interesting places, will be able to see the sights of the globe from the comfort of a box at the theatre. I saw a similar diorama in Paris, where Holyrood Palace and an ancient Carthusian church were displayed. The monk kneeling there seemed to be alive.

The diorama in London is decorated with portraits of some eminent painters, including Joshua Reynolds, West, Poussin, Ruisdeal, Rembrandt, Vernet, Claude Lorraine, Berghem, Leonardo da Vinci, Teniers, Rubens, Raphael and Gainsborough. No better location could be found for this group of masters than next to a new triumph of the art of painting. Dioramas, however, are too costly to be as numerous as panoramas: excellent painting and the patenting of the technology are essential. It will be long before they will be found beyond the borders of large capitals, where connoisseurs and opulence abound.

Several days later, on November 18th 1823, Leonard Horner and I visited the sculptor Chantrey,[6] who is the English Phidias. The courtyard was filled with scattered blocks of alabaster and marble, many from Carrara. These were completely raw and destined to be tamed and imparted with shape and meaning by the sculptor's chisel. While examining them I imagined what they would become: what deeds, what feelings might they represent? Perhaps they concealed the features of some philosopher, poet, hero, or defender of humanity, or perhaps one of the contemporaries by whom I had been befriended, a kindred spirit whose light I had been allowed to share? The paths to glory are many. A monument is a trifle but it is, notwithstanding, the only just reward that one can accept from the world.

But let us enter the sculptor's house. Although he was not yet there he was expected. We were taken to his studio where the subjects of his work were important national people and events. When we entered, the sculptor's apprentices were working on the statue of General Gillespie,[7] which was intended for St Paul's Cathedral. It had been commissioned by Parliament (a rare event) to commemorate his victories in the East Indies. I also saw there fine busts of the King and Wellington and many other people – some attired in judges' gowns, with wigs, books and holding quills in their hands and others wearing uniforms or seated in comfortable chairs. The sculptor frequently has to conform to the wishes of his living models and downgrade his art from the heights of imagination to the mundane. He has even to accept that in sculpture, detrimental though it may be to art, nationality should be expressed. His bust of Walter Scott, which we saw there, had had the poet's features beautified but, in order to establish his nationality, his shoulders had been covered with a plaid. By virtue of its folds, however, it was quite a pleasing sight so that the symbol of nationality did not disfigure the ideal of the poet; on the contrary, it enhanced it.

It is particularly with the statues of ladies that Chantrey allows himself to perform those innocent improvements. At that time he was finishing a wonderfully beautiful effigy for the tomb of Lady Winchester. Her figure radiated sweetness and charm: she was depicted in the first bloom of her youth, clad in light Greek drapery, and kneeling with her head bent. Her face, like an opening rose, was half veiled. Looking at the statue I uttered inadvertently: 'She must have been young when she died.' 'On the contrary,' retorted Chantrey, who by this time had joined us, 'She died at an advanced age.' I was amazed at the liberties which the sculptor took in transforming the reality of the appearance of his subject; but as it was, the figure was much more pleasing than it would have been had the marble been creased with wrinkles. Painting can represent all ages equally well, for by means of colour it can improve and modify what offends the eye. Sculpture is not so fortunate: it is happiest when depicting youth. It was such liberties, ignoring the realities of human life, which the sculptor had taken when executing the statues of women. Were we to form an opinion about English women on the basis of these, we would be forced to believe that they were all beautiful and died young. All the statues of women that we saw there were in the attitude of prayer, which was most appropriate since all effigies are destined for tombs. The artist covered each with a light veil which almost concealed their countenances. In such a posture we saw the relief of the Princess of York, the daughter of the King of Prussia: she was kneeling with her eyes raised towards the heavens, her hands crossed upon her bosom and above her head three stars were engraved. She resembled Urania from the poem by Mr Tiedge.[8] A similar but more sumptuous wreath adorned the head of Lady Ilchester. Looking at the relief I recalled the poem by Sarbiewski:[9]

> ... cui vigiles comam
> Flammae coronavere et albo
> Sidera circumiere gyro.

Incomparable among all the sculptures seemed to me to be the one of Miss Bradshire who died in the first flush of youth. Chantrey represented her gliding towards Heaven where her trusting eyes are turned. Over her face spreads a sweet smile, which resembled what the English poets call a foretaste of Heaven. A light gown and a veil are streaming behind her and, as a token of her virginal modesty, she is shielding her bosom with her hands. There was also a magnificent tomb made of white marble and erected for Mr Bold of Boldhall, the father of Count Sapieha's[10] wife, which was intended for the church where his body rested. Upon it were engraved his name, his family's coat-of-arms and a kneeling figure in a penitent attitude which was supposed to represent his daughter, whose face the sculptor had veiled.

The monuments which express family feeling do not usually allow much variety but even there the artist was able to express his ideas. Testimony to this is borne out by the group depicting the death of Marianne Jones. She was the only child of her parents and died in the flower of her youth. The father is portrayed in the blackest despair, holding his dying daughter's head, while the mother, at the foot of the effigy, is shedding tears upon the child's hand. The mother's countenance is invisible; the sculptor followed the example of the Greeks

Chantrey's James Watt. Chantrey was as famous for his portrait busts as for the church memorials described by Lach-Szyrma.

and concealed it to convey her boundless sorrow. In order to indicate the virtues of the dying daughter he sculpted her with her hand resting on a pile of books, one of which bears the inscription *The Bible.* Beside her is a lute, a musical score and a slate with sketching tools. It would be difficult to render a scene of the utmost grief and of so many wrecked hopes in a more masterly way.

How far Chantrey is able to go beyond the commonplace is shown by a similar group for the Watt family. There are six figures. The most important is an old man giving his blessing to his dying daughter-in-law. She is kneeling in front of him with two children, and the third one, well-nigh an infant, cannot comprehend the gravity of the sad scene but is nestling against the mother's bosom as if he wanted to share the blessing. Their father, overcome with grief, is standing behind them awaiting the final blessing of the old man.

Chantrey occasionally records the history of his nation. Among his historical works is a superb monument of General Haughton which I saw in St Paul's Cathedral. The commander perished in the Battle of Albuera and is portrayed in the posture of a dying man who is facing the foe, surrounded by soldiers wielding their bayonets. The figure of a winged Victory is holding a standard in one hand and with the other is decorating the hero's temples with a wreath.

At times Chantrey is a poet. His genius is influenced by the beauty of Greek concepts but he does not copy them and is always original. In his studio we saw two beautiful reliefs, the ideas for which he derived from verses by Homer. One of these was Penelope, holding a bow on her lap, surrounded by her slaves and longing for the return of Ulysses; the other was the parting of Hector and Andromache. Both were created for the Duke of Bedford who at Woburn, the family residence situated a few miles from the metropolis, collects masterpieces of painting and sculpture. It is well worth a visit. The statue of Louise Russell, his daughter, as a child is considered by experts to bear comparison with the most outstanding achievements of Greek sculpture. Chantrey is peerless in portraying guileless simplicity and is perhaps the only great sculptor of children. His 'Sleeping Children', which in 1815 was on display in the Royal Academy, is renowned. It stood between Canova's 'Terpsichore' and 'Hebe' but the Greek goddesses, who symbolised the ideal of youthful beauty, did not succeed in drawing as much admiration as those sweet slumbering children. The artist represented them embracing one another in their sleep. The younger is holding a narcissus, which nearly slips away from her tiny, sleep-benumbed hand. So agreeable and graceful a combination of slumber, beauty and innocence had never been seen in sculpture before. Mothers looking at them are said to have been moved to tears. Had he not executed any other works, this one would suffice to place him in the first rank of sculptors. He is a direct descendant of the Greeks. In his works he conveys a faithful picture of the nation's emotions, its character and the events of the age in which he lives.

Chantrey was born in Norton, Derbyshire, of peasant parents. He lost his father very early and from the age of seventeen had to share his time between education, provided by the village school in Norton and the agricultural labour which he had to undertake after his father's death. He was already modelling figures in clay and later on, during his apprenticeship to a glazier, in putty but he did not recognise the dawn of his developing genius. It was when walking along a street in Sheffield that he saw a shop whose window was filled with plaster figures. He experienced a secret feeling of enchantment which made him realise what his vocation would be. At that moment he decided to be a sculptor and, ignoring his relatives' and friends' advice, went into the service of the owner of the figures. After three years of assiduous but unprofitable work he was advised to go to London in order to cultivate his talent. It took him several years of probation in the capital before he created busts of some of his friends and it was not until he took part in the competition for executing the statue of George II that the public learnt about him. In 1814 he made a trip to Paris in order to examine the monuments of antiquity in the Louvre. On his return, he was commissioned by the church in Lichfield to sculpt a colossal figure of Satan. This was inspired by the description of the fallen angel in Milton's *Paradise Lost*.

The art of the sculptor is widely supported in England not only because it perpetuates the memory of people distinguished in service to their country but also on account of affection for deceased friends and relatives. Hence, in churches and in graveyards, one finds the most impressive monuments and tombs. The same is true of imaginative work, which wealthy Englishmen order from their sculptors, while other works are brought from Italy or Greece. But it comes as no surprise in a country which has achieved such a level of affluence and where the taste for the fine arts waxes every day. Like painters, sculptors also accumulate vast fortunes. Of great repute were Roubilliac,[11] Nollekens,[12] Bacon,[13] Westmacott[14] and Flaxman.[15] It is to them that Westminster Abbey and St Paul's Cathedral owe most of their ornaments. The principal work by Westmacott represents Psyche opening a box offered to her by Venus. 'Psyche', the experts say, could stand comparison with the accomplishments of ancient Greek artists. Flaxman's masterpiece is deemed to be his statue of Fox.[16] The statesman is offering his spirit to Liberty, to whom his dying gaze is turned. At his feet stand Peace, for whom he always strove, and a kneeling African for, during his short tenure of office as prime minister, he abolished the slave trade. Less successful was Flaxman's figure of the victor of Waterloo. Wellington is portrayed as Achilles but without the attributes appropriate for the vanquisher of the Trojans. The English Achilles is a colossal figure of a man cast in bronze and standing upon a tall pedestal in an open square (which they happen to call a garden). He is so devoid of grace that one would be more likely to interpret it as a statue of some common boxer than that of light-footed Achilles. In the posture of a fencer, the English Achilles would not have been able to hide among Lykomedes's daughters and remain unrecognised. It was commissioned by women patriots after the victory of Waterloo. As a memorable mark of honour from women it ought to be an embodiment of grace. Unfortunately, it seems that the artist made haste with the completion of his work and did not take into consideration either the exquisite taste or the modesty of his countrywomen. Had he done so he would have covered the statue with a tunic. As this national Achilles stands now, he deservedly earned the jibe that he is not 'Wellington' but 'villain tone'. In an age and a climate in which we customarily shield ourselves from the cold, as well as from other people's eyes, nothing can justify the nudity of statues. Gone are the times of Theseus, Achilles or even Apollo as presented to the less demure viewers of antiquity. Much more successful nowadays are those sculptors who cover with apparel their ignorance of human anatomy. Although it puts them to the inconvenience of having to be acquainted with the crafts of tailoring, wig-making and haberdashery, it also protects them from the reproach that the representation is at variance with the model. Chantrey firmly believed in the necessity of preserving the attributes of age and nationality, and strongly criticised the statue of Johnson in St Paul's Cathedral for the absence of a national costume.

In sculpture it is habitual to introduce allegories, a kind of national mythology. Even though it facilitates the comprehension of the concept and meaning of a monument, it is not always advantageous as regards art. It is helpful to surround the statues of commanders with cannons, pikes and standards – it allows the observer to recognise at first glance the occupation in which the person commemorated distinguished himself. But what advantage is it to art when monuments, especially reliefs, are as symbolic as stamps? In some cases the winged Victory is decorating the hero with a wreath, which may well be correct but does not allow for variety. Britannia[17] is occasionally placed beside celebrated admirals. She has the national features of English women and their stiffness of posture and on her head they put Minerva's helmet. As a metaphor for her rule over the sea she holds Neptune's trident and as a metaphor for industry and trade she holds Mercury's rod. In what way do these allegories borrowed from antiquity advance the art of sculpture? National sentiments may also be represented by inanimate objects; a boat might be added to a relief in order to perpetuate the memory of a victorious fleet. Many elements are difficult to reconcile with art and logic but they are there nonetheless. For example, the German Ocean, the Mediterranean, England's domination over settlements in America and Asia, and larger and smaller rivers in India are represented as well as fame, hypocrisy, freedom, lions, eagles, geniuses, etc. These are virtually incomprehensible but at the same time evoke events which are grave and significant for the British. Their statues have been criticised for being too large but I believe they were sculpted in this way so that the person represented could be raised above the commonplace. This was the practice of Greek sculptors. The vastness of buildings such as

Westminster Abbey or St Paul's Cathedral, where most of them are exhibited, was also taken into consideration. In addition, the visitor was expected to observe the monument from an appropriate distance. This is commonly disregarded, as though the pleasure derived from the art of sculpture was contingent upon the viewer's proximity to the work.

On the whole, like their poetry and painting, their sculpture reflects their nationality. Attention is directed to thought and only to a lesser extent to outward form and, since thought is very difficult to convey, discordances are frequent. Where a religious or family feeling is to be expressed, the English sculptors are peerless. This can be seen most clearly in Westminster Abbey and St Paul's Cathedral, which house many a monument. Let us pay a visit then to those shrines of national glory and national art.

NOTES:

1 The most socially exclusive club in London, Almack's was founded by William Macall in 1765. During the season, from March to June, the seven patronesses organised balls on Wednesday evenings. These were known as the 'Marriage Market' and Almack's became 'a temple of insipid propriety'. Bored bachelors so frequently escaped to a pub near Smithfield Market that it became known as 'All-Max in the East'. Throughout the year, Almack's was an equally exclusive gambling club.

2 Richard Tattersall (1724-93), English auctioneer. The mart for the sale of thoroughbred horses which he set up at Hyde Park Corner in 1776 became a centre for gambling.

3 Thomas Moore (1779-1852), Irish poet, writer and musician. His *Irish Melodies* were published between 1807 and 1834.

4 Richard Porson (1759-1808), English classical scholar and Regius Professor of Greek at Cambridge.

5 Philippe Loutherbourg (1740-1813), German-born British painter, stage designer and illustrator. Employed by Garrick as artistic advisor at Drury Lane, his transparent backdrops and the eidophusikon are believed to have influenced Gainsborough and other artists.

6 Sir Francis Legatt Chantrey (1781-1841), English sculptor. The bulk of his fortune was left to the Royal Academy for the purchase of British works of art which are now exhibited in the Tate Gallery.

7 Sir Robert Rollo Gillespie (1706-1814), Scottish general.

8 Christoph August Tiedge (1752-1841), German poet.

9 Maciej Kazimierz Sarbiewski (d. 1851), Polish poet.

10 Eustachy Sapieha (1797-1860). One of the three Polish princes for whom Lach-Szyrma acted as tutor during the Grand Tour which had started with two years' study at Edinburgh University.

11 Louis-François Roubilliac (1708-1762), French sculptor. In London from 1750, his best known statues are of Handel, Newton and Shakespeare.

12 Joseph Nollekens (1737-1823), English sculptor, known for his statues of George III, Fox, Pitt, Garrick, Goldsmith and Sterne.

13 John Bacon (1740-99), English sculptor. One of the first students at the Royal Academy, his monument to Chatham is in Westminster Abbey and to Dr Johnson in St Paul's.

14 Sir Richard Westmacott (1775-1856), English sculptor.

15 John Flaxman (1755-1826), English sculptor and painter. Director of the Wedgwood design studio in Rome from 1787-94, he became the first professor of sculpture at the Royal Academy in 1810. His statue of Nelson is in St Paul's and those of Robert Burns and John Kemble are in Westminster Abbey.

16 Charles James Fox (1749-1806), see Chapter 12, Note 14.

17 The model for Britannia was a Scottish noblewoman, Francis Stewart, Duchess of Richmond and Lennox. A great beauty and known as 'La Belle Stewart', she was a Lady-in-Waiting to Catherine of Braganza and possibly a mistress of Charles II.

Chapter Nineteen

St Paul's Cathedral. Wren. Wolsey. Nelson. Johnson. Howard. The Dome. History of the Cathedral. The Clergy. Sects.

St Paul's Cathedral significantly enhances the splendour of London. It is built in the shape of a cross and it resembles St Peter's Cathedral in Rome. Its architect was a native Englishman, Christopher Wren, to whom London owed its reconstruction and adornment after the Great Fire in the year 1666. The Cathedral stands third among the great churches of Europe: the first is St Peter's in Rome, which is 227,069 English square feet in area, the second is St Mary's in Florence, 84,802 square feet, then comes the cathedral in question, which is 84,025 square feet, and finally the church of St Geneviève, the Pantheon, in Paris, which is 60,287 square feet. The erection of St Paul's Cathedral took thirty-five years and that of St Peter's Cathedral in Rome an hundred years longer. The former is 340 feet high, the latter 437. All things considered, in spite of the immensity of St Paul's Cathedral, in spite of the magnificent dome which dominates the whole metropolis, in spite of the two lofty steeples and the two grand transepts resting on their Corinthian columns, its aspect is not as splendid as it would be were it located in an open space without being enclosed by the neighbouring buildings. Great edifices like great men require suitable positions to reveal their full grandeur; it is only mediocrity that benefits from concealment. Although impressive at first sight, the architectural dimensions of the cathedral are blurred by an excess of detail. The very marble of which it was built does not help its appearance. A sombre black, it is covered here and there with huge white spots, as though snow had drifted against the dark background of walls and pillars. The impressiveness of a building does not depend solely upon its architecture; the quality of the materials with which it has been built are of almost equal importance.

Although it has many merits the interior of the cathedral is not without flaws. It is generally believed that the arms of the cross lack breadth and the capitals of the pillars are too heavily ornamented. Nonetheless, the lofty vaults of the towers rest upon the pillars in a

St Paul's Cathedral. Sir Christopher Wren's plan to raze the area devastated by the Great Fire and to rebuild on a new street plan appropriate for a great city was never seriously considered but his design for the Cathedral was accepted. He laid the first stone in 1675 and the building was completed, the fifth on the site, in 1710. Its great dome and the 51 churches whose building, as Principal Architect, he supervised, still dominate the skyscape of London.

most agreeable manner. The light falling through the dome illuminates the centre of the cathedral well, leaving other parts of it in solemn shade. Looking from below at the bright soaring curve of the dome it seems as though there were yet another sky above one's head. Solitude and stillness pervading such an immense interior make a most profound impression; a man's stature is dwarfed to that of an ant. His very step interrupting the dignified silence seems sacrilegious, his presence there an importunity, and subconsciously he alters the tone of his speech. The eye wanders from one object to another in astonishment and, with no previous experience of so vast a building, cannot comprehend it at once. It seems as if the eye were overwhelmed. An unsophisticated American who entered this stupendous cathedral is reputed to have enquired: 'Was it all erected by man?' What would he have said had he visited St Peter's Basilica in Rome?

A visitor coming here might well ask himself what is the actual purpose of this construction? Upon entry he anticipates a sumptuously decorated church, as is usual in cathedrals. But what does he find? A large well-planned space which is uninhabited, empty, stark and devoid of any embellishment, not bearing the slightest resemblance to a Christian church. Here and there the flags hoisted on the bare walls commemorate victories won by English regiments but, since they are in tatters, they disfigure rather than decorate the sanctuary. The statues of famous people surrounded by divers allegorical figures do not succeed in filling the void of so huge an edifice: the deviation from its original purpose is apparent everywhere. I do not intend to discuss the propriety of placing such statues in churches designed for religious worship, for this has become customary. But how can we accept in a Christian church the mythological deities of the Greeks; the accompanying of human statues with the figures of Neptunes with their tridents, Herculeses with their clubs, Minervas with shields, goddesses of Victory in the shape of winged women garlanding the heroes of Britain? Does it not imply restoring those Greek divinities to the status of cult figures? Where are the altars or other indications of holy ceremonies? The concept of a cathedral, with which the visitor entered, disappears and he is left with the unanswered question: what is the purpose of this seemingly religious building in which so much is contradictory? Admittedly, a service is held in one of its chapels which is separated from the remainder of the church by an iron grille, but this does little to reduce the feeling of emptiness or impart the construction with some unity of character. The services of the Protestant denominations are too simple; they resemble an assembly of a large family rather than religious rites and cannot fill the entire cathedral. This would be more suitable for the sumptuous ceremonies of the Catholic Church. As it is now, the cathedral can by no means win approval, for it is diminished by a motley collection of human, pagan and Christian elements. In order to be inspiring, works of architecture must reflect their purpose. Failure to do this is as diminishing as are mean proportions.

St Paul's Cathedral may be regarded as a Pantheon; for the English it is a second Westminster Abbey in which those in public life may hope to be laid, for its gates open solely for the renowned. Westminster is the resting place of so many great men that without encroaching upon the peace of its old dwellers one could not find room for the great of this generation. St Paul's Cathedral was chosen as a new resting place for the distinguished and there are already numerous graves and effigies there.

One should mention the tomb of Wren, its architect. It is located in the crypt under the church and upon it is this plain inscription: 'Lector, si monumentum requires, circumspice.' And indeed there could not be a more splendid mausoleum. It is also in St Paul's that Cardinal Wolsey is buried. Archbishop of York during the reign of Henry VIII, he held the highest offices in the country but ultimately fell out of favour with the king. The words spoken on his deathbed are unforgettable: 'Had I but served my God with half the zeal I served my king, he would not in mine age have left me naked to mine enemies.' How unlike Wren who, having suffered in a similar way, said to his friends upon his premature retirement: 'Well, I must philosophise a little sooner than I intended.' But Wren was no courtier so he could scorn a career at court.

Next to Wren's there is the tomb of Nelson, to whom there are memorials throughout the country. Normally gratitude impels people to erect only one monument to distinguished citizens and those who are forgotten are merely buried in their graves. The tomb is square and built of bricks. Nelson rests in a coffin which, during his lifetime, he had ordered to be made from the mast of a French ship, 'L'Orient'. The admiral's hatred of the French is best illustrated by a piece of advice which he gave to his friend's son when admitting him to naval service. 'Firstly you must always obey orders implicitly, without attempting to form any opinion of your own regarding their propriety. Secondly, you must consider every man your enemy who speaks ill of your king; and thirdly you must hate a Frenchman as you hate the devil.' Near to the hero of Aboukir is buried his friend and comrade in arms Collingwood who, after Nelson's death at Trafalgar, took over the command of the victorious fleet. Apart from the tomb, there is also a statue of Nelson in the church itself. On his right stands Britannia, pointing him out to two young naval cadets as an example to be followed; on his left there is a lion, the symbol of fortitude and perseverance. The inscription upon the base of the memorial is simple: 'Copenhagen Nile Trafalgar', the scenes of his victories. Nelson was born in 1758, the son of a Protestant vicar.

Among the statues in the church one's attention is attracted to an exceptionally fine representation of Dr Johnson, the famed grammarian of the English language, the author of an exemplary dictionary and a work on the lives of the English poets. He is depicted in the robes of a Greek philosopher. Even more attractive is the memorial to Howard, the friend of humanity to whom prisoners owe so many improvements in their conditions. He is depicted with his right hand leaning against the prison door while in his left he holds a rolled parchment with an inscription which reads 'Proposal for the Improvement of Prisons and Hospitals'. Under his feet are fetters. As was mentioned previously, he died abroad and only his memorial is in St Paul's. There are many other statues, frequently representing those distinguished in battles on land and sea, but it would be difficult to enumerate them all.

Having examined what was interesting on the floor of the church, we ascended the stairs leading to the gallery in the dome. The dome is so immense that it seemed as though there were yet another church above the first. The floor upon which we looked down is made of large quadrangular blocks of white and black marble and resembles a fine chessboard on which people were barely visible. The gallery which skirts the dome is known as the Whispering Gallery, for words spoken on one side so quietly that even a person standing beside the speaker is not able to hear them can be heard not only clearly but also loudly on the opposite side. One has only to put one's ear to the wall. Slamming a door produces a rumble equal to that of thunder. The dome is 112 feet in breadth and is covered in its entirety with paintings representing scenes from the life of St Paul. They were executed by Thornhill[1] but they have already become somewhat faded.

Anyone who wishes may climb up from there to the so-called lantern, the glass sphere situated just above the dome. A superb panorama of the whole of London, its suburbs and environs can be enjoyed from there. However, a mild day and a time when the city is least obscured by smoke should be chosen. One shudders when looking down from such an elevation but deckhands will wager on their ability to climb to the highest cross when, having reached it safely, they win their bets. It seems that ascending wobbly masts and sitting in a swinging crow's-nest can make one immune to vertigo. After all, the seabed and the pavement in front of the church are equally fraught with danger.

One of the transepts of the church houses a library which, like most church libraries, is of no particular interest. Guides, however, do not fail to praise it on account of the register of visitors which forms the basis of their remuneration: one is charged in St Paul's for visiting each part of the church and well-nigh for each step one takes and one can see the library for twenty groszy. An equal amount is charged to view an immense bell which can be heard only on important occasions such as the death of a member of the royal family, the mayor or the bishop of London. Its tone is reputed to be extraordinarily pure and it can be heard within twenty English miles. It is sixteen feet in diameter.

On the very place where the Cathedral now stands there used to be a Gothic church which perished in the Great Fire of London, and before that it had been occupied by other churches which had been destroyed by the foes of Christianity, the Romans and the Saxons. The temple of Diana is said to have stood there originally. The construction of one of these churches is connected with the year 604 when St Augustine,[2] sent to England by Pope Gregory, converted Æthelbert, the king of the Saxons. According to the chroniclers it was on his orders that a church, dedicated to St Paul, the apostle of the gospel among the pagans, was erected. And since the apostle had preached not in churches but in the open, there was a pulpit in front of the church from which not only were sermons delivered but also important announcements made to the people. It was referred to as St Paul's Cross.

Every day a choral service is held in the Cathedral, during which the magnificent compositions of Tallis,[3] Gibbons,[4] Purcell,[5] Boyce[6] and Handel[7] are performed to great effect. Each year in May an oratorio is given on behalf of the impoverished widows and orphans of the clergy. All the distinguished musicians of the capital can then be heard displaying their talents in the church orchestra. A similar oratorio (for this is how they differentiate church from secular concerts) is organised in June, when not less than 8,000 penurious children who receive education, maintenance and apparel within the parish of St Paul's are gathered there in order to venerate and offer thanks to the Creator for imbuing human hearts with pity and mercy. The most important among the schools, St Paul's, was founded by Dr Colet.[8]

St Paul's Cathedral has its bishop, dean, precentor, chancellor, treasurer, five archdeacons, twenty canons, six vicars and a considerable number of servants. Reading a list of these titles one would be tempted to think that it was a Catholic Church but, not at all, it is Protestant and, as I write this, its members may be the fiercest objectors to the independence of Catholic Ireland. The Anglican denomination has preserved not only bishops and the offices of the Catholic Church but also a substantial number of church rituals. It is, therefore, called the Episcopal Church and, in its internal organisation, differs from the Presbyterian denomination established in Scotland. In this all ministers are equal and each year they choose a senior minister from among themselves who acts as Moderator.[9] As was the case before the Reformation, the privilege of conferring livings is usually vested in the aristocratic families. Since the handsome salaries associated with them provide significant incomes, the patrons usually bestow them upon members of their own families, principally on one of their younger sons or on some impoverished distant relative. The recipients frequently draw benefits from their parishes without performing their duties, spending most of their time enjoying the social life of the metropolis. They may even repair to France or Italy and thus abandon their fold to some deputy, a vicar or curate. How badly they are remunerated and the extent to which they are subjected to the caprice of their principals will be familiar to readers of Goldsmith's *The Vicar of Wakefield.* It is one of those blatant abuses from which English society is not free and which, being historically established, is not only tolerated but also considered to be just. Such a state of affairs does not lead to zealous work in the Lord's vineyard but rather encourages intrigues and an obsession with worldly possessions which should be alien to a servant of the Church.

As things are today, many crave a profitable post so as to be financially independent as soon as possible. In no other country did I observe as much sloth among the clergy as in the Anglican church. It fulfils its duties solely out of necessity but apparently without any sense of vocation or divine inspiration for so high an office. Their service itself, which for the most part is based upon reading the *Liturgy (the Book of Common Prayer),* is exceedingly convenient for them, as it does not require the least exertion of intellect or even memory since it may be read. Perpetual reiteration of the same prayers, beautiful as they may be, has led to mindless repetitions by priests no longer alive to their content and spirit. The same numb indifference is characteristic of their sermons, which are also devoid of soul and are routinely read from notes. Hardly any, like the Scottish ministers, deliver them from memory and such a one would be esteemed a marvellous preacher. Very few of them acquired literary renown; those who distinguished themselves included Tillotson[10] and Sherlock[11] and, from contemporaries, Alison. The Church of Scotland, whose requirements for entry into the ministry are much more stringent, can boast far more such clergymen among whom are the eminent orators Chalmers,[12] Thomson and Irving.[13]

The said lack of vocation among the clergy as well as the inadequacy or total neglect of theological education has resulted in many

London from Strand Bridge. One of the three bridges built by private companies during the Peninsular War, Rennie's Strand Bridge was renamed Waterloo Bridge and opened by the Duke of Wellington in 1815. With its approach roads it was completed in 1817 at a cost of £1,050,000. In the foreground is Somerset House, originally Protector Somerset's London palace. It was replaced in 1775 by Sir William Chambers to house the Royal Society, the Royal Academy and a number of government offices.

bachelors receiving church benefices due to aristocratic favour alone. This has led to a situation in which, in spite of the considerable privileges enjoyed by the dominant Church, large sections of the populace have renounced it. Man's innate search for understanding and the unrestricted freedom of the press have contributed to the burgeoning of religious sects on a scale unprecedented in any other country. An expert theologian would be required to summarise and evaluate their tenets; so numerous and subtle are the differences between them. The most distinct and clear cut characteristics are those of the Methodists, Quakers, Unitarians and Moravian Brethren; the divergence of other groups is over minor matters and subtleties of wording. It is to these non-conformist sects rather than to the Anglicans that the fervour displayed by the English in the promulgation of the Holy Scripture, the establishments of schools for the poor and other charitable institutions can be ascribed. Religious zeal and constant striving for improvement are preserved among them, contrary to the practice of many members of the dominant Church. The majority of Methodists and Quakers are to be found in North America, where Methodism is well-nigh a dominant religion. The founders of the Methodist sect were Wesley[14] and Whitefield.[15] The former would at times address up to twelve thousand listeners; there were no churches spacious enough to accommodate them all. Thus the custom arose of preaching in the open, in the fields, in the streets and at the markets. Occasionally they would appear at public celebrations to reprehend immorality and impiety. By virtue of its religious severity the sect has adherents in England even among those who are not open members of their congregation.

NOTES:

1 Sir James Thornhill MP (1675-1734), English painter and the father-in-law of Hogarth, one of his pupils. His baroque paintings have survived at Hampton Court, Greenwich Hospital and Blenheim Palace.

2 St Augustine (d. 604), Italian churchman and first Bishop of Canterbury. In 596 he landed at Thanet with forty monks and was welcomed by Aethelbert whose wife Bertha, daughter of the Frankish king, was a Christian. He converted the king and many of the people of Kent.

3 Thomas Tallis (c.1505-85), English musician and composer. 'The father of English church music', he was organist at Waltham Abbey before its dissolution in 1540. He became a gentleman of the Chapel Royal and shared with William Byrd (1543-1623) a monopoly of music printing.

4 Orlando Gibbons (1583-1625), English composer. Organist at the Chapel Royal in 1604 and at Westminster Abbey in 1623.

5 Henry Purcell (1659-95), English composer. Recognised by contemporaries as the greatest composer of his time, his choral work is outstanding. He was influenced by developments in both Italy and France.

6 William Boyce (1711-79), English composer, best known for his choral and orchestral work.

7 George Friederic Handel (1685-1759), German musician and composer. Appointed to the Court of Hanover in 1710, he was working in England before the Elector became King George I in 1815. He composed 46 operas and 32 oratorios, a form of sacred music which he invented.

8 Dr John Collet (1467-1519), English scholar and theologian. Influenced by Savonarola and Erasmus, his Oxford lectures on the Epistles of St Paul challenged the interpretion of contemporary scholastic theologians. In 1505 he became Dean of St Paul's. With the fortune inherited from his father, a former Lord Mayor of London, he founded the first school in England to be based on humanist principles.

9 The Moderator is elected to preside for one year over the annual General Assembly of the ministers and elders of the Church of Scotland. The monarch, usually represented by the Lord High Commissioner, may be invited to attend but has no authority over the Church.

10 John Tillotson (1630-94), English prelate. Although sympathetic to Presbyterianism he accepted the Act of Uniformity in 1663 and became Archbishop of Canterbury in 1691. He was reputed to be the finest preacher of his generation.

11 William Sherlock (1641-1707), English prelate and, until 1690, a nonjuror. Master of the Temple and Dean of St Paul's, his sixty published works were controversial.

12 Thomas Chalmers (1780-1847), Scottish theologian and preacher. His 34 published volumes deal with natural theology, apologetics and social economy. A brilliant orator, he led the 270 minsters who left the established Church in the Disruption of 1843. In the Free Church which he founded ministers were chosen by the congregation and not by the landowners of the parish.

13 Edward Irving (1793-1834), Scottish clergyman and mystic. Trained as assis-

tant to Chalmers, he moved to London to the Caledonian church in Hatton Gardens. His preaching attracted large congregations, many of whom followed him to found the Catholic Apostolic Church in 1833. His stress on the human attributes of Christ and the imminence of his second coming were considered to be heretical.

14 John Wesley (1703-91), English evangelist and founder of Methodism. He was one of a group of devout Oxford students brought together by Charles Wesley, his hymn writing brother. The resistance of many of the eastablished Anglican clergy to his attempts to reform the church from within led to the creation of the break-away Methodist Church.

15 George Whitefield (1714-70), English evangelist and one of the founders of Methodism. A rigid Calvinist, he broke away from Wesley's Arminian Church in which some emphasis was placed on ceremony. He preached to huge congregations, often in the open air, thoughout Britain and America.

Chapter Twenty

Westminster Abbey. Tombs of the Kings. Wax Figures. Henry's Chapel. Graves of Famous People. The Anniversary of the Gunpowder Plot. Poets' Corner. Shakespeare. Memorials of Poets and Artists. Funerals and Graveyards.

One day in autumn I decided to visit Westminster Abbey. As is widely known it is the place where the kings of England are buried and where genius, bravery and service are commemorated. There is no other nation in possession of such holy ground which, for centuries, has gathered together so many memorials to the great. The day was grey and misty. I entered a large cemetery which, because of the buildings surrounding it, seemed to me too narrow in relation to the size of the church. It was covered with marble tombstones, many sunk into the earth. I tried to avoid treading on them so as not to rub out inscriptions which were already half worn away. Telling of friendship, gratitude or vanity, they were so eroded that they were failing to immortalise them.[1]

I stopped from time to time and tried to read them but the dead leaves, blown from nearby trees, hid the illegible inscriptions as though they would wish to erase them entirely. It showed the futility of man's fame and mocked my curiosity. This little leaf, I thought to myself, after being touched by autumn's cold will never be green again; these blades of grass growing among the graves will soon wither; how similar they are to us when the merciless hand of death takes us from life – they also have to pay their debt to nature and earth covers us together!

Busied with such thoughts I raised my eyes above the tombstones to the magnificent church, the abode of earthly splendour. The two high towers were like fingers pointing to the sky. The building is made of hewn stone in the purest and most restrained Gothic style. Its windows, as in all Gothic buildings, were narrow, reaching to the vault; the panes were made of stained glass. Through a wide but rather sunken gate people were entering the building. They were going into the church in groups of ten so I joined one of these groups and we went in together.

The seriousness of my thoughts became overwhelming when I found myself standing among the tombs of people of centuries long past. I felt that I was standing in the presence of their immortal spirits when I gazed on their features and recollected the greatness of their genius and the glory of the deeds they had done for the sake of their country and humanity. Lost in the past, I thought I had entered the land of shadows to talk with the dead. This communication with the past was strengthened by the bleakness of a place overshadowed by towering pillars and numerous sculptures. The place where the dead rest is awe inspiring; in its silence, you walk there slowly and shyly, respect banning any lightheartedness and leaving one almost breathless. When our guide talked to us his voice seemed to be a whisper which faded under the Gothic vault and which blended with the grave-like atmosphere. Harpokrat,[2] the god of silence, seemed to dwell there and order silence with his finger raised to his lips. Those in their graves hate to be disturbed; whether resting on a bed of virtuous or evil deeds the dead wish to sleep on.

We were wandering as if we were in a forest of marble and bronze tombs, memorials and statues which, having survived through the centuries, will survive many more. The guide reeled off the names and nearly forgotten deeds of the kings, magnates, courtiers and commanders as though he were reading from a register, indifferent and sometimes half asleep. This he could not have done with impunity had they been alive but almighty death, having taken their lives away, also took their power of revenge. A passer-by looking at their images discovers only how fleeting is the greatness of this world and the guide, not giving time for reflection, leads him from one grave to another, from one statue to another, reducing their long inscriptions to a few laconic words. These guides are so bored with the story they tell every day that the only thing they care about is the end of the tour, thus their interests and those of the visitor always conflict. In the mass of fleetingly presented memorials one can remember only a few. Not all the inscriptions are characterised by relevance and brevity; of many of them a man can repeat after Pope:

Friend! For your Epitaphs I'm griev'd
Where still so much is said,
One half will never be believ'd,
The other never read.

Man's desire to leave some memorial behind him will never fade: a peasant will have a mound over his grave and a monarch will raise for himself a magnificent mausoleum. In twelve side-chapels there were the tombs of kings and magnates. They were usually of rectangular shape and lying upon them were the figures of dead kings in their crowns and sceptres, knights in armour with swords by their sides and hands clasped on their breasts, all resembling the dead person's appearance and clothing. However the true features of their faces could hardly be recognised, having been erased by rust just as time had turned to dust the bodies of those whom they were depicting. Some of them, even after death, have not escaped the plots against them. Henry V, called the scourge of France, lies without his head because it was made of silver. Elizabeth, who had taken the sceptre away from others, lies without her sceptre because the value of the metal had attracted a thief. Strongholds are not strong enough nor sanctuaries holy enough to keep the insatiable thief from breaking in.

On one of the tombs lies brave Edward I and by his side Eleanor of Castile, his wife. Visitors look at them with pleasure. When in 1279 Edward went on a crusade to Palestine Eleanor accompanied him. He was wounded by a poisoned arrow but, for fear of their own lives, none of the courtiers dared to suck the poison out. This was the only possible cure in such a case. Not caring about her own life she sucked the poison out, an example of virtue rare in the history of mankind. Inseparable in life they were not separated by death.

A bit further on one can see a very different image. The duke of Leicester[3] lies on a magnificent tomb with his first wife at his right side but the left side of the wide tomb is empty. It was meant for his second wife but she scorned the place and preferred to be buried away from her husband and her rival. It would be hard to find a more extreme example of a woman taking offence at something. Nobody would ever have remembered her if her vanity had not made her immortal.

In one of the chapels we were shown wax figures of Elizabeth, Queen Anne and Nelson dressed in the costume of their times and looking, we were told, as they had done in their lives. They stand in a showcase behind a glass door. It is as well that they are kept under lock and key because such statues would be better fitted to a waxwork than a hall of fame. The costumes, reminding one of ever-changing fashion, and colour, reminding one of life, are inappropriate in a place where everything earthly disappears and eternity rules. Copper or even pale or colourless marble are the most appropriate materials to use. In some way I always find wax figures disgusting and was disgusted to see Elizabeth and Nelson, looking neither alive nor dead and reduced to mere spectacles. Where everything is serious laughter is painful. Elizabeth, as was the custom of the kings who preceded her, has an elaborate and magnificent tomb but after her no king was buried in this chapel and there were only a number of statues of famous people.

The chapel of Henry VII is regarded as a masterpiece of Gothic architecture. The standards of the Knights of the Bath hang on the walls and a name and a coat of arms are placed by each of them. The standards of those who have acted dishonourably are torn off; the place previously occupied by that of Lord Cochrane[4] remains bare. He was deprived of this honour and exiled because of his greed. During the Installation the knights sit in the stalls together with their three esquires. The stalls are beautifully carved and the whole chapel decorated with biblical figures. One writer said about this wonderful building that God himself had made the plans and angels had carried them out. The construction cost 7,000,000 francs which for Henry VII, for whom such lavishness was abnormal, must have been a great sacrifice. But what will not be sacrificed when one's vanity is involved? He built this chapel for his own burial: anyone who was not of royal blood was to be excluded. To this day the will of the founder has not been violated. Proof of this lies in the long inscription on the tomb of Margaret Douglas.[5] At least fourteen ancestors, including monarchs of England, Scotland and France, beginning with her great-grandfather Edward IV, are listed to prove that her ashes have the right to be buried in the chapel.

Having seen the chair on which the kings are crowned and this fantastic stone to which the country's fate is bound – only an ordinary grey stone – we entered the part of the church which is intended for memorials to renowned men of war, government and science. There the ashes of the commanders Howe[6] and Wolfe,[7] of the poet Congreve,[8] of the orator Grattan[9] and of many other famous men were honoured. Some of them have fine memorials made by the best woodcarvers. The memorial to General Hargrave is noticeable for its size. The commander is depicted rising out of the tomb while Time, in the form of an old man, breaks the spearhead of Death and the crown, fallen from the head of the sceptre, is thrown into a chasm. Lord Mansfield[10] is depicted sitting on a judge's chair, wearing a robe and a wig, and gazing on the Scales of Justice. Wisdom and Justice are sitting at his feet and behind them is Death – the first time I have seen her represented as a woman of great beauty and not as a gruesome and scarifying figure. The Greeks showed Death and his brother Sleep as young men laying down their torches. In the Middle Ages this beautiful image was replaced by Death as an ugly and terrifying skeleton. But in this tomb the original, ancient image was restored. It is hard to imagine that a man as noble as Mansfield, whose mind and pure character made him adored when he lived, could be in the power of such a fearsome monster; no, for him Death must be a pleasant sleep after his work and toil. That is the message that the artist wanted to convey and nobody has found fault with him. This memorial was made by Flaxman.

Pitt and Fox are lying side by side, almost as though they had been laid in one grave. Walter Scott had reason to say:

> Drop upon Fox's grave the tear,
> 'twill trickle to his rival's bier.

The fame of both ministers is so great that their tombs do not need inscriptions; only the first letters of their names had been written down: P. and F. Opposing each other in matters of principle they joined together when it was a matter of their country's good. Their consistency won the sympathy of their fellow citizens: Fox became the leader of the Whigs and Pitt of the Tories.

Newton also has his memorial here. Under his tomb deities are placing planets at measured distances from the sun. The inscription, which is rather long, ends with the words: 'Let mortal men deem themselves to be blessed by the birth of so great and good a man who became an honour to the race of men.' Among great men honoured by monuments is George Stepney[11] who in 1699, during the reign of August II, was a legate to Poland.

Two coffins are standing in one of the corners in this chapel: in one of them is supposed to be the body of a Spanish legate, in the second that of a Sardinian diplomat of the same rank; they came to this abode of fame by the simple means of not paying their debts. Their bodies, which after their deaths lost diplomatic immunity, were handed to their creditors who laid them in the chapel. It is a partially serious yet ridiculous way of gaining back one's property but it shows how severe are the English laws concerning debt. In St Ann's church lies an even greater debtor – Theodore of Corsica - who died in 1756, shortly after being released from the King's Bench prison. He left his kingdom Corsica to the creditors. All this has been written on the tombstone together with these lines:

> The grave, great Teacher, to a level brings
> Heroes and beggars, galley-slaves and kings!
> But Theodore, this moral learn'd ere dead.
> Fate pour'd its lessons on his living head,
> Bestow'd a kingdom and denied him bread.

Among great people an honourable place in Westminster Abbey is taken by Pascal Paoli,[12] the Corsican leader who, having released his country from French rule, gave it into the hands of the English. Finally, troubled by misfortune, he died in 1807, still collecting from the treasury £2,000 annually. A marble bust immortalises his features and brave deeds. Frederick the Great called him the first warrior of his time, presumably meaning the second after the king.

But the Abbey is not devoted solely to the fame of men; family affection is recorded there too. I saw a few memorials to women with inscriptions like 'pia, casta, prudens' and even 'untrique marito bona uxor', quite unlike those on the graves of warriors and sages. The most spectacular is the one built for Lady Nightingale. She died in her twenty-seventh year, in the springtime of her life. The woodcarver depicted her as she was sheltered from Death in the arms of her husband who, supporting her on one arm tried to protect her from Death's spear with the other. Death leans out from the open grave at the base of the monument. This is covered with a shroud like veil beneath which you can see a skeleton. The fearsome reaper rests one hand on the scythe and threatens its victim with the other. It is a faithful reproduction of most people's image of death or as it is represented in romantic ballads. Totally different is the memorial raised to honour the memory of Lady Walpole. Her figure, made of white marble, stands on a simple base. It is so classically correct that it might be taken for the work of a Greek wood carver. Veiled from head to foot, she has the appearance of a vestal virgin but her features, dignity and modesty could only be those of an English matron. It is a beautiful statue but more appropriate in a gallery than as a memorial in a graveyard.

As I was wandering among the memorials discovering for whom they had been erected I heard the solemn notes of a pipe organ echoing under the vault of the church. It was a weekday so I asked the guide what it meant. He replied that it was the anniversary of the discovery of the Gunpowder Plot which had planned to blow up Parliament. It is celebrated on the 5th of November. I entered the chapel which was within the church. This, because of its size, had been partitioned. The singing of the choir and the sound of the organ made a deep impression as the music faded away into walls consecrated by the memories of the great. It was pleasant to think that this centre of faith had become the last resting place of the famous. Religion in England too often mixes with politics and has little influence on the behaviour of people and the course of government. Nelson during the battle of Trafalgar was reported to have said: 'Victory or a grave in Westminster' – and he gained the latter. The clergy who were conducting the ceremony were sitting in stalls just as Catholic priests do; the choristers, in white gowns, were on seats below; students occupied the middle benches. There were few spectators for, on a weekday, everyone is going about his own business.

Religious ceremonies of the Anglican Church are simpler than those of the Catholics but are no less impressive and the intermingling of the voices of the clergy and the congregation gives them an added significance. The autumn fog spreading through the church seemed to carry the prayers away, while mild sunlight breaking through the stained glass threw a mysterious light over the interior. The shadows of the pillars on which the Gothic vault rested created a gloomy dusk in the church and everything seemed to direct one's thoughts to eternity and the incomprehensible. Finally, two priests dressed in white ceremonial robes, who had been kneeling on either side of the altar, began to read the liturgy from a great, richly ornamented book. The choir, and the young people, repeating after the clergy, intermingled their responses with the prayer. The ceremony reached its climax when, during the prayers for the king and the royal family, I heard the sound of cannons mingling with the words of the prayer. In this building so many monarchs were anointed and their bodies laid to rest, so many ministers and leaders, whose council and courage have added to the glory of their country lie, so many wise men, poets, geniuses of all kinds who, like constellations of stars will be known for ever, have found a place of rest and remembrance. What Englishmen would not love his country in such a place? Who would not dedicate his life to her service? How many great deeds have originated from seeds sown in this place?

Entrance to the tombs of kings and famous people is through the Poets' Corner, as if through their lips people gain immortality. When I visited Westminster Abbey for the first time the Corner was closed due to renovation works; it was on the 3rd of December 1823 that I saw it for the first time in the company of my friend, Mr D, a Frenchman who was visiting England. After paying the usual entrance fee of one shilling and sixpence we walked into the Corner, accustomed now to the English practice of charging visitors wishing to stand on sacred ground and perhaps not resenting it on this occasion because I was about to salute the immortal spirits of men of genius. My comrade Mr D also seemed to be serious though perhaps not as earnest as I. Having not yet reached the place from which one can see the monuments, with the speed characteristic of his nation with

Poet's Corner, Westminster Abbey. By the nineteenth century a tradition had developed of burying or erecting memorials to poets in the south transept and to prominent statesmen in the north transept of the Abbey.

whom speech always precedes thought, he said: 'Voilà Shakespeare!' Hearing these unexpected words I was breathless with astonishment. I stared at the monuments and, not having managed to find one that could be his and having regained my breath, I managed to stammer 'Où est-ce?' To which the Frenchman answered 'I'm looking for him just now.' The mere mention of the great genius made such an impression on me that I was moved to a depth beyond description. There are people incapable of such an experience, whose defence is 'nil mirari' and who barricade themselves against anything that delights, surprises or elevates. What is only insensitivity and lack of feeling they take for strength of mind. Standing before Shakespeare's memorial I did not identify with those strong-minded 'esprits forts' and I would have been ashamed if, standing there, I had not been conscious of his greatness. The memorial to Shakespeare is made of white marble. He is depicted standing, his head resting on three books held in one hand while the other points to a parchment on which are those profound words which, at the entrance, prepare the visitors for the nature of the place they are visiting:

> The cloud capped towers, the gorgeous palaces,
> The solemn temples, the great globe itself,
> Yea, all which inherit, shall dissolve
> And like this unsubstantial pageant faded
> Leave not a rack behind. We are such stuff
> As dreams are made on, and our little life
> Is rounded with a sleep.

Only his monument stands in Westminster; his body is buried in Stratford upon Avon, in the parish church, where he was baptised. He was born on the 23rd of April 1564 and died in 1616, also on the 23rd April. He wrote 42 plays.

Next to Shakespeare is the memorial to Thomson, the author of *The Seasons*, with the following inscription on the base:

> Tutored by thee, the sweet Poetry exalts
> Her voice to ages and informs the pages

With music, image, sentiment and thought
Never to die!

Thomson is the only Scottish poet given a place in this temple of fame, for up to this time it seemed to be committed only to Englishman. Pope, Swift and Sterne who were Irishmen do not have memorials here. No decision has yet been made about Moore, Campbell and Walter Scott but their genius is such that it could not diminish the fame of any place. Lord Byron, due to his religious opinions, was excluded by the commission. In the past anyone who paid enough could be buried there and many tombstones appeared which might have found more appropriate homes. Today neither vanity nor money alone could find one a place amongst the illustrious dead.

Among those who are honoured with well-earned memorials are Chaucer, the father of English poetry who died in 1400; and Gray,[13] Davenant,[14] Goldsmith,[15] and Cowley.[16] Memorials of some of these are very modest. Cowley has only an urn encircled with a wreath of bay leaves and Dryden a marble head inscribed 'Dryden'. The inscriptions are simple and characteristic of the style of the writers. Beneath Ben Jonson's memorial, the inscription reads just: 'O rare Ben Jonson!' To be remembered in the words of another poet is the greatest of honours. Next to him is a bust of Butler, author of the famous poem '*Hudibras*'. The inscription beneath describes the sad fate of Butler[17] and of so many other poets.

Ne cui vivo deerant fere omnia
Deesset etiam mortuo tumulus.

This modest memorial was funded by an admirer of his poetic genius, a Londoner. A genius has to have friends if he is not to be forgotten.

Fame is a twofaced creature; it may be a blessing or a curse. In an inconspicuous corner stands the tomb of Spencer, prince of English poets and author of the *Faerie Queene*. It is unadorned in any way in the belief that a godlike genius needs no memorial other than his own works. Spencer was born in 1552 and died in 1596. He was a contemporary of Jan Kochanowski, but while our poet's works constitute the model of good Polish language, Spencer's are now barely comprehensible for Englishmen and even more obscure are the works of his predecessor, Chaucer.

England at that time could not boast such authors as Rej from Nagłowice or Górnicki. Other memorials are also simple and inconspicuous as were the quiet and modest lives of those whom they commemorate. The head of the poet Gay[18] is presented as though it were a symbol. Above it are musical instruments and masks, one of which is pierced with a knife to represent the type of poetry for which the poet was famous. On the base is an inscription which, because of its triviality, is inappropriate for the place:

> Life is a jest, and all things show it;
> I thought so once, but now I know it.

Over Milton's bust, which is made of white marble, stands an urn of black marble from which fire flares. The face of the poet, framed by his long hair, expresses gentleness. In his childhood this poet of the *Paradise* is reported to have been so pretty that his fellow students called him miss. The features of his face become more manly when he grew up but the sweet expression remained. Prior,[19] although not one of the finest of poets, has been given a more impressive memorial than many others. On a coffin of black marble stands his bust. Over it hovers the head of a cherub, surrounded by wings; on the top of the memorial is a figure with an hourglass and a second holds a fading torch of life. Beneath, on the base, stand two Muses. Addison's memorial is classical and completely different in style. This author of the play *Cato* and publisher of the *Spectator* is depicted as a Greek philosopher, in a long full robe and holding a scroll of parchment. On the base are bas-reliefs of mourning Muses. This masterpiece is by Westmacott and is deservedly honoured. Standing in the centre of the vestibule, this memorial seems to over-shadow others and resembles the author's style in its correctness. Despite this the author's play *Cato* did not last long on the English stage and has had few performances.

However, the memorial to the Duke of Argyll[20] is the most magnificent of them all and it might be said that it is too grandiloquent for a place where even the great should be reminded of man's mortality. Yet the duke rests there not because of his literary fame but because of his military achievements. He is shown resting on the weapons of war. Beside him the standing figure of Fame has already written down all his deeds while the figure of Minerva symbolises the prudence of the commander, and Britannia mourns over the loss of her brave son. This masterpiece was created by Roubilliac.[21]

Although named Poets' Corner this is also the resting-place of scientists and artists, both English and foreign. Among the scientists is the famous philologist, Casaubon,[22] who came to England in the time of James I. Grabius,[23] the Prussian, is shown with a quill pen and other writing instruments by his hand and Kneller the painter and Handel the musician, both Germans, are there too. Thomas Parr[24] is remembered because, an expert on prolonging life by abstinence, he lived for 152 years. There are memorials to Taylor the architect and to Garrick the actor. Garrick is shown coming on stage after the curtain had gone up. Over his head is an image of Shakespeare and on either side the Muses of Tragedy and Comedy. The first is masked and mournfully veiled; dagger in hand, his heavy clothes express sadness: the latter is also masked but his pipes and light and airy clothes represent joy. Particularly beautiful is the bas-relief honouring Handel. The musician stands with his eyes turned toward heaven as though he were listening to the harp of the heavenly angel hovering above him. Before him lies the score of the *Messiah,* open at the famous aria: 'I know that my Redeemer liveth.' This has great significance for the English, associated as it is with the ceremony of burial. Handel died in an unusual manner. He was playing the *Messiah* in Lent when his strength left him and he fainted over the keys. He recovered sufficiently to finish the music but died soon after returning home.

However, to see the tombs of all of the most famous people one must go beyond these two ancient churches, for many are situated elsewhere. Akenside,[25] the author of a beautiful poem about the delights of imagination, has his memorial in the Church of St Jacob, Sterne's is at St George's, Otway's,[26] the author of the drama '*Venice Preserved*', who died in 1685, is at St Clement's. Fletcher[27] and Massinger,[28] dramatic writers of old, share a grave at St Saviour's and the painter Holbein was buried at St Katherine's. Bacon,[29] the greatest of philosophers, lies at Stowe, as do Locke[30] and Alfred the Great,[31] the greatest of English Kings. The author of *Paradise Lost*[32] is honoured with a memorial in Westminster but also has one in the Church of St Giles's. Here he was buried in the parish now best known as the haunt of thieves. In the Catholic graveyard of St Pancras there are many stones on the graves of foreigners who died in England. Amongst them are the modest memorials to those Frenchmen who sought shelter in England during the revolution, including those of seven bishops. Behind the altar at St Clement's there is to be an interesting painting of the Pretender and of his wife, who was born a Sobieski princess, and of their children. It is a strange memento for a Pole. In almost every graveyard there is something worth seeing which illustrates the character of this nation. For centuries tombstones have recorded important moments in history; their details cannot fail to be of interest to the stranger trying to build up a picture of the people of another country.

Finally, it would be proper to say a few words about funerals and customs associated with them. These are less ostentatious than in other countries but social rank, dignity and wealth are clearly expressed. Death, who abolishes all differences, triumphs but at the tomb she is surrounded by symbols of earthly magnificence. No one wants to descend to an unmarked grave; the vanity which has been with him through life accompanies him to the tomb. Amidst the turmoil and rush of everyday life in the capital you are likely to see funeral processions. Walking after the hearse there may be a group of friends. Wearing black for this sad ceremony, they will have white scarves round their necks (not black, as is our customs) crepe on their hats and white trims, which they call weepers, on their sleeves. A man buried in such a manner is usually of a lower class, a good craftsman, a baker or a merchant. Another coffin will be followed by a procession of vehicles, usually rented, covered with black cloth, with people sitting in many of them. The deceased would have been a rich merchant, a financier or an important official. And following another will be a long line of magnificent carriages, whose design establishes the social standing and importance of the deceased. But these vehicles are usually empty and they accompany the burial only for ceremony. The hearse is pulled by four horses covered with black cloth, their heads adorned with black feathers.

Paying the last respects to the deceased is left wholly to a hired undertaker, as if he were his kinsman and most faithful friend. If the man had been of a noble family his coat of arms would be displayed on his house and would stay there for a considerable period of time. All this happens in appropriate silence, but that is all. There is no singing and neither speeches nor a funeral sermon. At the gates of the graveyard the minister admits the body with the words: 'I know that my Redeemer liveth.' He continues: 'And he shall descend to Earth on the last day. We brought nothing into this world and it is certain we can carry nothing out. The Lord gave and the Lord has taken away. Blessed be the name of the Lord.' In the church Psalms 39 and 9 are read and then Corinthians 1, 15 about the Resurrection. When the body is lowered into the grave the priest says: 'Man that is born of woman hath but a short time to live and is full of misery. He cometh up and is cut down like a flower. He fleeth as it were a shadow and never continueth in one stay. In the midst of life we are in death. Of whom may we seek for succour but of thee, O Lord, who for our sins art justly displeased?'

In Scotland this ceremony differs little from the English one. Friends of the deceased are invited to his house. The minister in whose parish the man lived should be there. After a short speech, which is not meant to praise the deceased but to comfort the living, they serve bread and wine. Meanwhile the coffin, which was not in the room with the guests, is carried to a hearse and the friends accompany the deceased to the graveyard; they go on foot or ride in vehicles. Only men of the family take part in the ceremony, women, who are more sensitive, stay at home. The grave is not left until it is filled and covered with sod. The minister is the last to leave. The Scottish clergy fulfil this duty without any payment, neither do they take anything for weddings and baptisms.

Graveyards in England do not have the attractive appearance which is common in France or Germany. I have never seen anything more beautiful than the graveyard in Lipsk or anything more magnificent than Père-Lachaise in Paris; Englishmen honour only great people and raise splendid memorials for them but, generally, they seem to have little veneration for the dead. Thus their graveyards are not adorned with splendid family tombs as happens elsewhere. The simplicity of their religion seems to reject surface splendour and, in some sects, even forbids it. The Christian and family name, the date of birth and death, sometimes its cause, an appropriate verse from the Bible; these are all possible inscriptions on a grave and perhaps most appropriate for a Christian for whom faith is more important than worldly glory.

Among the monuments in London it is difficult to find one that is more than twenty years old. Overcrowding reduces the area of land available for cemeteries and does not allow the dead an undisturbed place of rest. A certain Mr Gilbert wished to be buried in an iron coffin but because it would have been more enduring than a wooden one this was not allowed. Where approximately 27,000 people die every year a place to bury them is needed but it is hard to allow the dead an eternal lease of the land. Parents have to give up their own lair to their children, as if they again admitted them to the womb. If there is anywhere that you can say: 'Peace be to his ashes' when you walk away from the grave of your friend, it is not in England. Death has filled the old graveyards with its victims to such an extent that the ground had risen and there is little left of the original soil. If it were not for the thick sod which covers them it would be painful to look at the graves or even think about the people buried there.

No one is so cynical as to be indifferent about the soil which will one day cover him. Thus for centuries the most beautiful places were chosen for the graveyards. There is also a bad habit in England of burying people in the graveyard of their parish church. I suppose it is important for a man to be buried near the place where he acquired his faith but when those cemeteries lie in such a crowded capital as London, it must be that the health of the city will suffer and the graves will fill up fast.

NOTES:

1 The cemetery was on the west side of St Margaret's Chapel. It was grassed over in 1880.

2 Harpokrat or Harpocrates was rhe child of Osiris and one of the forms taken by Horus, the Egyptian sun god. Represented as a child with a finger in his mouth, the Greeks and Romans misinterpreted the symbolism and thaught he was the god of silence.

3 An extraordinary mistake. The tomb is that of Thomas Cecil, 1st Earl of Exeter, 2nd Baron Burghley (1542-1623) English soldier. He suppressed the Northern Rebellion in 1569, Essex's Rebellion in 1601 and fought in the Low Countries. His first wife was Dorothy Nevil (d. 1609). His second, Frances Brydges (d. 1649), was buried in Winchester Cathedral.

4 Thomas Cochrane, 1st Earl of Dundonald (1775-1860), Scottish naval commander and campaigner against corruption in the navy. He made £75,000 in prize money after the capture of over fifty French ships off the Azores and £10,000 on the stock exchange in 1814, after a fraudulent rumour that Napoleon had been overthrown sent prices soaring. In disgrace, he went to South America to command the Chilean and Peruvian navies in their wars to gain independence from Spain. He commanded the Brazilian navy from 1823- 25 and the Greek navy from 1827-28. In 1832 he was granted a free pardon and was buried in Westminster Abbey in 1860 .

5 Margaret Douglas, Countess of Lennox, was the daughter of Margaret Tudor, the widow of James IV, by her second husband. Her son, Henry Darnley, married Mary, Queen of Scots.

6 Richard Howe,1st Earl (1726-99), English naval commander and 1st Lord of the Admiralty. He distinguished himself in the Seven Years War and the American War of Independence and, on 'The Glorious 1st of June' 1794 defeated the French at the Battle of Ushant.

7 James Wolfe (1727-59), English military commander. His second attempt to capture Quebec by storming the Heights of Abraham was successful and led to the eviction of France from Canada.

8 William Congreve (1650-1729), English dramatist and poet. A comedian and a satirist, he is best remembered for *Love for Love* and *The Way of the World*.

9 Henry Grattan MP (1746-1820), Irish statesman. One of the leaders of the struggle for Irish independence, he secured the abolition of claims by the Westminster parliament to legislate for Ireland in 1782 but failed to prevent the Act of Union of 1800. He sat in the united parliament till his death.

10 William Murray MP, 1st Earl of Mansfield (1705-93), Scottish judge. Chief Justice of the King's Bench, he made important contributions to mercantile, insurance and international law.

11 George Stepney (1663-1767), English diplomat and poet.

12 Pasquale de Paoli (1725-1807), Corsican patriot and commander of the struggle for independence from the Genoese. A friend of James Boswell, he escaped to England when the island was sold to the French, returning as governor in 1790.

13 Thomas Gray (1716-71), English poet. An early romantic, he studied

Icelandic and Celtic poetry. He is remembered for his *Elegy Written in a Country Churchyard.*

14 Sir William D'Avenant (1606-68), English poet and playwright. In 1638 he succeeded Ben Jonson as poet laureate His *Siege of Rhodes* (1648) is considered to be the first English opera. He opened a theatre, 'The Cockpit', two years later.

15 Oliver Goldsmith (1722-74), Irish novelist, playwright and poet. A gambler, he made several false starts before starting his literary career as editor and founder of *The Bee, The Vicar of Wakefield, the Deserted Village* and *She Stoops to Conquer* followed. The memorial in the Abbey was paid for by members of the Literary Club of which he had been a founder.

16 Abraham Cowley (1616-67), English poet. His epic poem *Davideis* was published before the Civil War when he followed Henrietta Maria into exile and became her secretary.

17 Samuel Butler (1612-80), English satirist. *Hudibras*, a burlesque satire on Puritanism, was published after the Restoration. He died in poverty.

18 John Gay (1685-1732), English poet and playwright. *The Beggar's Opera* was inspired by Swift and set to music by the German composer Pepusch (1667-1725).

19 Matthew Prior (1664-1721), English poet and diplomat. A Tory under Queen Anne, he was imprisoned for two years for his share in negotiating the unpopular Treaty of Utrcht in 1713. His poetry was witty but slight.

20 John Campbell, 2nd Duke of Argyll (1678-1743), Scottish politician and soldier. A supporter of the Act of Union, he commanded the Hanoverian troops during the Jacobite Rising of 1715 and fought with distinction in the War of the Spanish Succession. He was the main agent of government control over Scotland after the Union.

21 See Chapter 18, note 11.

22 Isaac Casaubon (1559-1614), French scholar and humanist. Born in Geneva, he held chairs in Greek in universities in Switzerland and France. He moved to England when persecution of Huguenots started after the death of Henry IV in 1610.

23 John Ernst Grabius (1666-1741), German Protestant writer.

24 Thomas Parr (c. 1483-1635), English farm servant. He died in his 152nd year after being feted at the court of Charles I. His biography was written by John Taylon (1580-1653), the Water Poet.

25 Mark Akenside (1721-70), English poet and physician. His *Pleasures of Imagination* was published in 1744. Appointed a physician to the Queen, his haughty and pedantic manner was cariacatured by *Smollet in The Adventures of Peregrine Pickle.*

26 Thomas Otway (1652-85). An English dramatist, he translated Racine's *Berenice* and Moliere's *Cheats of Scapin*. His own best known work is *Venice Preserved, or a Plot Discovered.*

27 John Fletcher (1579-1625), English dramatist. He collaborated with Beaumont and, to a lesser extent, with Massinger, Rowley and Shakespeare. His best known plays are *The Faithful Shepherdess, The Humorous Lieutenant*,and *Rule a Wife and Have a Wife.*

28 Philip Massinger (1583-1640), English dramatist. *The City Madam* and *A New Way to Pay Old Debts* are satirical comedies.
29 Roger Bacon (1214-92), English philosopher and scientist. His interests extended to alchemy and earned him the title 'De mirabilis.' A Franciscan, his belief in the importance of esperimental and mathematical proof led to his imprisonment by the Order. He was buried in Oxford.
30 John Locke (1632-1704), English philosopher and physician. A Fellow of the Royal Society, his *Two Treatises of Government* challenged Hobbes' assertion of the theories of Absolutism and Divine Right. He was buried in High Laver, Essex.
31 Alfred the Great (849-99), Anglo-Saxon King of Wessex. His successful resistance to the Vikings led to the creation of the Danelaw and, a century later, to the unification of England. He was buried in Winchester.
32 John Milton (1608-74), English poet and politician. *Paradise Lost* was published in 1667, after the Restoration. A founder Fellow of the Royal Society, he was Latin secretary to the Council of State during the Commonwealth.

Chapter Twenty-One

Famous People. John Bowring. Lord Erskine. Cartwright. The Reverend Fox. Robert Owen. William Allen. The Settlement for the Poor. Elizabeth Fry. The Quakers.

In the preceding two chapters we have taken a closer look at the tombs and monuments of prominent people; in this one we shall turn our attention to the living people who contribute to the present greatness of the nation. The distinguished people of Britain are easy to recognise because, having been entrusted with state affairs, their lives are public rather than private and their thoughts and deeds are the subject of conversation throughout the country. By articles in the newspapers and other journals they become common property. This sort of familiarity with their ideas had made me almost uninterested in meeting them, despite the frequent and convenient opportunities to do so which presented themselves. In what way would the reader benefit had I started to describe the blond or dark hair, the lively, dazzling eyes and the stature of some prominent person. What can be stated for certain about famous men after a casual encounter? What can be stated after a brief conversation which might present them in a most unfavourable light? It is not unlikely that they might experience what once happened to the famous Hume upon his arrival in Paris. At a magnificent dinner he found himself unable to say anything either witty or even sensible. The distinguished guests who had gathered to honour him started to smile and exchange knowing looks. I am not sure what the effect would have been on the reputation of this great historian and philosopher if it had not been for the help of a Paris humorist who addressed his disappointed compatriots: 'C'est que M. Hume a fourré tout son esprit dans ses livres.'

To get a true impression of great people one needs to observe them from a distance and form judgements by criteria which are specific to them. Brief reminiscences from a journey should be set in the context of the literature and morality of the nation. One might mention Coleridge, an authentic poetical genius and a philosopher who was the first to acquaint his compatriots with the ideas of

German philosophy; Campbell,[1] author of the poem *The Pleasures of Hope,* one of the first poets to combine a taste for the ancient with the energy of the romantic school. He wrote a history of English literature and is now a professor of literature at the University of London. Hazlitt combines originality of literary judgement with rare sensitivity, and there are Shelley, Lamb, Croly,[2] Wiffen,[3] all poets, and Irving,[4] a preacher. Mention should also be made of Bentham, who has clarified the area of constitutional legislation, Doctor Lyell,[5] who was then publishing his *A Journey to Russia*, and Blaquiere,[6] a known Philhellenist, who had travelled to Greece several times and was writing about the contemporary condition of the Greeks and is now fighting for their independence. I have met a few of them personally but, as I have already said, the reader would gain nothing from a superficial description. I will mention only those who may be of interest to the reader due to their specific character or through their link to the history or needs of his country.

Among the figures connected to the history of our own literature is John Bowring,[7] an author of several original and translated writings in verse and prose, to whom the Slavonic people owe gratitude. He was the first to turn the attention of his compatriots to education in Slavonic countries in this century and to Slavonic poetry. First, he published an English translation of *The Russian Anthology*, with a short description of the lives of the finest of the Russian poets. For this work he was honoured by the late Tsar Alexander with the gift of a precious ring. Recognition by his Majesty must have encouraged him to undertake a similar translation of Polish literature, whose fame had been revived under the protective sceptre of the monarch. He worked in London and published under the title: *Specimens of the Polish Poets*. Bowring speaks several modern languages, which is rare among the English who dislike learning foreign languages. He speaks fluent Spanish, French, and German, others he understands. He has travelled a lot and has developed a particular love for Slavonic culture. He has recently published some Serbian songs and at the moment is said to be working on the poetry of the Czech language and to have started corresponding with Czech scholars. He is about thirty six years old. He was the secretary of a committee established for the purpose of

Lord Erskine (1750-1823) Born in Edinburgh, Thomas, Ist Baron Erskine was called to the Bar in 1778. He joined 'The Friends of the People' and was a brilliant defender of those who sympathised with the ideals of the French Revolution. Lach-Szyrma seems to have had little contact with the English aristocracy but reached London armed with introductions to people of the calibre of Erskine.

supporting the Greeks and was involved in the supervision of the Greek youths who were receiving their education in England.

It was at a dinner in his house that I met Lord Erskine[8] who had been Lord Chancellor during Fox's term in office and who, due to his eloquence in court, was called the Eagle of the English Bar. The English apply to him Shakespeare's lines:

> Turn him to any cause of policy,
> the Gordian knot of it he will unloose
> familiar as his garter that, when he speaks,
> the air, a charter'd libertine, is still
> and the mute wonder lurketh in men's ears,
> to steal his sweet and honey'd sentences.

He is a native of Scotland, the cradle of great people. In his youth he had served in the army and in the navy but, having grown weary of this occupation, he entered the legal profession and, in 1778, became a barrister. Due to his extraordinary talents he was soon appointed Attorney General and finally Lord Chancellor. He was short and slim; at the time he could have been seventy years old but he was vigorous and seemed younger than in fact he was. He received no deferential treatment in Mr. Bowring's house apart from normal politeness. One could tell that both in public as well as in his private life he behaved with the utmost simplicity. He wore a black tailcoat like the other guests and there was nothing unusual about him. No one could have told that he was such a high official of state. He did not even have his own carriage. As the company slowly started to leave and everyone was wondering how to get from Hackney, where Mr Bowring lived, to London, he and his son, together with other guests, went by stage coach. Since its route and stops were predetermined it did not take him to his house but let him off with several other passengers, including myself, in the middle of a street. He continued on foot and, as I happened to be going in the same direction, I accompanied him for a while. In the end, according to the native custom, we shook hands and he left me thinking about the extent to which superficial pomp can be renounced by the truly great who do not need it. This distinguished man died the next year and, as is often the case with the highest state officials in this country, I do not know whether the family could afford the expenses of the funeral.

It was at a dinner in Mr G.'s house that I met Major Cartwright,[9] well known for his specific political and moral views. At the time he was an elderly man of eighty years of age and, as I was introduced to him as a Pole, he took me kindly by the hand and asked whether people in Poland still remember Kociuszko.[10] The tone of his voice suggested that he believed that such things were easily forgotten in our country. I told him that in order to commemorate him a mound of stones, modelled on the graves of the ancients, had been erected. I attempted to describe its shape, since the British are unfamiliar with this kind of monument. He was glad to hear this. He told me that he had met Kociuszko during the latter's stay in England.

When around ten o'clock the guests started to leave, he asked me where I lived and, as this was nearby, he offered me a lift with him and his wife in their carriage. Having arrived, I gladly accepted the invitation to visit them since I particularly wanted to see this man in his home. The house was furnished in the wealthiest possible English manner, although the demagogue was famous for his hatred of riches. Similarly, he loathed the high offices which, due to his talents, were offered to him at various stages of his life. His revolutionary ideas about parliamentary reform, which were second only to the payment of the national debt as the problem the English would have to cudgel their brains upon, were considered by Fox to be impossible to carry out. This gave Cartwright reason to doubt the sincerity of the intentions of this liberal minister and he came to view him with utter disgust. Among the reported peculiarities of his behaviour, for the most part made up by his enemies, many revealed some of the most praiseworthy features of his character. During the war with America he did not want to use information obtained from others which might have made him quite a fortune. He did this on the principle that equal access to information is the essential basis of personal agreements. Retention of a secret by one party brings about unequal conditions and to obtain profit in a contract by withholding information he considered to be fraudulent. As an example of his humanity, I would mention his dismissal of a servant who had watched the hanging of a criminal. He wished to assert that he could not live in the same house as a man who took pleasure in observing the death of his neighbour. He used to say that all that was good in the English constitution came from the Anglo-Saxons and all that was bad from the Normans, whom he simply called bandits. I met many who shared his opinion. I have learned from journals that he died in 1825. An account of his life was written by his daughter.

In the same circumstances I met a minister of the Unitarian sect named Fox.[11] Once he learned I came from Poland he enquired about the state and condition of his co-religionists in our country. I have heard several times that a belief persists in England that there are many Socinian[12] communities in Poland. They are misled by the numerous works that were printed in Raków in the seventeenth century, which

Robert Owen. A Welshman, not a Scot, Owen sold his shares in the model factory at New Lanark shortly after his meetings with Lach-Szyrma in London. He devoted the rest of his life to the Trade Union and Co-operative movements.

include the great volumes of the Polish Socinian community's library. The Reverend Fox was surprised when I told him that this sect no longer existed in our country and that out of all dissenting beliefs this one was subject to the greatest persecutions, its followers having been deprived of civil rights and banned from the country.

In the house of Mr A.[13] I had the opportunity of meeting Robert Owen,[14] whose exemplary factory and educational institution in Lanark have been mentioned in the *Reminiscences* of my stay in Scotland. I have spent many pleasant moments conversing with him about how people's lives might be made happier. He had the honour of presenting to Tsar Alexander his ideas in this matter, but they would be impossible to implement without significant changes because of their revolutionary nature. In Owen's opinion, centuries of barbarism and the power of the rich have turned humanity from the roads it was meant to follow. Starting from the principle that all men are equal, he believes that everyone should be given equal chances to increase their own and other people's happiness. The possession of greater opportunities by one class of people must be causing harm to others. He thinks that governments should divide the people into communities composed of seven or eight hundred families, for greater communities are more prone to corruption and more difficult to organise. Any government could arrange such communities and the form of government does not really matter. Each community would live in separate buildings – parallelograms he called them – and for easier communication they would be alongside each other. Each would have its own farmers, craftsmen, tradesmen, church and schools so as to be entirely self-sufficient. The produce and all profits would be common property and this would be increased by an appropriate division of labour and the use of machines. Only in this way could greed and theft be prevented, for no one would either desire or steal what was their own. The seeds of many crimes would be rooted out and poverty and penury would be eliminated. A Dunkard Christian sect is said to live in this way in Georgia.

As for the punishments for theft in England, Owen, like Thomas More, thinks their severity is neither just nor fair, for robbery, even the greatest, is not a crime which merits the death penalty. The fear of punishment, however severe, cannot prevent theft by those who have no way of earning a living. England, like many other countries, imitates the bad school teachers who, instead of educating, flog their pupils. Instead of making strict laws, it would be better to think of some measures which would prevent crime.

In an industrialised country, where the division of people into communes would prove impossible, Mr Owen has other plans. He suggested devising work houses, a fixed wage for a job, introduction of moderate food prices and, finally, providing them with an appropriate education that would eradicate false ideas. He believed that one should not give prizes at schools to encourage children to learn, not to mention financial rewards. The spirit of emulation fostered by the pedagogues only kills the purer motives. Like the finest of scientists they should not work to outdo each other but only for love of truth and learning. He advises the teachers to be kind and even friendly to their pupils, to have their trust and to excite their curiosity by presenting new ideas and stimulating questions. There should be the maximum of freedom as long as order is maintained. All elementary subjects should be taught, integrated with dancing, singing and practical exercises. The study of languages he considered unnecessary for workers. Girls, he believed, should also learn needlework, sewing, making stockings and embroidery. As Mr Owen told me, most difficulties were encountered with teaching reading either because of the obstacles connected to the English language, with its words written one way and pronounced the other, or because of the lack of elementary books which accorded with his system. In counting they adhere to the method of Pestalozzi[15] and they pay particular attention to the teaching of mental arithmetic. Mr Owen is so convinced of the positive influence of education on human happiness that he finds it needless to refute the accusations of those who see its propagation as a threat. He adheres strongly to his views, and, although his projects seem alarming due to their originality, he speaks of their beneficial character with such absolute certainty that once, as he was enumerating the benefits they might possibly bring, he

New Lanark School. By 1800 there were 2,000 workers in the mills. Children attending school at the end of a 12 hour working day were given lessons in singing and dancing as well as reading and writing. Owen's great reform was to stop employing children under the age of ten and to provide schooling for five to ten year olds.

added with great ardour that, if four or five thousand people agreed to implement his plans, in less than two decades Europe would see changes which even Napoleon with all his power would not have been able to introduce.

In a country like England, with a complex society in which so many immemorial laws and customs intertwine and obstruct the implementing of new ones, Mr Owen had to encounter numerous insurmountable obstacles. However, his persistence sowed the seed of many improvements. The first was the creation of societies which tackle poverty among craftsmen; the second the opening of schools for the poor, although with modifications of his plans which have been necessary in order to win people's support. Teaching the established religion was introduced in them despite Owen's conviction that the mysteries of faith should be left to students of a more mature age. The very perception of these matters from a new perspective has led to many useful improvements.

However, Owen did not confine his reforming zeal to his homeland. He has visited America, wishing to develop his ideas in the new world. His fame went before him. The President of the United States and important state officials received him with great respect and, when he was to hold a lecture in the church of a county town, the enthusiasm was so great, and so much importance was given to his ideas, that the courts suspended their sessions. A settlement called Harmony, which he founded at his own cost, was the first attempt to implement his plans. At the moment (1828) he is in Mexico, where he is being received with similar enthusiasm by the government authorities.

Mr Owen is of middle height and slim, with an oval face and swarthy complexion. He may now be some forty-eight years old. He is neither very lively nor very serious. He does not express himself with ease and he speaks with a slightly Scottish accent since he is a native of Scotland. Starting as an apprentice in a cotton factory, he made a fortune through his own efforts and high intelligence and increased this by marriage. He uses this for the benefit of humanity, undeterred by difficulties and adversity. Inspired by the hope that one day his projects will be successful, he seems to live and breathe for them. He is eager to explain his principles to everyone and listens to any criticisms willingly, as he believes it is only through discussion that he can make his plans clear. He depends entirely on principles; they are the stronghold from which he attacks his adversaries and defends himself. In a country where everything is subject to strict analysis and investigation one can base and defend one's reasoning only on principles. It is the only way to gain trust; timidity is unacceptable. Speaking in Parliament the best orators and even the ministers refer to their principles, thus winning trust and convincing the audience of their honesty.

One day I was invited to dinner by William Allen, a Quaker, at his country house in Newington near London. My readers are sure to know to what extent the adherents of his sect differ from others. The invitation was in their customary form. 'Come to me, if you like' – said Allen – 'on Saturday to Newington. Here is a card with the house number on it. I am a simple man and you shall have a homely dinner with me and my family. We eat at four o'clock.' I came at the set time and found no difference between the said simple dinner and the dinners in other wealthy English homes. But there were fewer decanters on the table and no drinking of anyone's health. This is a custom that is not observed by the Quakers both because of the modesty of their life and to avoid the worldly habits which are contrary to the rules of their religion. I found a few 'Friends' (this is what they call themselves) already present. All of them wore their everyday clothes; men wore old fashioned coffee-coloured tail coats; women wore black dresses with wide sleeves, a wide white scarf on their necks and smooth, white batiste bonnets without any embroidery or embellishment on their heads. They spoke little, for simplicity, submissiveness and humbleness are the rules of this sect. Also present at the dinner was Mr Schmidt from Wirtemberg, who was travelling at the expense of his government and was at the time on his way back from America. After dinner, which was shorter than is usual because there was no prolonged conversation over the wine, we followed our host to his library. It was quite substantial and consisted mainly of books on chemistry, physics, mechanics and crafts because, according to the rules of the sect, scientific and all other work should be aimed at usefulness. If the fine arts, painting, music and poetry were left to the Quakers, they would remain uncultivated. Whatever William Allen did, it could be characterised as useful. What we found interesting in his collection was a hand mill which ground flour, not with the help of a stone but of two rotating barrels. The mill was not expensive and it would be helpful everywhere for domestic use; it was set in motion with a crank. Inappropriate for the adherent of such a strict religion was the observatory which, for a private workshop, was well equipped with all the instruments necessary for observation. But William Allen is very fond of the sciences; he believes that they are interlinked and support each other and so he embraces them all. He is known as a skilled chemist and has a large laboratory where he prepares medicinal ingredients. He had travelled all over Europe, visited Russia and was in Tsar Alexander's good graces. In London he had been in charge of Lancaster's[16] schools, their founder also being a Quaker, and he was pleased to hear from me (for such honest people are glad to hear about good things) that we had schools organised according to Lancaster's method in our country. As I was unable to provide him with more detailed information he asked me to send him a report on their state. Does this sound like the egoism of which the English are usually accused? If we are to assess the relative selfishness of nations, should we not take into account the number of their charitable institutions which are the best evidence of humanitarian action? Is there a place with a greater number and variety of such institutions than England? Which nation could immediately point to people who sacrifice themselves for the good of their neighbours with such eagerness as Mrs Fry, Owen and Allen, let alone the many philanthropists who had preceded them and those of their contemporaries who make up the unbroken humanitarian chain?. If there are charity institutions elsewhere, are they not modelled on the English ones and was England not the country where the first ideas and incentives originated? Accusations aimed at the egoism of the English nation are unjustifiable.

In Newington we visited an early settlement for the poor with William Allen. The houses which were being built all had three acres of land which, according to their calculations, was sufficient to maintain a poor family with four children and to pay a small rent. The aim of this institution is to prevent the poverty of many families who, being unable to find work, are yet unwilling to register as poor, so becoming a burden on the country. The institution owes its existence to the Society of Friends, the Quakers, whose religion is known for its eagerness to support the needy and alleviate all human suffering. Allen was entrusted with the supervision and accomplishment of this plan. Similar settlements have been erected in Fredriksoord in the Netherlands and in the Kingdom of Wirtemberg. In the latter country settlers are given land free for ten years and only then are they obliged to pay a rent. How beneficial would that prove in diminishing the poor and unemployed in our country?

A few days later, on 12 December 1823, I spent two days at Plashet House, Mrs Fry's country home. I mentioned her before in connection with her noble work for the benefit of the public; here I was to be a witness to her home life. Mrs Fry, who might be called an apostle of prisons, is a Quaker and the wife of a wealthy London banker. She is tall, with a strong but gentle face. Her grey eyes and fair hair suggest a Saxon origin. However, the origins of her ancestors would bring her no respect from the Quakers. They do not allow pride in their antecedents and she adhered strictly to the rules of her religion. She would set out on her charitable visits in the company of a few of her Quaker friends. With their clothing and peaceful conduct they resemble nuns and among them Mrs Fry, with her tall figure and winsome sweetness, seems like a prioress.

The houses of Quakers, as far as I could judge from Elisabeth Fry's, William Allen's and some other houses I happened to have been to, do not differ much from other private houses. These wealthy people have the same amenities and furnishings, only with less superficial splendour. Life in them is orderly, simple and gentle. All this was true of Mrs Fry's house. Children, of whom she apparently had eleven, the servants and Mr and Mrs Fry all used familiar forms of address. They referred to me in the same way, which made me feel as if I were an old acquaintance of theirs and almost a member of their patriarchal family. All in all, this unusual way of speaking in England, where even servants are addressed as 'you', is observed only by the Quakers to stress friendly equality among them. It is quite specific and uncomfortable in conversation, in particular with people whom one respects. I experienced it personally each time I had to address Mrs. Fry; it was unthinkable for me to say to her 'Elizabeth' instead of 'you', 'Elizabeth Fry'; instead of 'Mrs Fry', although the first manner of address seemed more appropriate to her and in accordance with the high dignity of this honourable matron. Neither could I start addressing the others without adding 'Mr' or 'Mrs' It was only the little ones in the family that I called by their Christian names. Clearly, I could not immediately become a Quaker.

Since Mrs Fry's preoccupation at that time was prison reform, this was her main topic of conversation. She enquired about the kinds of crimes committed most often in our country, about their causes, about the level of education among the common people and about the number of country schools. She believed that without education there can be neither knowledge nor love of duty and that education is indispensable in diminishing crime. Thus, they were increasing the number of schools simply to decrease the number of criminals. The positive results achieved in this way can be seen among the Quakers; there are no vagrants, thieves or beggars among them and a Quaker-bandit is something unheard of.

The number of followers of this sect in England is said to be 70,000 and in the United States of America up to 400,000 It was founded in the mid seventeenth century by Fox,[17] a shoemaker's apprentice. When he was summoned to court for spreading his religious opinions which, in those intolerant times was dangerous, he started his bold speech to the judges with the word: 'Quake!' This is said to have awakened laughter and to be the origin of the name of his followers, the Quakers. Others believe they derive their name from the convulsions they would fall into in moments of spiritual exultation. This, however, does not seem to be true, since I did not see any sudden movements when I observed their religious practices. On the contrary, they conducted their services with exemplary tranquillity. They call themselves the Christian Society of Friends. The only basis for their religious and moral teachings is the Bible, in which they believe literally, rejecting any interpretation or explanation. They do not depart from the principle that every man who sincerely wishes to enter a relationship with God may do so. This they believe is possible thanks to seeds sown in the human soul. They have no ministers and meet together in churches which have neither altar nor pulpit nor any paintings. They sit in silence on simple benches, their heads covered, waiting for the Holy Spirit to move someone among them to speak. Someone who feels the presence of the Spirit indicates this with a loud sigh and, when everybody is standing, he or she tells them the words which have been revealed. The belief that women may also have this experience is validated by the testimonies in the Old and New Testaments to women who had the gift of prophecy. These include Miriam, Deborah, Huldah and Anna. Others, like Phoebe, Priscilla, Aquila and Persis, rendered apostolic services in the early Church and the apostles address them as servants and sisters in Christ. The Catholic Church, in accordance with the spirit of the Holy Scriptures, preserved their memory as nuns. For these important reasons the Quakers do not exclude women from participating in their services.

One Sunday I happened to witness the performing of ministerial duties by a woman. Breaking the total silence, as everyone was immersed in reflection, a voice coming from deep within someone's chest could be heard. I believe that someone fainted. A young woman stood up and said a few pious words in a slow and sad voice, admonishing the congregation in a gentle manner to trust in God's grace, to persist in the love of one's neighbour and to do good to others. I did not hear the rest for the preacher had a very quiet voice. Then she sat down, as did everyone else, and once again everybody remained silent. Sometimes a few people, both men and women, speak one after another but this happens extremely rarely. Usually no one speaks and, as they came to church in silence, they remain silent and depart in silence. One could imagine them as the apprentices of Pythagoras who cannot speak until they have passed the test of silence. The inner feeling of prayer, the prayer of the heart, is sufficient for their religion. They call it the inner light and they compare its power to that experienced by the apostles. They concentrate on it and do not practice any church rites. They have neither baptism nor communion, nor is there any singing in their churches, nor music or bell ringing. They bury their dead without any ceremony or funeral speeches and they erect no memorials.

The stringent character of some of their rules may conflict with social order but measures have been taken to prevent the resultant absurdities. For instance, Quakers must not swear or take an oath but another rule of their sect forbids them to lie. Thus, where the representatives of other confessions are required to take an oath, in the case of a Quaker it is sufficient to make a statement. Their religion forbids paying taxes but at the same time it forbids putting up resistance, so when taxes are payable the taxman seals their shops and wares and seizes the movables. A Quaker knows what this means and buys himself out without resisting. They do not serve in the army but purchase their exemption from duty from the government, for they hold war as contradictory to the love of one's neighbour. They were also one of the first Christian denominations to establish a state in America without shedding any blood. The Europeans were not oppressors, nor were Americans slaves,and it remained peaceful and happy until they were corrupted by outside influences. I am talking of Pennsylvania which was named by the Quaker Penn,[18] its founder and legislator.

Despite the ridicule aroused by some of the customs of this sect, there is no doubt that the moral character of its adherents is outstanding. They may be characterised as diligent, orderly, thrifty and honest. Anyone unfamiliar with current prices should go to Quakers' shops and be sure he will not be cheated, for their prices are fixed. What is attractive in their actions is their simplicity, a reliable sign of their honesty, their manner of speaking, which is unsophisticated and open, and their home life which is full of family virtues, clarity of morals and reciprocity of attachment. Above all, they win people's respect through their love of humanity and philanthropic activity in the founding of schools, charity homes and hospitals. In these anyone who is in need, regardless of their faith, is accepted. They prevent vagrancy and homelessness by training their young from their early years to work and by teaching them only subjects and skills which will be of use. They work in crafts and in trade. From the sciences they cultivate only the arts of medicine, pharmacy and chemistry. Musicians, dancers and painters are not revered by them and they never hunt, go to balls or to the theatre. There are no suicides among them, for only idle people get bored with life and therefore cut it short; active people never have enough time and for them – life is too short. Criminals in their sect are only admonished: if they do not reform they are excluded from the society by a simple statement that from now on they cease to be members of the Society of Friends. However, everything that was considered too outlandish in their character is slowly disappearing, only the main rules, whose basis is good, remain. The elders view with disapproval this departure from former strictness and expect it to lead to a future decrease in the number of the sect's adherents and its ultimate fall. The strict ones are called dry Quakers, the less strict the wet Quakers. Particular issues concerning their community, such as marriages, educational institutions or hospitals, are settled at the monthly and quarterly meetings. Issues concerning the overall organisation of the entire Society are settled at the main meeting, which takes place annually at a set time in the seven provinces into which the Quakers are divided. The European Quakers meet in London.

NOTES:

1 Thomas Campbell (1777-1844), Scottish poet and journalist.

2 George Croly (1780-1860), Irish poet and rector of St Stephen's Church, Walbrook. His best known work is *Salathiel*, a poem based on the legend of the wandering Jew.

3 Jeremiah Holmes Wiffen (1792-1836).

4 See Chapter 19, note 13.

5 Sir Charles Lyell (1797-1875), Scottish geologist, who became Professor of Geology at University College, London.

6 Edward Blaquiere (1779-1832), whose *Narative of a Second Visit to Greece, including Facts Connected with the Last Days of Lord Byron* was published in 1825.

7 Sir John Bowering (1792-1872), British diplomat, linguist and friend of Jeremy Bentham. He was reputed to have some understanding of 200 languages.

8 Thomas Erskine 1st baron (1756-1823). A Scottish jurist and MP, he was famed for his defence of political radicals and his sympathy with the ideals of the French revolutionaries.

9 Major John Cartwright (1746-1834), English reformer, the brother of the Rev Edward Cartwright, inventor of the power loom. Known as 'the Father of Reform', he advocated the abolition of slavery. His ideas on parliamentary reform were adopted by the Chartists.

10 Taduez Ko ciuszko (1746-1817), Polish patriot and soldier. Trained in France, he became a brilliant commander and fought for the colonists in the American War of Independence. He was commander-in-chief of the armies resisting Russia's 2nd and 3rd Partitions of Poland He visited England in 1796 and died in Switzerland when his horse fell over a cliff.

11 William Johnson Fox (1786-1864) English orator and political writer, his sermons from the pulpit of the Unitarian chapel at Finsbury aroused public support for the Anti-Corn Law League and the movement for free trade.

12 The Socinian sect was founded by the Italian Protestant reformers Laelius (1525-62) and Faustus (1539-1604) Socinus. Their Unitarian doctrine tried to reconcile Christianity with humanism.

13 Aytoun of Muiriston was a Writer to the Signet and one of the Scottish friends with whom Lach-Szyrma had frequently stayed during the two years he had spent in Scotland.

14 Robert Owen (1771-1858), Welsh industrialist, educationist and social reformer. In 1799 he bought the cotton mill at New Lanark from his father-in-law David Dale and, continuing Dale's work, made it a model industrial community. The Institute for the Formation of Character included the first nursery school and playground for children, and evening classes for employees, to be provided by the owners of a factory.

15 Juhann Heinrich Pestalozzi (1746-1827), Swiss educationist and idealist. Devoted to the education of the poor and believing in the moralising virtues of agricultural occupations, he set up schools in rural environments. Most of these failed through incompetent management but the principles he developed in *How Gertrude Educated her Child* were supported by the Swiss government.

16 Joseph Lancaster (1772-1833), English educationist. He introduced the monitorial system into interdominational schools in London in 1798 and founded the Royal Lancastrian Society. This became the British and Foreign Bible Society. In1818 he went to the USA where he lectured and founded several schools.

17 George Fox (1624-91), English religious leader and founder of the Society of Friends. His rebellion against the social conventions and the formalism of the church attracted thousands of followers, many of whom were imprisoned. He preached throughout the British Isles, Germany, Holland, Jamaica, Barbados and the American colonies.

18 William Penn (1644-1718), English reformer and colonialist. The son of Admiral Sir William Penn, in honour of whom the colony was named, Penn sailed with his persecuted co-religionists to found a colony on land granted in lieu of payments due to his father. The model constitution he drew up recognised the rights of the native Indians and any behaviour not considered wicked by puritan standards was tolerated.

Chapter Twenty-Two

Education. Bell's and Lancaster's Method. The Model School. Infant Schools. The need to Educate Common People. Higher Education. Academies. Universities. Comments on the Approach to Teaching.

In the preceding chapter and in other places in my reminiscences I introduced the reader to some prominent people, alive and dead. It would be appropriate to add a few words about education, which is the only way of achieving and guaranteeing the greatness of both an individual and an entire nation. Natural disposition may be more equally allocated among people than it seems to be, for there is no doubt that the best land left unploughed and without sowing yields nothing but weeds. To learn about the education of a nation is to know the basis of its present and the bud of its future power. It is where the present and the future combine in an inseparable relation of cause and effect.

Thinkers who have reflected on education in England have divided it into physical and moral. There could be no fairer division; it is in these two areas that the hopes for the well-being of future generations are developed. Infants remain under the tender care of mothers who have the praiseworthy habit of feeding their children themselves; exceptions from this motherly love are rare. Further development of physical strength is left, more than elsewhere, to the forces of nature without the help of books or restricting systems which are an unbearable yoke for a child born to be free. England is also quite poor in theories of education but rich in the strength of its citizens' constitutions. Despite the severity of the climate an old man, the tenth part of Methuselah's age, is not a rare sight and, in Scotland, a ninety-year-old man calls his sixty-year old son 'his boy'. In the upper classes, despite dissolute habits and an irregular lifestyle, old age is not rare. The health of the parents lays the foundation for their children's health. It is strengthened by the clean strong air and by the emphasis on physical rather than intellectual exercise in the early years. This continues in later years. They start to teach children quite late, that is, not before the age of seven, and any earlier teach-

Christ's Hospital. In what had been the cloisters of the Greyfriar's priory a school for 300 boys, 'The children of poor distressed men and poor distressed women', was founded by Alderman Sir John Moor. John Shaw's Tudor building was restored by Wren after the Fire. By the nineteenth century the school had become so fashionable that its governors were selling places for £30 a head and the notice 'This is Christ's Hospital where Blue Coat Boys are harboured and educated' was removed.

ing is done in an easy way, more in the form of entertainment than as serious study.

School education may be divided into elementary and secondary. One receives the first in Bell's[1] or Lancaster's schools and then in grammar schools; higher education is offered at universities. The method of teaching in groups accelerates learning and makes education less costly but there are still schools which have not substituted the new method for the old, for the English are not eager to pursue novelty. The most obvious proof of this is at the universities of Oxford and Cambridge, which continue in the very form they had taken in the Middle Ages. None of the changes in government nor those in the Church have managed to cause any alterations in these seats of the ancient Muses. If it were not for the modern and up-to-date state of the Scottish universities, and if higher education depended solely on them, sciences in England would be pervaded by obsolete scholasticism. But let us first take a closer look at the lower schools.

Almost all of them without exception organise teaching by the methods of Bell and Lancaster, which are, in fact, the same method introduced simultaneously by Bell and Lancaster, so that nobody knows who was its inventor. They differ solely in religious teaching. This is taught by Bell according to the Catechism of the Anglican Church and by Lancaster by the use of appropriate passages from the Bible. The latter, who was a Quaker and taught Quakers, would not allow the teaching of a strange Catechism and, having introduced Bible teaching into the school, made it accessible to the young of all confessions. Due to the greater number of students using it, the practice of group teaching was named Lancaster's method and under this name it spread all over Europe.

Out of curiosity I visited one of the schools in London in which teachers were trained to use this method which was regarded as excellent. It was in Borough Road. Its government and supervision were in the hands of the British and Foreign School Society, whose influence also embraces foreign countries. Thus, in addition to the English, I encountered Germans, Jews and Greeks. I asked the teacher which of them, in his opinion, revealed the greatest aptitude. He responded that the Greeks excelled in clarity of apprehension, the Jews in arithmetic, for which they seemed to have an additional faculty, and that the English and Germans were remarkable for morality and thrift rather than any extraordinary clarity of thought. Both boys and girls were accepted into the schools. They were taught in identical halls, which were rectangular, high and spacious and all able to accommodate 1,000 students. At that time there were 700 boys and slightly fewer girls. The benches were placed in the middle and at one end of the hall there was a platform resembling a balcony. From this position the teacher could see all the students. To prevent the voice from resounding in these lofty and spacious halls a green cloth was hung at some distance below the ceiling. On the walls there were blackboards on which excerpts from the Bible were written. Each bench accommodated seventeen children and had a monitor who supervised study and kept order. The students sat in the lower or higher benches according to their level of achievement, the beginners being closest to the teacher. The girls' school remains under the supervision of a guardian who is also their teacher. In addition to reading, writing and arithmetic they are taught needlework and, as in other subjects, there are several levels. The girls learn hemming, quilting, marking and embroidering and nothing is missed out. This method does not tolerate change so little or nothing has been changed in it since its creation. It is confined to teaching basic things like reading, writing and arithmetic. Thus its value lies not in the study itself but in the inculcation of system and order by the quickest method possible, for the poor have neither money nor time to spend on learning. In this respect the school resembled a handicraft workshop, with the master controlling all the actions of the apprentices. Everything proceeded at the teacher's signal with the precision and character of military drill. At his command books were taken up, opened and read; boards were wiped, slate pencil lifted, numbers written and equations checked – all to a regular rhythm. There were even commands for leaving school: a sign was given for the pupils to get up, tie up their books, lift their hats, put them on, leave the benches, stand in pairs and finally to go out by the door. There was even a drill for how to grasp each thing, whether with one hand or with both, how to lift it up and how to put it down. These details, though small and at first sight unnecessary, are of priceless value: they teach skilfulness, obedience, and concentration, the mother of thrift and discovery. They also prevent the loss of time when teaching, as well as many other difficulties which it would be hard to avoid with such a large number of students. Pupils become accustomed to order, which is absolutely necessary for everyone, especially in a trading and industrial country. A tradesman needs it in his shop and at the till, a craftsman needs it in supervising his workshop and machines, a helmsman needs it at the helm where the smallest negligence or omission could cause irreparable loss of life or property. To meet these needs the introduction of this method is more important than knowledge itself. This could be gained and mental faculties developed by more efficient and less mechanical means, but there is no better method for the education of the common people. This requires more practice than theory; unlike the methods of such pedagogues as

Pestalozzi, Rousseau,[2] Niemayer,[3] and others of their kind. Its authors, Bell and Lancaster, were not philosophers, but simple teachers, moreover, teachers of poor children, for whom the skills necessary for them to earn their bread were more important than the systematic development of their mental faculties. Everything was calculated accurately so that time and effort were spared. One teacher and one guardian, with the help of monitors, sufficed for such an enormous school; everything proceeded like clockwork, for each child knew what to do. Order was the main requirement and over the door in golden letters were the golden words: 'A place for everything and everything in its place.'

It is thirty years since Lancaster's method was first known, but only fifteen years since it was first applied. At the moment most schools, especially those for the common people, are organised according to its principles. It has been introduced in America, the East Indies and in all English settlements and, thanks to its unquestionably beneficial character, it has been introduced in all European states. Thus the words uttered by Lancaster, in his excitement when he overcame the first obstacles, came true. He is reported to have said: 'I am a mere tool in the hands of a higher will. The Omnipotent handed me a trumpet which will be heard in all the corners of the earth. The poor in Britain, in Europe and throughout the world shall receive the gift of education and no human force shall stop its salutary influence.' His enthusiasm overcame all obstacles. Amongst its supporters were Charles James Fox and George III. On a visit to Lancaster's school he uttered the memorable words which have been repeated with reverence by every English child: 'I would wish' – said the monarch – 'that the least of my subjects should be able to read the Bible in his native tongue.' This was when the British and Foreign Bible Society was founded.

It is difficult to describe the extent to which the education of the common people in England had previously been neglected. There had been no local schools and the teachers had moved from place to place to give lessons. It was not until the year 1783 that a few well intentioned citizens established a society for the introduction of Sunday Schools for craftsmen. Their number grew every year and it now exceeds the expectations of its early supporters. In the capital alone there are 55,000 children being educated and up to 5,000 men and women who give lessons without any remuneration. Lancaster's method accelerates education quite incredibly. From its establishment in 1817, the model school mentioned previously has educated 24,000 children within nine years. The foundation of these schools has been made possible thanks to donations from the king, the clergy, the nobility and the tradesmen. The peasants and the workmen pay a quarterly sum for their children. Despite the high prices for printing and paper, the books used for teaching are so cheap that they do not cost more than one Polish złoty annually. Since a frugal approach makes one book serve six children, the real cost of books per child may be calculated as five groszy. The school fee for one child is four to six shillings annually.

Gentleness was not a feature of the early provision of schooling in England. There have long been small canes for children and bigger ones for youths. Parents sending their children to school were not unlike the Polish nobleman who, in Kraski's *Mikołaja Do wiadczy skiego przypadki* said 'Beat him; that is what I pay you for.' It is to Lancaster that schools owe the abandonment of corporal punishment. He introduced milder measures, but since he knew little about pedagogy they are equally ineffective and sometimes quite ridiculous. One wonders how they could make any improvement. For instance, he put an indolent child into a cradle; those playing truant were hung in a basket; the wayward were yoked like oxen and crosspatches had iron hoops weighing from four to six pounds placed on their necks. Grimy hands were washed publicly in a not too delicate manner; they were rubbed with a brick. For minor offences labels bearing the following inscriptions were hung on their necks: Gossip, Frolicker, Fidget, etc. Such punishments have been abolished and, instead of harshness towards the badly behaved pupils, which usually occasions embitterment rather than improvement, rewards for the good and the diligent have been introduced. The latter are promoted to become monitors, for the honour of teaching and supervising is very flattering for children. They are rewarded with tokens which serve as bills of exchange; eight such bills are worth one penny. The two head monitors are paid four pence for their week's service. Each quarter, tokens are exchanged for money, for which books, caps, shirts, stockings, penknives and similar useful articles are purchased for the children. They are then distributed by the teacher who summons pupils by reading their names from a book. He starts with the monitors who, on this occasion, take precedence over the others. The monitors choose whatever they like not exceeding, however, the value of their tokens. The remaining students come after them. The head monitors lead those rewarded around the hall announcing, like heralds, what the rewards were given for; for example, decency, regular attendance at school, diligence and good progress. The pupils can buy themselves out of punishment by relinquishing the tokens which had been awarded. The forms of punishment are as follows: a public reprimand and staying behind at school for a quarter of an hour or longer and, for those who wilfully do not attend classes, the punishment is extended to three hours, so that they can learn what has been missed as a result of negligence. Should the monitors trespass in any way they are disciplined with the utmost severity since they have abused the trust placed in them. The misdemeanours include inattention, insubordination and partiality; false incrimination and lies are chastised most harshly. Therefore, it is at school that the foundations of a man's future character are laid; from the school a pupil takes home not only education but also concepts of morality. One generation follows another, each better educated and more enlightened than the first and thus welding society together.

The common people constitute the majority of every nation, so all reforms should commence with the people. Living in a nation as educated as the English are, I have never heard any complaints about the detrimental effects of learning; on the contrary, with such a multitude of academic institutions there are still constant complaints that their number is not sufficient. It is the general opinion that the deformed mind is always accompanied by a perfidious heart. Hence, they educate the mind in order to improve the heart or at least raise man to such a level of perfection that the heart cannot reproach the mind. But of all the schools I visited I was most amazed by the infants' school at Spitalfields. It was founded on principles similar to those of Owen's elementary school in Lanark, but the most successful institution cannot last more than a few years without being improved in some way. Its purpose is the superintendence and education of the children of poor workers who, earning their livelihoods with their own hands and sometimes staying the whole day in factories, are not able to attend to their children and consequently have to leave them without supervision at home. This exposes them to miscellaneous perils and corruption or at least fills the parents with perpetual fear and trepidation. The humaneness of the proprietors of factories as well as the enthusiasm of citizens gave rise to these schools of which, in 1823, several already existed in London. Children between the ages of two and seven years were admitted there and tended with solicitude surpassing even that enjoyed by them at home. Commensurate with their intellectual faculties and age, they were taught to read and pictures were used to acquaint them with biblical, national and natural history. They were taught about various farm implements and craft tools and even the rules of geometry. Who would have believed this was possible in a school in which the oldest pupil was not older than five or six years? I observed their progress. This is how, in time, the young shoots are skilfully straightened and tended so that one day some of them may develop into huge trees. I became convinced at this school that, as regards knowledge, nothing is premature and everything depends on the selection of appropriate teaching methods.

Public opinion in England is in favour of education. Whatever stance we assume when reflecting upon education, be it its influence upon the poorer classes or on society as a whole, it is always a matter of the utmost importance. 'On the grounds of the dependence of the destitute upon the affluent' (says the preface to an elementary English book) 'the destitute ought to be provided for with particular care by the affluent.' What is more, responsibility for their physical and moral welfare seems to rest with the opulent, for there is no doubt that vice and crime follow in the wake of ignorance. The cultivation of morality, which can be aided by literacy, opens the mind, organises the intellect, and gives children a clear idea of their social and religious obligations. It prepares pupils for the effortless acceptance of a higher culture, develops an inclination towards virtue, and accustoms children to subordination and obedience. Reports submitted from all schools prove without exception the beneficial consequences of elementary education. In addition, those parents whose reprehensible way of living had been common knowledge have become more orderly since their children began to attend schools. For example, great importance is attached in schools to cleanliness, so parents endeavour to send their children to school looking as clean as possible. Thus they themselves become used to cleanliness and adopt a neatness of clothing and behaviour which aids a pauper, for it prevents his privation from becoming loathsome.

The middle classes have even more contact with the poor than do the wealthy. It is to their work and ability that we owe our bread, clothing and the amenities of life; we therefore attach much more importance to their moral education than we probably realise. We frequently entrust our fortunes to their care, relying solely upon their fidelity. Furthermore, they can exert a good or a bad influence upon our children when charged with their protection and supervision. Having once become accustomed to order and moderation, they will reject begging and vice and will not be useless burdens on the shoulders of the workers in society. The effects of teaching institutions, when spread among the whole population, will surely be more conducive to diminishing vice and crime than the severity of the penal code. Together with the rise of religious sentiments and charitable institutions, they may lead to a situation which could originate only in the dreams of a most dedicated friend of his country and humanity.

The commendation which England justly deserves by virtue of its elementary schools cannot, however, be extended to her secondary schools. I do not intend to say that there are none noteworthy among them; on the contrary, I have already described one which is on a par with the best schools in Europe. But the majority leave much to be desired and the English themselves do not spare them censure. The aristocracy, similar in this respect to their Polish peers, have acquired the habit of educating their children at home or sending them to live with and be tutored by some enlightened minister. Such schooling, though the domestic life of the vicarage may be exemplary, tends to be exceedingly poor in terms of knowledge. A single man, however learned he may be, can never be an adequate teacher for a youth who is supposed to be preparing for higher studies. This is particularly true of a tutor encumbered with religious duties. Such an education does not produce great people. Those whose sons are destined for public life send them to grammar schools, of which the most famous are Eton, Westminster and Harrow, where Latin, Greek and the rules of English grammar are taught. These schools, which are ranked next to the universities, can hardly be compared to gymnasia in Germany, let alone our schools where, in addition to mathematics and natural sciences, modern languages are taught, although the standards reached in the classics are far below those reached in English schools. On many accounts their schools would not bear comparison with our district schools. The method of teaching classical languages is obsolete and bears no resemblance to newer, improved practices. What was laid down by the founders of the schools, which at the time may have been ideal, is still strictly adhered to without any alteration. The instructors cleave to old books and do not produce new, more appropriate ones; if anyone dared to introduce a modification it would be considered an encroachment upon the privileges enjoyed by the school. The adherence to old ways impedes the teachers and creates a situation in which, although much Latin and Greek is taught, England cannot boast philologists as eminent as those in Germany; the most renowned are Bentley[4] and Potter.[5] German editions of classical works are esteemed to be the best and are reprinted. I observed their philologists pestering the students with vain and verbose elaborations, grammatical trifles and prosody, instead of rendering the spirit of the works of classical authors. I did not encounter a single lecturer who approached the subject from a philosophical standpoint. The education I have described is referred to as classical, that is learned, but it is limited to the translation of ancient authors whom they call the classics.

Apart from such schools there is a profusion of others, dedicated to specific vocations and fields of learning. They bear the grandiose appellation of academies. Hence, there are academies of painting, commerce, navigation, arithmetic, dancing, fencing and swimming – even riding, where the horseman (occasionally replaced by his deputy, a stable lad) fills the role of Plato. These academies resemble in some

Francis Bacon's Study, Oxford. Francis Bacon went from Oxford to Paris where his interest in Philosophy, alchemy and magic earned him the title 'Doctor Mirabilis'. Returning in 1247, he became one of the teachers who attracted students to what became England's oldest university. His teaching emphasised the importance of mathematical or experimental proof: a Renaissance man 200 years before his time.

ways our boarding schools and are separate for boys and girls. They are not public institutions but commonly remain under the supervision of the families for whose children they were set up. The large gilded inscriptions which can be observed above their doors, must also attract random students and benefactors. They are advertised like other products. It is in the same papers and well-nigh the same columns that advertisements for miscellaneous goods, silken garments, iron wares and herrings are placed next to notices concerned with academies and boarding schools for upper class girls and boys. These include long lists of subjects being taught and do not fail to mention the excellence of the teaching as well as the patronage of those noble families who had managed to persuade the teacher to establish the school. Also advertised are solicitous supervision, elaborate conveniences and most moderate prices – those who swallow the bait will have to pay! None of these academies or boarding schools is superintended by the government, nor are public examinations organised. How much circumspection is required from parents when making their choice! How many risks the rash ones incur! But the government merely opens the path to education and leaves it to each person's discernment what to avoid and how.

Having acquired the rudiments of knowledge in lower-level schools, the young go to universities in Oxford or Cambridge.[6] These revered institutions are age-old, for the former originated during the reign of Alfred the Great, and the latter, as some people maintain, in the pre-Christian epoch. It is said to have been established by Cantaber of Spain, the son-in-law of the king of Britain, who lived 375 years before Christ. Formerly they were legitimately famed for their learning but it seems now that they have become antiquated. A foreigner entering the imposing Gothic walls is filled with veneration for their ancient glory, but all he will find within them is a record of pensioned pedagogues and little learning. There is not even a list of lectures to be given or subjects taught. The so-called faculties are organised differently from those in other countries and do not embrace the full scope of human knowledge. At Cambridge, for instance, there is a course in casuistry, which is unheard of elsewhere, but there is no zoology; there is a course in modern history but not in ancient; there are two departments of astronomy and one for the Arabic language but none for English literature. Incongruities of this nature abound at both universities. They proceed from the fact that at the time of their founding there was no overall plan and benefactors established departments only in the subjects in which they were interested. Many of the fields of knowledge familiar to us did not exist then. The number of lectures assigned to a particular department varies. The limited state of human knowledge in the past did not necessitate a whole year's lecturing, so fewer hours than now seem necessary were allotted to it. A large number of professors are allocated not more than forty lectures a year. One professor of history, Professor Dodwell, delivered only twenty of them in the course of three years. The superannuated form in which these universities have survived makes it impossible for them to contribute to the development of knowledge. It is quite the reverse. They are much criticised by the British themselves who observe that the young frequently forget what they learnt at school and instead of polishing their manners they become even more unruly. Any progress in learning is dependent on the individual effort and wisdom of the younger members of the university staff who are called Fellows and give tuition in exchange for payment. These are tutors, which means the same as private teachers, and, if not Doctors, bear the learned titles of Masters or Bachelors and are members of one of the colleges.

Students learn everything with equal intensity, they read a lot, they write a lot, they almost become universal experts in diverse fields of knowledge, which renders English universities truly universal in character. Since their alumni are acquainted equally with the entire scope of human knowledge, they are protected from one-sidedness and unbearable pedantry. None of them chooses a particular department; it is only through practice or a longer sojourn at the university that a student discovers in himself the exclusive proclivities for a given subject, which he selects for his domain. Universities constitute only a general preparation for academic studies and a test of perseverance. Both universities comprise of a number of colleges and halls. They date from different centuries and, like the halls at the old university at Cracow, were established by kings and aristocrats. Some of them are named after their founders. Each person who wishes to be admitted to the university must dwell in one of these colleges and pay at least £300 annually. This, in addition to other expenses connected with apparel, supervision and private tuition, amounts each year to a considerable sum. A penurious person would in vain seek education at Oxford or Cambridge: these major schools were established in the centuries when not everyone was granted entrance to the temple of the Muses and the enlightenment of the people was not a general concern. It is easy to comprehend the inconvenience resulting from this in the present age. An attempt has recently been made to remedy this by establishing a university in London where, in a big city, it would be easier for students to support themselves. Moreover, a system of learning in keeping with the progress in contemporary education has been introduced there and all difficulties arising from various religious denominations have been surmounted. At Oxford and Cambridge students have to swear to the Thirty-nine Articles, the dogma of the

Anglican Church, before they can register. Dissenters are not permitted to enjoy the privileges accorded to the universities.

Those academic institutions are governed by their own laws; they have their own judicature which, following the example of former universities, is extended not only over the city but also its environs. Two representatives are sent from among their members to sit in Parliament. Their election ought to serve as a model for all elections in the country, for it is held without much ado and excessive expenditure on the part of the person chosen in recognition of services to the community. Once elected they may regard themselves as perpetual members of Parliament unless they become Lords or, which seems most unlikely, turn out to be mindless of the welfare and honour of the country. It is appropriate that a circle to whom the education of future citizens is entrusted is not excluded from matters pertaining to the country and that it combines learning with the affairs of daily life.

The highest official at universities is the Chancellor, with which office a wealthy aristocrat who is an alumnus of the university is honoured. At Cambridge this position has been occupied since 1811 by the king's brother, the Duke of Gloucester. He remains in office for the period of two years, but *tacito consensu* can hold it for life provided that the University Council does not proceed in time with the election of a new one. The Chancellor nominates a Vice-Chancellor, who represents him at the university and is always head of one of the colleges. The third official is the High Steward. He is also appointed by the Chancellor but confirmed by the University Council. This office at Cambridge has been held since 1806 by Lord Hardwicke, Magister Artium. The post is for life and involves the obligation to guard the rights and liberties of the university. The Proctors are charged with preserving internal order, watching over the good conduct of the young as well as eliminating the means of corruption. They are therefore permitted to enter students' lodgings at any time, detain suspect persons, drive them out of the city, mediate in disputes between townspeople and students and expel students either permanently or temporarily. This is termed 'rusticatio'. There is a multitude of other officials who, save for the so-called Fellows, work towards the development of various facilities within the institutions rather than exert any influence upon the youth studying there. Each college has at its disposal servants, such as the caretaker, the cook, the cellarman and even its own barber and constitutes in itself an independent community.

The University Council, which in Oxford is referred to as Convocation, comprises heads of colleges, Doctors, Masters and Fellows; their number at Oxford approaches 1,200. The latter dwell in colleges and their annual income varies from £50 to £1,000. This is received for life unless they marry. If they do so, they are awarded benefices which, as is the case with chapters, are owned by each college and can be managed at its discretion. Having won these scholarly laurels, they usually rest upon them: surrounded by wealth, they lose sight of glory and focus solely on the comforts of life. Every college has such fellows whose number is dependent upon its organisation; the smallest number is twelve and at Christ Church in Oxford, where there are 101 of them, the bell in the tower tolls that many times at nine o'clock in the evening before sleep. To them are apportioned the students; it is they rather than the professors who supervise their education by assigning to them authors to read and advising them on their written tasks.

The number of students always exceeds 1,000. They can be divided according to their condition and birth into noblemen, gentlemen-commoners and commoners. The first group includes sons of lords and hereditary gentry; the second those from less important but affluent families; the final group comprises those who, not being of noble origin, go there only to study. They are charged less than the others but, as regards learning or discipline, there are no differences between them save for apparel, which is distinct. They all wear gowns with broad sleeves. The sons of lords are clad in gowns made of purple damask, with lavish gold embroidery, others are attired in black gowns with silvery embroidery or, like ordinary students, without any embellishment. They wear caps with a square top and golden or silvery tassels. Every academic degree and every university official is marked by a gown of a different cut and colour and distinct decoration. Especially superb are the gowns of Doctors: each of them has three such garments, and the gala one, which is donned for great ceremonies, is most magnificent. It is said that nothing can surpass the sight of the university staff when gathered in large numbers. Such a situation is reputed to have occurred in the year 1814, during the sojourn of the monarchs in Oxford, when the degree of Doctor of Law was conferred upon the Emperor Alexander, the King of Prussia, Prince Blücher, Prince Metternich, Count Lieven and Platov, the Hetman of the Cossacks. Chairs, upon which the crowned guests were seated during the ceremony, are still preserved there and their portraits by Gérard,[7] a Frenchman, ornament the conference room. Eight speeches were delivered on that occasion, the Latin one was made from a rostrum by a public orator. Four thousand people are said to have attended the ceremony.

The entire outward form as well as the internal organisation of those two universities, for there are no others in England, is permeated with a cloistral atmosphere. The Gothic architecture of the colleges transports a foreigner into the Middle Ages. As in monasteries, students live in cell shaped rooms. There is a dining-hall, which resembles a refectory, where they eat in the company of their teachers and take their seats at the table according to an order determined by the rank of degrees and offices. Meals are announced by means of a bell and, in the case of one college, a horn. They begin and end their meals with a Latin prayer. The use of Latin formulae in examinations and marking, the habit of syllogistic disputations, giving written homework, assigning Latin or Greek poems to be learnt by heart as punishment to those who are not sufficiently diligent or do not attend church, were all transferred from the monasteries to which we owe so many ancient writers and manuscripts. What is more, the very oddity of clothes, which remind one of monastic apparel, transports a visitor preoccupied with the ancient glory of the institute to the murky gloom in which the first foundation of the university is shrouded. He would be totally immersed in the depths of Gothicism were he not abruptly roused from his reverie by the medley of old and modern behaviour which abounds there. Here is one example: a student admitted to the university swears as solemn an oath as if he were entering some clandestine organisation. But the content of the oath is comical rather than solemn. For, having pledged himself to believe in the Thirty-nine Articles of the Anglican

Church, he renounces the Pretender and the Devil; he promises to wear black and dark clothes (*coloris nigri et suffusci*), not to have a moustache or grow whiskers and to be ashamed of the ignoble and disgraceful habit of wearing shoes (*absurdo illo et fatuoso publice in ocreis ambulandi more*). They all wear boots and are not permitted to appear publicly without their gowns.

These two abodes of the Muses are also centres of merry living and the young are not at all loath to spend several years in these halls of learning. After dinner, when, in keeping with an English custom, decanters are passed around the High Table in order to aid digestion, the students, not allowed to meddle and drink wine in Hall, repair to their own quarters where, one after another, they organise parties. Hence, numerous strict defenders of morals castigate the universities for being nests of carousing, gambling and debauchery. In spite of copious supervision, not everything is noticed and a blind eye is turned to much of it, for it is in the colleges' interest to have as many students as possible. Stringency, well intentioned though it might be, would not attract them. Students constitute one body and form a close community. Like the German ones, who refer to themselves as Burschen and others as philistines, the Oxford students call themselves the Gown and the others the Town. Those words serve them as watchwords by which they recognise one another at night or occasionally, as in Germany, as a cue for brawls. Like the Germans, they also have their songs whose lyrics originate in the deepest antiquity, proof that mirth has dwelt in the temples of the Muses for a very long time. Nothing else ought to be expected where so many opulent youths live together. The beautiful environs of Oxford and Cambridge, which are so attractive for walkers, establish friendships amongst contemporaries and leave them with happy memories of the years spent at the universities.

It is a real strength of education in England that the young are not inordinately burdened with lessons. They have enough time for their own studies, to which they would not have been inclined by coercion and constant harassment. Nothing develops the intellectual faculties as much as one's own work; other people's thoughts can divest one of the ability to think independently. Many examples from the history of science demonstrate that it was to their own efforts that the greatest geniuses owed their renown, and not to the careful education enjoyed by the rich. Only one's own commitment will establish once and for all respect for science and the ideals of one's youth.

The private libraries of the English are full of works by Greek and Latin authors, for their entire school education is based upon ancient literature. They quote passages from them during their meetings, a habit which elsewhere would be deemed pedantic. What is more, their most celebrated speakers, knowing that they will be comprehended, quote them in Parliament in order to support their arguments. The study of those dead languages is so advanced that not only do they acquaint themselves with the major thoughts of the ancients but they also examine the minutiae of their grammar and prosody. One Latin word mispronounced once inspired such universal laughter in Parliament that the person responsible was so ashamed that he did not venture to take the floor again.

The acquisition of knowledge in England is largely dependent on the efforts of the students. They read a lot, prepare extracts from books, write treatises and hold discussions in societies founded specially for that purpose. The works they read are usually those which contain practical information rather than bold theories. The principle behind their reading is 'non multa, sed multum'. The best mind will deteriorate if overwhelmed by the study of a multiplicity of subjects. The words of Jean Paul[8] seem to be apposite here: 'Nur der Hunger verdauet, nur die Liebe befruchtet, nur der Seufzer der Sehnsucht ist die belebende aura seminalis für das Orpheus-Ei der Wissenschaften.'

There is nothing systematic in their education and its relevance to the vocation chosen by a student is of the utmost importance. Examinations, if any, are organised to gratify parents and reports are not submitted to any higher authority. In schools there is no elaborate schedule of study, nor is there any prescribed plan of teaching; teachers adhere to the methods formerly practised in their schools or are guided by common sense, shunning any novelties. The exception is the system devised by Bell and Lancaster, if we regard as a system something which does not contain anything philosophical. The colleges are in complete disarray: some are so obsolete that their structures are inappropriate for our century, others too modern, and old traditions are not respected. There are neither identical departments nor a systematic division of study. Other than for medicine, studying for scientific degrees is not practised. They are conferred upon scientists, without examinations, as honorary distinctions. The departments themselves are by no means systematic. The most proficient professors deliver lectures for the sake of money and not in order to develop their field of knowledge. I knew several who, although they had numerous students, had never published anything connected with their subjects. Many of them utterly neglect a subject which they consider to be a school one, and publish works which are more in harmony with the spirit of the age. The universities, therefore, are not, as in other countries, centres of literature – they house academics accomplished in their skills but no eminent writers. The latter live independently or occupy positions unrelated to schools. Ability is judged on the basis of achievement and not the number of courses attended or certificates gained. English philosophy is also exclusively practical: it is distinguished by exactness, thoroughness, modesty and a sensible approach to the natural order, but it lacks the breadth of vision evident in the systems of Leibniz,[9] Kant[10] and Schelling.[11] Their boldest philosophers are down to earth and leave daydreaming to poets; hence, they exert a significant influence upon the social order and do not err. The desire to build systems and theories on the ruins of former ones does not, as in Germany, occupy English philosophers; they confine themselves to the analysis and rectification of the old theories. English education has no traditions of instilling into students a predilection for science for its own sake; science is for them a means, not the end, and each of its branches is practised only as long as it is of service.

By developing the intellect, education in England increases the number of active and diligent members of society, whereas in Germany, by affecting the heart, it begets enthusiasts. It seems that in England a maxim prevails that truth is embodied in the mind. The error, in Germany, is that truth is in the heart and the mind is its mere shadow: the heart cannot err morally and it is only in the mind that immorality dwells. The English do not know what 'this great desire, which has never been satisfied and cannot be named' is. It pervades German works and is a figment of their overactive philosophising imagination. Byron, Coleridge and Wordsworth were the first to have acquainted the English with it. It is the first recognised step from their utilitarian principles and the natural manner of perceiving things towards the philosophical mysticism of the Germans.

NOTES:

1 Rev Andrew Bell (1753-1832), Scottish educationist and episcopalian. Appointed superintendant of Madras Military Orphanage in 1789, he was unable to get teaching assistants and developed the monitorial system in order to use the ablest pupils as monitors. His *Experiment in Education* was published in India in 1797 but was less influential than Lancaster's tract, which was published in England in 1803. Bell became superintendant of the National Society for the Education of the Poor which was founded by the Anglican Church in 1811.

2 Jean-Jacques Rousseau (1712-78), French philosopher and educationist. His novel *Emile, ou de l'éducation* influenced Pestalozzi.

3 August Hermann Niemeyer (1754-1828), German theologian and educationist.

4 Richard Bentley (1662-1742), English classical scholar and philologist. Master of Trinity College Cambridge, his critical text of the Greek New Testament brought him a European reputation

5 John Potter (c1674-1747), English scholar and prelate. Archbishop of Canterbury in 1737, he edited classical texts and is remembered for his *Antiquities of Greece.*

6 Mythical dates for the foundation of the universities of Oxford and Cambridge became current in the fourteenth century. Oxford is first known to have been referred to as a 'Studium Generale' in 1163 and its first college was founded in 1249. The Chancellor of Cambridge University was recognised by the Pope and the Emperor in 1226. Its first college was founded in 1263.

7 Baron François-Pascal Simon Gérard (1770-1837), French painter. A pupil of David and portrait painter to Louis XVIII.

8 Jean Paul, the pseudonym of Johann Paul Friedrich Richter (1763-1825), German novelist, humorist and educationist.

9 Gottfried Wilhelm Leibniz (1646-1716), German philosopher and mathematician. His publication on infinitesimal calculus predated Newton's by three years and his genius was believed to span the whole of contemporary knowledge.

10 Immanuel Kant (1724-1804). A German philosopher and scientist, his *Critique of Pure Reason* challenged Hume's empiricism.

11 Friedrich Wilhelm Joseph von Schelling (1775-1854), German idealist and philosopher. Influenced by Kant, he studied the relationship of self to the objective world. His stress on the importance of art made him an important figure in the Romantic movement.

Chapter Twenty-Three

Environs of London. Greenwich. Orphans' School. The Painted Hall. The Observatory. Chelsea. Environs of Richmond. Slough. Kew Garden. Twickenham. Windsor. Eton. Highgate. Kent. Country. Sidney. Dover. The Shakespeare Rock. The Crossing. Calais. Ending.

London's environs have nothing in common with those of ordinary cities. Wherever you go wide suburbs surround you, they merge with once remote villages and absorb others. These villages are also unlike the average ones. They seem to be beautiful little towns adorned with the fine houses of wealthy bankers and the merchants who find peace at a distance from their business. Every road is shaded by trees and the fields are like gardens, providing vegetables, fruit and flowers for the capital. There is nothing more pleasant than to escape from London, evil smelling and dark with smoke, to these charming areas and to breathe the fresh balsamic air. I could describe plenty of such places in detail if only space did not restrict me to the major ones and to those that are connected to the history or institutions of the country.

Greenwich[1] is on the Thames, five miles from London, and is linked to the fame of the English navy. The magnificent palace built by Charles II was converted by William III into a home for retired sailors. It is so spacious and magnificent that it is considered by some to be the only building in England worthy of the name palace. It is certainly the only place where poverty and disability are placed together in such a palace. The most beautiful view of this hospital is from the Thames and the most beautiful view from the palace is of the river, on whose wide waters you can watch sailing ships from all the countries of the world. The eyes of the infirm sparkle as they remember the remote countries which they once visited and to which they may now only travel in thought. Staying in their peaceful shelter; they are like ships that survived a storm and now rest in a safe harbour under bare masts.

We arrived there at dinner-time. We were led into the dining-room where up to 800 sailors were sitting at the tables and, besides this hall, there were also other dining-rooms. Their supervisors, who had grown old in the same service, were sitting at the central table. One of them came to us and kindly offered us his meal, which consisted of barley groats and a square piece of fat beef. They ended the meal, as they had begun, with a prayer. After dinner they all went where they pleased for they live there without any restraint or occupation. Some sat on the benches under the pillars and basked in the sun, others gathered in groups in the gallery and talked about their lives' adventures. There were small wheel chairs for the sick and disabled. At the time there were 3,000 disabled in the hospital and 32,000 living outside to whom financial support was granted.

The charity of the nation does not restrict itself to the old sailors. The orphans left by the sailors who devoted their lives to the service of their country are also taken care of. The institute in which, at that time, up to 800 boys and 200 girls were brought up and supplied with everything they needed, was placed on a steep hill just by the Hospital. The girls who stayed there, under the supervision of a governess, are taught reading, writing, sewing, laundering, ironing and book-keeping. When they are fifteen they are sent into service. The boys also have their supervisors and teachers and we were present at one of their lessons. To start with they learn by Bell's method by which one teacher was able to occupy all the students. The school was divided into several classes and in each of them different lessons were taught. Silence and order prevailed in the school; only the voices of the teacher and controllers and the pupils' answers could be heard. A pupil who was disorderly or answered incorrectly was seized by the next one who instantly moved up and took his place. The teacher did not interfere. This system sharpens the students' attention and it accustoms them to progress in an orderly, disciplined and discerning way. All this was happening very seriously; I did not see any restlessness among the children nor any smiles on their faces. It was as though they knew that on their work their future happiness depended. I think that the reason for this was the method used; I had an opportunity to watch them playing after the lessons with normal childish enjoyment.

In the highest class boys are taught mathematics and navigation; how to determine the latitude and longitude of places at sea, use a compass and how to sail in variable winds. There is a ship used by the institute on which twenty pupils train every day. Having been taught the theory they are sent to serve at sea but they still remain under the protection of the institute. Usually they are taken on by merchant ships as helmsmen and they may finally become captains. The whole process of upbringing is meant to prepare them for their future job. Their clothes are of blue-black cloth and look like the typical clothing of a sailor; they even sleep as though they were already on a ship, on sails that are hung in such a way that they form cradles. Such beds are called hammocks. To improve their physical and mental state they are sometimes allowed to play outdoors. Teachers prepare them for every possible circumstance; how to sew shoes and clothes and any craft that might be useful someday, for a sailor's life is exposed to many adventures.

Greenwich Hospital is also visited because of its paintings. Its chapel is built in the most beautiful Greek style and adorned with pictures. The most interesting are in the Painted Hall in which are Thornhill's paintings, on which he worked for 24 years. The majority depict sea battles in which the Englishmen fought and portraits of their famous admirals. In the centre of the ceiling are portraits of King William and Queen Mary, the benefactors of the institution. They are surrounded by the four cardinal virtues, the four seasons and the signs of the zodiac. On the west side of the ceiling is the victorious battleship Blenheim and an image of London, with the rivers, industries and the arts; on the east side there is a galley flying the banners won from the Spaniards and also Tycho Brahe[2] and Flamsteed.[3] What would most interest Poles is Copernicus[4] holding the Sun in his hand, with the route with which the Earth encircles the Sun around it. Being curious I asked my guide who it was. 'A pope with a monstrance' he replied. I had not expected such ignorance. Having told him that he was mistaken I gave him a half crown and requested him, from now on, to tell visitors that it was Copernicus, the famous Polish astronomer, who was depicted. In one corner of the hall they keep the catafalque of Nelson, the greatest of admirals and a great man. Not far from the Hospital, on a high hill, is an astronomical observatory where the famous Flamsteed worked. The present astronomer's name is Pond. The line of longitude to which Englishmen relate all their

Chelsea Hospital. The hospital was founded by Charles II to provide an asylum for retired soldiers and for 700 boys and 300 girls, 'The children of Soldiers of the Army.' The boys wore red jackets and blue breeches and the girls red gowns and blue petticoats. The architects were Wren and his young assistant Nicholas Hawksmoor. Wren described it as 'Plain but not inelegant as the artist seems to have avoided all superfluous ornament in order to save expense.'

astronomical calculations runs through Greenwich. From here there is the fullest view of London, the Thames and its enchanting environs. Plenty of Londoners come here for fresh air and fun. Deptford, Woolwich and Chatham, the naval arsenals, are nearby.

On the other side of London, but also on the Thames, lies Chelsea – a village famous for the botanical garden of London's pharmaceutical society and even more so for a hospital for retired soldiers.[5] However, it is not as magnificent or as generously endowed as the Greenwich Hospital, as if England owed more to the navy than to the army, whose victories are achieved on land. There are places for only 476 patients but far more collect a decent pension from the government. The hospital is maintained by the money saved from the fund allocated to the army and a day's pay taken from the soldiers each year. If this is not sufficient Parliament provides the needed money from the public treasury. Near the Hospital there is a school for 700 boys and 300 girls – the soldiers' orphans – which is free. The school was founded by the late Duke of York, the Commander-in-Chief of the army.

Riding to Richmond by the banks of the Thames one discovers the most beautiful of London's environs. Hills, valleys, groves, mansions; everything has an inexpressible charm and seems to emerge from the smoke and rubble of the city in this pleasant and tranquil rural form. Beyond Richmond the land is even more beautiful; adorned with the works of both nature and art. Many elegant mansions catch the eye of a traveller and almost every house has a place in history. It is there that the politicians, poets and savants, whose names honoured their times, lived and found time to talk or relax with their friends.

In such charming settings one finds Fulham, the country residence of London's bishops, Kensington, a village with a magnificent royal palace and Holland House, where Addison lived after his marriage to the widowed Lady Holland. But it is sad to remember that this splendid dwelling became such an unhappy home. His aristocratic spouse turned out to be a stupid woman of the world whose only virtue was a good figure. As she was used to being admired, she resented the superiority of her husband's mind, believing that her social superiority and the glitter of her wealth outweighed his mental ability. Addison was far more sensitive than many another in such a position. Disappointed by her and finding worries instead of happiness, he lost his love of life and died, a hypochondriac, on 17 June 1719. He lived with her for only three years. The house has become a property of Fox's family and there the famous politician spent his childhood and he frequently visited it when he held office. He died at Chiswick in 1806.

The village of Richmond lies nine miles from London and for the beauty of its setting and the vastness of its park it is called the English Frascati and Montpellier. The garden is eight miles long and is surrounded by a wall. In the past there had been a palace there in which English kings often stayed and where Edward III died of grief upon the death of his brave son, the Black Prince. There too died Ann, the wife of Edward II. She was the first woman to use a side-saddle, a custom that has been adopted by other women and popularised by

Hampton Court. Built for Cardinal Wolsey by Henry Redman in 1514, it was enlarged by John Molton for Henry VIII and for William and Mary by Wren, To the left is Henry VIII's Great Hall and over the gateway Tompion's astronomical clock.

fashion in all countries. The views from Richmond Hill are enchanting. From the top of it Thompson,[6] the author of *The Seasons*, praised the beauty of the smiling valleys, cheerful groves, fertile fields and neat country houses. His own modest house was nearby and he was buried in the local churchyard. From the hill one can see Harrow, where Sheridan and Lord Byron were being educated and also Claremont, Windsor and Hampton Court, royal palaces where there are probably greater collections of artistic masterpieces than anywhere else in the world. At Hampton Court there is a particularly rich collection of paintings and also the famous labyrinth – the Maze. This is difficult to enter and then difficult to get out of, a relic of artificial French gardening and an amusing playground for the young.

At Slough, outside Windsor, there is the astronomical observatory in which Herschel[7] worked. He invented the longest known telescope, which is 40 feet long. With the help of it the commonly called Milky Way was discovered. It is a set of fixed stars of which the astronomer

Schoeter counted up to 12,000,000. The telescope is reported to weigh 4,000 pounds and it is kept in the open air because it would be difficult to build an adequate shelter. Under it stands a mirror that reflects the objects on which the telescope is directed. The stars in it are magnified 3,000 times. Hershel counted up to 50,000 which came before his eyes in an hour. He discovered the volcanoes on the Moon, the ring encircling Uranus and the six planets that accompany it. The astronomer was unmarried and died as an old man. It is widely claimed that mathematicians live long while those to die young are the poets. Works of imagination and intense feeling, says Jean Paul,[8] exhaust a man more than reasoning; in similar conditions a mathematician will always live longer than a poet of the same physique.

Only a mile and a half from Richmond is Kew – another beautiful garden with a splendid palace where King George III lived and the present king was brought up. The surroundings are flat and its only adornment is the garden which has a rich collection of plants and animals, particularly of birds, from every part of the world. A dozen or more temples are in the garden: temples dedicated to the Sun, to Aeolus, to Loneliness and to Victory. There is a replica of the hermitage of Confucius and a medley of ruins, Chinese pagodas and Turkish mosques; altogether too much for one garden.

Nearby is Twickenham, the village in which the famous poet Pope, the translator of Homer, lived and died. The house in which he entertained Swift, Gay and Lord Bolingbroke is no longer there. It has been replaced by one which is nicer but has no historical interest. There is still a trace of the grotto which Pope had adorned with moss, shells and small stones but these have now disappeared, mementoes of the pilgrimages made by worshippers of his genius. Even the willow that he planted has withered. Nearby a row of cypress trees leads to an obelisk which he raised as a memorial to his mother. Recently Pope found an editor and a severe critic of his works in the person of Mr Bowles.[9] We, respecting both the man and the poet, read his works with admiration. His *Abelard and Heloise* was inspired by his true but unrequited love. He was buried in the local church and because, as a Catholic, he could not be buried in Westminster the following inscription was written for him:

Heroes and kings, your distance keep,
In peace let one poet sleep.
Who never flatter'd folks like you,
Let Horace blush and Virgil too.

The entire district abounds in historical monuments. Nearby one can see the Gothic castle on Strawberry Hill which used to be the seat of Horace Walpole, the author of *The Castle of Otranto.* In his writings, particularly in his letters, he used to be as witty and biting as Voltaire and also, like Voltaire, idle and vengeful.

The furthest point I reached during my excursions outside London was Windsor, which is twenty-two miles away. The town itself, though beautiful and wealthy, is remarkable only for the castle which has been the seat of English kings since the Norman Conquest. It was also where the last King of England lived and died, insane, and where he is buried in the chapel with his wife and daughter. The magnificent St George's Hall, where the Order of the Garter was established, is 110 feet long. At one end there is a throne with the cross of St George, the patron saint of England, above it, encircled by a garter with the inscription 'Honi soit qui mal y pense'. The ends of the garter are held up by cupids: a strange concoction of worldliness, paganism and the Christian religion. In the chapel, which is the most beautiful example of Gothic architecture, new members are made Knights of the Garter and take their seats in the gallery. Their banners and coats of arms are displayed above them for as a long as they remain alive, for here, as in the graveyard, the dead have to give place to the living. The newest banners at the time were those of Tsar Alexander and the Prussian king who were knighted during their visits to England.

Windsor is situated on the Thames and on the opposite shore, in a pleasant valley, lies Eton, a place famous for the school where the sons of the most prominent families receive their education. The school was founded by Henry VI in 1440. Educated there and financed from a special fund, there is also quite a number of poorer students called the King's Scholars who, upon finishing school, proceed to the universities of Oxford or Cambridge and, having graduated, are appointed to lucrative posts in the colleges.

In the northern part of London, on the hills which dominate this area, one can see Hampstead with its spring of mineral water and the village of Highgate. It was on this estate that on April 19, 1626 Bacon, the Lord Chancellor, died. He was also known as the Lord of Verulam,[10] and, as is well known, dealt a blow to scholastic philosophy and is considered to be the father of knowledge based on experiment. His terminal illness developed from a cold caught while conducting physical experiments in wintertime. Since he was unable to return to London, he found temporary accommodation with his friend the Earl of Arundel. The state bed with which he was honoured had not been used for several months and was damp. This aggravated his condition and he died within three days. His body rests in St Michael's church in St Alban's. Over his grave he is represented, as he so often appeared in life, as a serious thinker.

It was just before New Year 1824 that the time of my return, when I would have to bid farewell to London, its environs and to England, came closer. I was to travel along a route which has already been described but at a different time of the year. It was winter, though this was not obvious, for there were only strong winds and ground frost. At one of the first stops I happened to meet Captain Parry,[11] who was at that time setting out on a new expedition to the North Pole. From the experience of air temperatures he had gathered during his voyages, and about which he published in 1825, he told us that on Melville Island it takes five months for quicksilver to freeze in the open air. However, even in such a severe climatic zone, deer, geese and ducks were able to live. With such extreme cold the sailors could remain on deck only as long as the air was still; the moment the smallest wind blew the frost was so biting that, despite the thickest clothing, they had to seek shelter within the ship. The cold caused severe headaches.

The county of Kent is famous for the fertility of its grounds but it was no longer summertime, which had previously made this area look so pleasant. Once again, in the wealthy towns I saw beautiful architecture, fortified castles and Gothic churches with their centuries-long histories – a pleasant sight from the road were the modest, unpretentious and spotless farm houses. The inhabitants of Kent seem to be practically all of a class which, elsewhere, would be called the middle class. They owe their prosperity to an unusual law called Gavelkind by which estates in the county are divided equally among all sons, whereas other counties follow the system of entail, whereby the oldest son inherits everything and siblings are either dependent on him or are limited to parental support or income from other property. The owners of such fragmented hereditary estates bear the name Kentish yeomen.

The hereditary castle of Penshurst in the county of Kent was the birthplace of Philip Sidney, the finest knight at the court of Queen Elizabeth and the author of the poem *Arcadia*, whose praises were sung by Waller and Ben Jonson. In the battle of Zutphen he was in command of a cavalry division when he was fatally wounded. As he lay on the battlefield, weakened by loss of blood, he was given water brought from a nearby spring. A dying soldier gazed upon it with longing and when his commander, Sidney, noticed this he took the water from his mouth and ordered it to be given to the soldier saying: 'Friend, I see that your need is greater than mine.' Historians note that in the last moments of his life he talked of the immortality of the soul. Addison is said to have had Sidney in mind as he was writing Cato's famous immortality monologue after the defeat at Utica. At the age of thirty-two he left the profession which he had embarked upon with great enthusiasm. I mention these details since this courtly and brave knight, whose life and deeds, according to the poet Campbell, are an image of the highest poetry, was, after the death of Stefan Batory, one of the candidates for the Polish crown. He refrained from perusing his ambitions in Poland due to Elizabeth's envy and perhaps fear of losing Sidney, who graced her court.

We arrived in Dover where we had to wait an entire day due to an unfavourable wind. Dover is one of the Cinque Ports which were once the most important of all the coastal towns. They were obliged to supply ships to defend the coast and in return were granted important privileges. Since it was decided that a regular navy was essential, the towns lost their former position. From time immemorial Dover has been considered an important strategic point, the island's key and shield against enemy attacks. The Normans were aware of this and built a defensive fortress on the hill which dominates the entire harbour and makes it inaccessible at any time. It covers an area of about six acres. The hill slopes towards the harbour and is like a precipice, with the sea 320 English feet below. Although the fortress is hard to seize by force, it was not able to resist cunning. A brave dare-devil and his twelve companions climbed the ramparts one night and made such an uproar that, believing that they had an entire army at their door, the defenders surrendered without drawing their arms. The name of this crafty conqueror has been preserved, it was Drake. The fortress may be reached from the sea by stairs carved in the rock. There is an interesting gun there called Anne's Pocket Pistol which the Queen received as a gift from the Dutch and which, as the tour guides assured us, is said to have a range of seven English miles. However, this is one of the marvels in which not everyone believes.

The town of Dover is sheltered on its three sides by high hills, among which the highest is called Shakespeare's Cliff. Its height is described in one of the poet's tragedies:

How fearful
And dizzy 'tis, to cast one's eyes so low!
The crows and choughs, that wing the midway air,
Show scarce so gross as beetles.

I stood on this hill during a great storm and as I looked at the high seas breaking at its foot and out to the turbulent sea, I could only express my feelings poetically:

Lucky the ships still in haven
Lucky the sailors where it's dry
From the sea over the land even
Whiter than the snow the terns fly
The wind harp is mourning today
And roaring on castaway's grave.

O mother, have you a son there,
Sister, a brother – for him pray

Francis Grose. It was of Grose, who explored Britain, notebook in hand in the 1790s, that Burns wrote 'a chiels amangst ye takin notes'. The lines could as happily be applied to Lach-Szyrma whose insatiable curiosity took him below the surface of late Georgian England.

No girl sobs, today, no despair
May recover her fiancée
Her prayers will fade in the storm
The wringing of hands not fathom.

You storms, indeed, you have no heart
The wind's wings truly flights are your
Always in a cloak that is dark
And not as Tatras cold, much more
The sun does never come your way,
Though cold Tatras enjoy its rays.

You sextons and ruffians in one
Who make seas turn into graveyards
Where lie the parentless children,
The fathers, and parted sweethearts
In depths does a man disappear
No tombstone, no prayer to hear.

A wave over the castaway
Builds as though a grave of a sort
That by the next one flat is made
By the sheer ruthlessness' effort
Among the depths where man will die
It makes an abyss open-wide.

Sea monsters behind the coffin
Stroll slowly in a burial rite
In undersea dens lead it in,
Conch and shell bedding be there might
In pearls, corals the grave'll lay
Seals and sharks as guardsmen'll stay.

Having spent a week at Dover waiting for propitious weather for the crossing, for during that week only the mail-boat risked crossing the Channel, we saw at last a day on which we could put to sea. We sailed on a steamer; on the two former occasions we had not risked this, for steam ships were looked upon with mistrust for a long time. As we sailed away from the land, we had a beautiful view of the hills and Shakespeare's Cliff. When we were some distance from the coast we looked at Albion whose shores seemed lower until, quite suddenly, they disappeared from sight as if they had been drowned in the sea. With them the real Britain vanished from our sight but not from our memory. Imagination paints a picture of these two islands between two obedient oceans, of the islands whose fields are more like fertile gardens, whose Arcadian valleys, shady woods and grazing flocks have been described by great poets. These are the islands where industry has brought wealth, the islands of rich cities, luxurious life and art. The islands are small yet they rule over the seas and over nations all over the world. And she rules solely by the justice and kindness of her laws and by her intellectual superiority which makes all of those nations look up to her and obey her. Her scientists, philosophers, artists and politicians are incomparable and the deep wisdom of the government and of the various institutions makes Great Britain the wonder and envy of the whole world.

As these and similar characteristics of England that distinguish it from other countries came to my head our ship arrived at the port of Calais. From the quay at which we landed we could hear loud calls – 'Meurice!' 'Desseign!' – they came from the *marqueurs* of two innkeepers who were inviting the newly arrived passengers to enter their doors. The officials in the French custom house proved to be very active, taking the passports, signing them and looking for contraband in chests and suitcases; I had not seen such strict searching before. There is no more important aspect of travelling than crossing the frontier from one country to another, for the history and conflicts of bordering nations provoke such strong feelings. One could write a few words about the similarities and differences between these two neighbouring and persistently jealous countries but this would exceed the frame of these reminiscences.

Here end my remarks about England and Scotland but not the remembrance of everything I have seen and witnessed. Many subjects which should have constituted further chapters have not been touched upon and yet they are important. They apply to the government, literature, religion and spirit of the nation. The picture of these is difficult to draw as it must contain a number of different items, dependent on innumerable coincidences, reasons, climate, forms of government, etc. As it would be difficult to put all this within these volumes about my journey yet it is very likely (let me not promise too much) that I shall publish another work on these countries, or at least publish the materials given here in a more adequate form.

NOTES:

1 Greenwich was the site of a Tudor royal palace. The Queen's House, Inigo Jones' masterpiece, was started for Anne of Denmark, James VI's wife, and completed for Herietta Maria, Charles I's wife. The Royal Naval Hospital was designed by Wren.

2 Tycho Brahe (1534-1601), Danish astronomer. The greatest pre-telescopic observer, he measured the position of 777 fixed stars, working in the observatory at Uraniborg and then, with Kepler, in Prague. He believed that the planets revolved round the sun and the sun round the earth.

3 John Flamsteed (1646-1719), English atronomer and clergyman. The first Astonomer Royal, he laid the foundations of the study of astronomy in England and made the first accurate catalogue of the fixed stars. His observations, made at the Greenwich Observatory, were published in the three volume *Historia Coelestis Britannica.*

4 Nicolas Copernicus (1473-1545). the Polish astronomer and founder of modern astronomy, his *De Revolutionibus*, which proved that the sun was the centre of the universe, was written in 1530 but not published till 1543.

5 Chelsea Hospital (1682-91), was also designed by Wren.

6 James Thompson (1700-48), Scottish poet and playwright. He is remembered for *The Seasons*, published in 1730, and *Rule Britannia.*

7 Sir Frederick William Herschel (1738-1822), German-born English astronomer. Appointed private astronomer to George III, he was assisted in his work by his sister Caroline. Lach-Szyrma was misinformed; Herschel's son, Sir John (1792-1871), continued his father's research and pioneered celestial photography.

8 See Chapter 22, note 8.

9 William Lisle Bowles (1763-1858), English clergyman and poet. An early Romantic and chaplain to the Prince Regent.

10 Francis Bacon, Baron Verulam of Verulam, Viscount St Albans (1561-1626). Verulam was the Latin name for St Albans near which was his estate at Gorhambury. He was one of James I's most obsequious courtiers but a distinguished philosopher. His *Advancement of Learning* was published in 1605.

11 Sir William Edward Parry (1790-1855), English Arctic explorer. As a young naval officer he was sent to the Arctic in 1810 to protect the whale fisheries. He returned five times between 1818 and 1827 and, attempting to reach the North Pole by sledge from Spitzbergen, went further north than anyone had been before.